COLUMNS

2009 — 2011

Murphy Givens

COLUMNS

2009 — 2011

Murphy Givens

www.nuecespress.com

Corpus Christi, Texas

Library of Congress Control Number 2014936212

Givens, Murphy

COLUMNS 2009 — 2011

Includes index.

  1. South Texas — History.
  2. Nueces County — History.
  3. Corpus Christi — History.

ISBN   978-0-9832565-5-7

Published by Nueces Press, Corpus Christi, Texas.

Cover design by Jeff Chilcoat
Cover photograph by Raymond Gray

www.nuecespress.com

PUBLISHER'S NOTE

When Murphy Givens and I published *1919 The Storm* five years ago, we were often asked when a collection of Murphy's columns from the *Corpus Christi Caller-Times* would be published. The columns until then were shorter and not as well-suited as a collection in a book. In the fall of 2009 Givens retired and began writing longer columns for the newspaper. After a review of these, we believed that these longer columns could be published as a collection. We have selected the best columns that were published from late October 2009 through 2011 in this volume. In some cases we added extra photographs to better illustrate the subject.

Murphy Givens has been writing history columns for the *Corpus Christi Caller-Times* since 1998. They have become a window into the history of Corpus Christi in particular and South Texas in general. Many of us cut out and save the columns for future reference. Even though I have nearly every column Murphy has written, sometimes I have been frustrated by trying to find a column on a particular subject. This volume will help alleviate that by including a comprehensive index of subject matter. Readers will be able to find a column dealing with a person or subject by looking it up in the index. I hope you enjoy this volume of Murphy Givens' columns as much as I have.

Jim Moloney
Nueces Press
www. nuecespress.com

INTRODUCTION

Gustave Flaubert said his favorite historical periods were those which were ending since that meant something new was being born. I realize that many columns in this compilation are about the beginning or end of some historical period — when Henry Kinney set up his trading post on Corpus Christi Bay, when Richard King bought his first 15,000 acres to begin a ranch on Santa Gertrudis Creek, when the Civil War began and ended and trail drives started to Kansas. But then, history is about change. This collection of columns is about the process of change and the people who made it happen. It's a cliché to emphasize how much things have changed, but that's why we find history so fascinating.

All the columns included in this collection first appeared on the Viewpoints Page of the Caller-Times. When I retired from the newspaper in 2009, it was agreed that I would continue to write a weekly column on Corpus Christi and South Texas history. These columns are part of the result. I have worked for newspapers since they used hot lead and linotypes, but I have never worked with an editor with as light a touch as Tom Whitehurst. The columns appeared in the newspaper almost exactly as written. Since then, they have been edited for this book. They appear here in the order they were published, so there was no attempt at any chronological progression based on subject matter.

I realized when I first began writing about history that people are more interested in historical events than in what I might think about them. So I keep myself out of the writing as much as I can. It is a useful discipline, one I had to break to write this introduction. A woman called me once to ask my advice. She said she was writing a book about her life, but didn't know what to say. Think of it. What a formidable task she faced, sitting down to a blank page with nothing to say. Sometimes I feel the same way, the fingers fairly itching to get started, but from the head nothing; the words refuse to come. Writer's block, they call it. But this book was made easy because all the columns were already written, the episodes of staring at a blank screen all past, leaving only the editing, the assembling, the putting together, for which I owe an enormous debt of gratitude to my publisher Jim Moloney. As always, any errors are my own.

Murphy Givens

TABLE OF CONTENTS

PRESIDENT TAFT'S VISIT

Oct. 22, 2009 marks the 100th anniversary of President William Howard Taft's visit to Corpus Christi. It was a big event in 1909. It gave the city more attention and publicity than it had received since "Blacksmith Bob" Fitzsimmons trained on North Beach in 1895 for his championship fight with "Gentleman" Jim Corbett.

President Taft dropped in because he was in the neighborhood. He came to South Texas to visit the ranch of his half-brother, Charles Taft, on the north side of Corpus Christi Bay. The president was a guest at the fancy ranch house, La Quinta. When the president arrived at La Quinta, according to the book "Taft Ranch" by A. Ray Stephens, the president turned to his half-brother and said, "Charley, old boy, you said 'Let's go to Texas and rough it.' I don't call this roughing it.'"

Corpus Christi officials had planned for the president's visit for some time. They wired Congressman John Nance Garner and got him to use his influence to have a Coast Guard cutter, the *Windom*, brought over from Galveston to ferry the president across the bay. They also ordered, after some debate, matching outfits that the welcoming committee would wear: Prince Albert coats, formal stovepipe hats, kid gloves and shoes of the same color.

On Oct. 22, the *Windom* picked up Taft on the north side of the bay and brought him to Corpus Christi's Central Wharf, where the welcoming committee members, dressed in their Prince Albert coats despite the unseasonably hot weather, were waiting. They were standing among the cotton bales on one of the hottest days that anyone could remember for an October. The portly president (his political opponents called him His Corpulence) made his way down the gangway.

There was quite a contrast between the president and the welcoming committee. He was wearing a battered old Panama hat, a well-worn alpaca coat and wrinkled gray trousers that looked as if they had never seen an iron. The members of the committee were immaculate in their swallow-tailed matching outfits, looking as trim and nifty and nervous as bridegrooms. An observer said the president was amused at the obvious discomfiture of the overdressed welcoming committee.

The president and entourage were taken for a parade down Chaparral. A stage with a roof over it (called a pergola) was built on the side of the bluff where Spohn Park is today. A crowd of thousands gathered to hear the president speak; some sat in their wagons to hear the president. Schools and businesses closed for the day. Taft noticed some men in the crowd wearing Civil War uniforms and he invited them to join him on the stage, in the shade, which displaced the welcoming committee, forcing them to stand under the hot sun. It was a sweltering day and several people fainted. A newsman, whose camera shutter made a loud click, had a bayonet shoved at him by one of the militia members policing the event. The president spoke of the city's need for harbor improvements and a deepwater port, subjects dear to Corpus Christi's heart.

Next on the president's agenda was a trip out to North Beach in a seven-passenger Rambler. The president struck the first ball at the Country Club's new golf course. His visit marked the club's formal opening. As Taft bent over to strike the golf ball, someone snapped a picture of the

2

Thomas Hickey dressed in top hat and tails as a member of President Taft's welcoming committee.

Corpus Christi citizens gathered below the bluff in front of Dr. Arthur Spohn's residence (left) to hear President Taft's speech on Oct. 22, 1909.

3

president's rear end, and for years afterwards, the Country Club displayed the golf club, ball, and photo in a glass case.

Next came a reception and lunch at Henrietta King's house on the bluff, just above where the president had delivered his speech. According to Tom Lea's "King Ranch," after lunch the president was given an extra-large saddle with a "Running W" brand, a bridle and pair of spurs.

Taft returned to La Quinta across the bay. He stayed at the ranch for four days. He saw one of the first gasoline-powered tractors in South Texas, a Hart-Parr. Cowhands on the Taft Ranch held a roping, branding and riding exhibition for the president. They dipped cattle to kill ticks. That 22-inch King Ranch saddle came in handy when the president was taken for a horseback ride around the ranch. They had found a large horse — Old Sam — for the 320-pound president to ride. The horse, according to "Taft Ranch," groaned when the president settled into the saddle. The *Dallas Morning News* made the horse famous when it asked the question: "Among your other troubles, how would you have liked to be the cow pony that Mr. Taft rode to the roundup?" It was said that as a reward for carrying Mr. Taft Old Sam was put out to pasture and never saddled again.

I suspect the welcoming committee never donned those Prince Albert coats and matching shoes and gloves again, either.

HARD TIMES

On Oct. 29, 1929 the stock market crashed. Shares lost half their value, then dropped to pennies on the dollar. Within days, $30 billion in paper value was lost. Banks closed, jobs vanished, families lost homes and were put on the road, farms were repossessed. The financial depression became the Great Depression.

Those were hard times, gloomy times. In Corpus Christi, Sunday, Monday and Tuesday were designated as "Prosperity Days" to encourage positive thinking. The newspaper said the difference between hard times and good times was 90 percent psychological: "If we can just actually feel that we are on the way back to prosperity, then, by golly, we are."

The news wasn't all about hard times. In January 1930, a new bakery opened at Leopard and Palm; Fehr Baking Co. made Fair-Made Bread. That summer of 1930, a dance marathon was held at the Crystal Beach Park Ballroom on North Beach. It lasted from July 24 until Aug. 25. One couple got married while they danced. The winning (and exhausted) couple received $675. That was a lot of money when you could have your shoes half-soled for 10 cents.

It was a lot of money. Farm laborers lucky enough to get work made about 40 cents a day. Bank tellers made $17.50 a week. A fireman in Corpus Christi earned $2 a day and he was on call 24 hours a day. But steak was 15 cents a pound, pork chops 10 cents a pound; you could get a room at the

Riggan Hotel for $3 a week and you could buy a new Erskine automobile at Winerich Motors for $895. At Roy Murray Ford, for $44.50 you could get a radio attached to the dashboard of your car so you could listen to the city's new radio station, KGFI, which some wag said stood for "Kome Get Fish Immediately."

Prohibition crime — bootlegging, smuggling, distilling whisky — was big news. Pint bottles of "Old Hospitality" were sealed in flat tin cans to resemble insect spray and brought in by the shipload. When Coast Guard cutters approached, the cargo of cans wrapped in burlap would be thrown over the side. Beachcombers found tins of "Old Hospitality" washed ashore on Mustang and Padre Island beaches. In Corpus Christi, welding shops made a profit by turning out small copper stills, small enough they could be moved when a raid was threatened. Moonshiners set up operations in backyards. Sometimes the stench from dumped mash led to their location. Law-enforcement officers would drive around sniffing the air. One bootlegger on the Hill kept track of the money owed him by making a mark on the wall by the name. The owner had the shack painted and the debts were all wiped clean. One of the town's best-known bootleggers was the bell-hop captain at the Nueces Hotel, Lincoln Daniels, known as "Old Dan."

If times were hard in 1930, they got harder in 1931, nationally, but Corpus Christi was like a man whistling in the graveyard. Oil had been discovered in the Saxet Field and the city's new port, five years old, led the nation in cotton tonnage, handling 216,000 bales in 1928, and 598,000 in 1931. Corpus Christi was the headquarters of cotton country. In cotton-picking time in the fall, fields of white stretched to the horizon. But in 1931, cotton prices fell from 18 cents to five cents a pound. Farm workers on the Chapman Ranch west of Corpus Christi were let go. The first farmer in the country to get paid for plowing under

Crystal Beach Park ballroom on North Beach was the site of a dance marathon in 1930 that lasted 31days. The couple that survived the ordeal won $675.

his cotton crop was a Nueces County farmer, W. E. Morris. He went to Washington and was presented the "plow-up" check by President Franklin D. Roosevelt.

Ranchers were hit hard when calf prices dropped from 9.3 cents a pound in 1929 to 3.6 cents a pound in 1933. On the Armstrong Ranch, Charlie Armstrong cut his salary almost in half and laid off most of the hands. On King Ranch, Robert J. Kleberg Jr. ordered 250 head of cattle rounded up to furnish meat for hungry families. The meat was distributed from the King Ranch warehouse in Kingsville.

Area banks were caught in the panic. The Odem State Bank and the Sinton State Bank closed in 1931 and the City National Bank in Corpus Christi went under in 1933. During the "bank holiday" in March 1933, the Chamber of Commerce issued trade certificates for $1 each that would be accepted by the town's merchants. Many were never redeemed; they were saved as souvenirs.

The New Deal began to take hold. The Works Progress Administration (WPA) opened a sewing room at 613 Waco where women were paid up to $43 a month to make overalls, underwear, shirts and dresses for the needy. Another WPA project was to terrace the slope and build a concrete base to keep Cole Park from eroding into the bay. Some 70 men worked in the park for six months in 1935.

Around the country, crude camps of the homeless and destitute sprouted on the outskirts of cities. They were called Hoovervilles and people who had made the economic plunge that landed them there were said to be Hooverizing. Corpus Christi's Hooverville was a migrant camp on North Beach, which consisted of tents and shacks, located past the tourist courts. When Corpus Christi won the competition for a new naval air station in 1939, the migrant camp on North Beach filled with workers and their families who came here from all over the country hoping to get work building the base. For Corpus Christi, that, and the beginning of World War II, brought the Great Depression to an end.

ELI MERRIMAN

Eli Merriman was born in 1852 and died in 1941. For much of nearly a century in between, he not only reported on the growth of Corpus Christi, but helped to make it happen. He was one of the great ones when they still had great ones.

Eli's father was a doctor-rancher who moved to Banquete in 1857. Dr. Merriman made his rounds to see patients by horseback. Young Eli, growing up in Banquete, climbed a tree once to watch two bulls on the prod, ready to fight, pawing the ground, running at each other and butting heads with terrific impact. Next day, he saw them eating cactus together like old friends. He saw the woman pistolero Sally Skull, who wore rawhide leggins and rode astride like a man (considered shocking); she carried pistols on the horn of her saddle and was not shy about using them. Merriman thought she had the fierce, staring eyes of a hawk.

One year during the Civil War, when he was 12, Merriman went to school at the Hidalgo Seminary in Corpus Christi, boarding at John Riggs' home. His teacher was "Little" Carroll, brother of Charles Carroll. (Charles' daughter also became an educator; Mary Carroll High School is named for her.)

One day Merriman's father took him out of class when surprising news arrived. At Col. Lovenskiold's home, Mrs. Lovenskiold relayed the news: "The war has ended, Gen. Lee has surrendered, and President Lincoln has been

9

assassinated." They rushed to Dr. Merriman's hospital in the Rabb home. Dr. Merriman told the news to sick soldiers. Then they set out for Banquete where another hospital was filled with sick soldiers.

They met Col. Lovenskiold with his sisters-in-law about where Robstown is now. They were surrounded by wild-looking men ready to kill the colonel. Dr. Merriman pleaded with them to let the Confederate official go. The angry Confederate soldiers said they had been turned loose without a dollar, hundreds of miles from home. Dr. Merriman told them to take the colonel's money, but let him go on to Corpus Christi. They agreed; the time for killing was over, and Lovenskiold escaped with his life.

Occupation authorities opened an office in the Russell home where Confederates were required to take the oath of allegiance. Some took the oath, but many refused. "There were several regiments of U.S. colored troops sent to Corpus Christi, pitching their tents with Old Glory waving in the breezes."

In 1867, a yellow fever epidemic claimed the life of Dr. Merriman. He had worked day and night with little rest before he got the fever. After his father's death, his mother sold her land at Banquete and sent 15-year-old Eli to get the money. He met the buyer at the Byington Hotel in Banquete and was paid in $20 gold pieces. Eli put the money in a sack and rode back to Corpus Christi, holding his six-gun "with a vigorous grip the whole way back." His mother opened a boarding house on Chaparral.

In 1870, at age 18, Merriman was in Professor McOmber's school. During recess, he went to Benjamin Neal's publishing office above Atwood's tin shop and asked for a job. Neal, publisher of the *Nueces Valley*, hired Merriman as a typesetter.

Merriman was there when the first spike was driven by Uriah Lott for the Tex-Mex Railroad on Thanksgiving Day,

Eli Merriman, the son of a pioneer doctor, was one of the founders of the Corpus Christi Caller in 1883.

1876. The gilded spike glittered like gold; it was stolen that night. Grading started the next day west of Blucherville.

After a stint with the *Galveston News*, Merriman returned and took a job with the *Gazette*. During an economic downturn (they called it a "money panic") he was laid off; they couldn't pay him his $12 a week salary.

In 1877, Merriman and Bill Maltby started the *Free Press*. Merriman rode the countryside, from Nuecestown to Oakville, selling subscriptions. He would fill out the form on the horn of his saddle. In 1881, Merriman married Ellen Robertson. They shared a tragedy; her father, a pharmacist, also died in the 1867 epidemic that claimed Eli's father.

After a trip to California, Merriman returned to learn that J. P. Caruthers and Ed Williams planned to start a new paper. He sold them the *Free Press* for $2,500 and joined the venture. They named the paper the *Caller*. The significance of the name, Merriman wrote, "was that as newsboys called out the paper for sale, the hearer would get the conception of the paper being a 'caller' of news, just as in earlier times a town crier would 'cry out' the news." They rented the Noessel building and the first issue came out in January 1883.

Merriman sold his interest in the *Caller* to Henrietta King in 1912, but he continued to write for the paper. He died on Jan. 25, 1941 when he was **88**. A former newsboy, J. W. Falvella, said Merriman "was always heart and soul behind every movement that had for its purpose the making of a greater city of Corpus Christi." Before he died, Merriman wrote that his father and mother were buried in old Bayview and that was where he would be buried when he joined them beyond the river. "You know, that's one of my favorite hymns. At night, if I can't go to sleep, I sing that old song, 'Shall we gather at the river' and I just drop off to sleep."

LIFE ON THE RANCH

The Truitt family packed up and left Corpus Christi in the summer of 1902 for the Rio Grande Valley. The Truitts were moving to Rancho Capisallo owned by Brownsville political boss James B. Wells, who was also the attorney for King Ranch. Alfred Levi Truitt had been hired to manage Wells' ranch.

The Truitts left with two wagons, a buggy, eight mules, two buggy horses, and four saddle horses. From Corpus Christi they traveled west for 10 miles, then turned south. They followed the same route Zachary Taylor's army took when it left Corpus Christi in 1846. After they passed King Ranch headquarters, they came across a flock of geese and the vaqueros accompanying them raced among the geese, using rawhide bullwhips to bring down several as they took flight. The popping of the bullwhips sounded like gunshots. The mother, Molly Truitt, cooked the geese, seasoned with salt and pepper, flour and water, in a Dutch oven covered with hot coals. For supper they ate roasted goose with pan gravy, camp bread and coffee.

Going south, they saw cattle bones bleaching in the sun, skeletons from an old drought. They watched as the Alice-Brownsville stage passed and at one point saw the stagecoach driver change horses at Encino del Poso. They traveled through isolated country; there was not a village or post office between Sinton and Brownsville in 1902, before the coming of the "Brownie" railroad. They stopped at El

13

Sauz, a division of King Ranch, where they were guests of "Uncle Josh" Durham, ranch foreman and former member of the famous McNelly's Rangers.

They turned southwest to reach Rancho Capisallo, straddling Hidalgo and Cameron counties. Rancho Capisallo was 100 miles from the nearest railroad. Not long after they arrived the ranch was sold to Lon C. Hill and the Truitts moved on to another owned by Wells, the 146,000-acre ranch in Starr and Hidalgo counties named Rincon Medio.

The ranch house at Rincon, built in the shape of a T, had 18 rooms but no indoor plumbing. Each bedroom had a washstand and white enamel chamber pot. When the weather was cold the Truitt children bathed by the fireplace. On the ranch everything stopped for siesta at 2 p.m., the hottest time of the day, when horses stood under a big mesquite, lazily switching at flies. About 3 p.m., they would awake to the sharp smell of mesquite smoke mixed with the odor of roasted coffee beans coming to a boil.

They got mail by horseback from Sam Fordyce 35 miles south. They would get the Sears Roebuck catalogue and the *Kansas City Packer*. For entertainment, they had a gramophone on which they played the songs of Enrico Caruso and the band music of John Phillips Sousa. Later, a salesman whose mission in life was to sell pianos to Texas ranchers brought them a piano. Mrs. Truitt could play; she had taken music lessons from the Catholic sisters in Corpus Christi. She would play "Give My Love to Nell" and "A Package of Old Letters." They got books for Christmas, Kipling's works, "The Light That Failed," "Captains Courageous," "Kim."

Ranch days began early, at 4:30 or 5, with the sound of the coffee mill grinding followed by the smell of freshly brewed coffee. The coffee mill was nailed to the wall. The green Peaberry coffee beans came in 100-pound sacks and

Maude T. Gilliland wrote about life on a South Texas ranch in her book "Rincon."

the beans were roasted in black bread pans. They had venison, cabrito and beef. The beef was cut in thin strips and hung out to dry in the sun for beef jerky. Crusty loaves of bread were baked in an old wood stove. There were *tortillas, pan dulce* and *bunuelos.*

On wash day, mesquite wood fed a fire under a big black wash pot in the yard. Shavings from a bar of Crystal White soap were added to the boiling water. As clothes boiled in the pot, they were punched down with a broom stick. For ironing, rows of flat irons were heated on the wood stove. Even after washing and ironing, the clothes gave off the strong odor of mesquite smoke.

Those were the ranch times described by Maude T. Gilliland in "Rincon (Remote Dwelling Place)," published in 1964 about her life when she was young Maude Truitt, the daughter of Alfred and Molly Truitt. The book has long been out of print, but if you are lucky you may run across

15

one on eBay or at some garage sale. I found mine at Half-Price Books. There is much more to "Rincon" than what I have condensed here, more about the influx of wealthy refugees from Mexico after the Madero Revolution in 1910, more about John J. Pershing's Expeditionary Force and the mobilization of U.S. troops on the border, more about the bandit troubles of that era. Mostly, though, Gilliland's book is about the unique life on a South Texas ranch after the turn of the century.

Maude Gilliland captures a unique sense of time and place. She writes that those who have never lived on a ranch have missed something in life. "It is nice to have ranch memories stored away to draw on when the looking-back period comes . . . memories such as the lace-like shadows of the mesquite under a noonday sun . . . the paisano folding back his wings as he skims across the road . . . the yip-yip of coyotes . . . thirsty horses drinking from a wooden trough . . . the sound of creaking saddle leather and the clinking-clanking of spurs. All these make looking back a pleasure."

MEMORIAL COLISEUM

People ask me what I have been doing since I retired. I have been busy trying to avoid thinking about what to do with the Memorial Coliseum. I have spent entire days trying to clear my mind of the subject. It is hard to do and the paper has been no help at all.

The news has not been worth repeating, but it is repeated anyway. The coliseum should have its own section of the paper: Coliseum Only. The other day the paper criticized the City Council for not discussing what to do with the coliseum. The position was that the suffering must continue until some kind of decision is reached. That was followed by a kite's tail of posted comments to prove that opinions are like asterisks; everyone has one.

I have an opinion, too, but nobody asks us out in the retired world. Tear it down. You can't attract new money with old eyesores. The City Council could make a decision before breakfast (OK, before supper) and let the men with the hard hats go to work. Make it a park. Green lawn with pink daffodils. Or yellow as the case may be.

Don't like that idea? All right, fix it up. As the man said, it may not be our best coliseum, but it's our only one. Make it a mercado. Make it a place where merchants can sell obscene books. Anything.

It would be a great expense to rehab the building and keep it up. Of course, the city is always broke until it comes time to raise the salaries of top officials at City Haul, but the

Council could come up with the money by the simple expedient of raising taxes on all those who want to keep it.

Why is this such a hard decision? Because half the town are Tear-It-Downers and half are Fix-It-Uppers, half Big Endians and half Little Endians. The Council is torn between them. There is hemming one day, hawing the next, a constant beating around the oleanders, clockwise one day, counterclockwise the next. They say, "Rome wasn't dismantled in a day." Surely there is a way out of this.

Here in the retired world, between getting up, going to bed and taking the dog for a walk, I have been giving this some thought, at those odd times when I can't avoid the issue. Maybe we're too close to it. Maybe we could trade civic problems with, say, San Antonio. Let San Antonio voters decide what to do with the coliseum and, in return, we could decide any problems they may have in the future with the Alamodome.

Don't like that? You say San Antonio might use the opportunity to score some civic one-upmanship. OK, let some disinterested people in Corpus Christi make the call. Let third graders at Chula Vista decide. Not enough experience? All right, let the fourth graders do it. They couldn't do any worse than we have.

A story the other day explained why the City Council didn't discuss the coliseum at the weekly meeting. The story said the city manager was not prepared to discuss the issue. Not prepared? In the memory of man, has this ever stopped the City Council from discussing an issue? That is setting the bar high. The City Council is under no requirement — by statute, by ordinance or in equity — to discuss the issue, or if it comes to it, make a sensible decision, or any decision at all. Nothing in the City Charter says they must fish or cut bait.

But they need to make a decision. Maybe they could put the ideas in a jar and pull one out. Make it a casino (with the

Memorial Coliseum in its early days. It was razed in 2010.

help of our crack legislators). Make it a mercado, or a Mikado for that matter, with Nanki-Poo and Yum-Yum in the wings. Make it an Olympic swimming venue, with or without alligators. Return it to the IceRays, or just raze it. Tear down half and restore the other half. Cover it with dirt and rent out dirt bikes. Plant kudzu and watch the vines cover that peeling green roof. Clear out a space near the front (leave those rats alone) and let the City Chiselers (er, City Council members) meet in that dark cavern until they make a decision.

I am afraid we have become like Sisyphus. You know the story. For all his misdeeds, Sisyphus, the King of Corinth, was given an unusual punishment by the Judges of the Dead. They gave him a huge stone and ordered him to roll it to the top of a steep hill, then topple it down the other side. But as soon as Sisyphus gets close to the top of the hill, the weight of the stone becomes too much for him and it rolls back down again and he starts all over, onward and upward. ("The Greek Myths," Robert Graves.)

The coliseum is our colossal stone. Our punishment comes from an inability to make decisions. Some years after the Civil War, the city was told that it couldn't demolish the old derelict lighthouse on the bluff, as it was federal property. One dark night, persons unknown dismantled the old lighthouse, presumably at the pay of the city, and thanks for your advice, Washington.

Which means that this is a place where decisions used to be made, maybe in a backroom with a shot of whisky and a seegar. Walter Timon or Roy Miller would have made the decision to fix it up or tear it down and we would have moved on. Now it's up to *vox populi*. Or is it that the *populi* have too much *vox*? Whether it is the fault of *vox populi* or City Haul or the City Chiselers or you or me, what has happened to the Memorial Coliseum is a crime. And we all know that what is needed with any crime is some kind of closure.

OLD TRADING GROUNDS

Before it was Corpus Christi, or Kinney's Rancho, this place was called the old Indian trading grounds. It was where traders landed contraband goods on the beach to avoid paying customs duties, then loaded them on pack trains to carry into Mexico. A more fitting name would have been the smugglers' old trading grounds.

Trader John J. Linn in 1829 landed a cargo of tobacco at the site, planning to meet a man named Wright with a mule train to haul the tobacco to Camargo in Mexico. Linn found no settlement here ("Reminiscences of Fifty Years in Texas"). H. A. Gilpin landed that year with goods for sale in Mexico. He saw no signs of civilization.

The written record citing Corpus Christi during this time is scant. Manuel de Mier y Terán made a tour of Mexico's province of Texas ("Texas by Terán") in 1828. Terán noted that some officials favored Corpus Christi for a port, referring to a place on the bay since there was no settlement called Corpus Christi.

Bill Walraven in a column ("Which came first: Kinney or the city?") wrote that Mexican Gen. Juan Nepomuceno Almonte mentioned Corpus Christi as a port in 1834 and Lt. Col. Enrique de la Pena, with the retreating Mexican army after San Jacinto, datelined the stop of June 2, 1836 as "Corpus Christi." Like Terán, the colonel was probably referring to the vicinity of the bay. As for Almonte mentioning it as a port, he no doubt meant it was place where shallow-draft vessels could unload goods, not that there was a settlement at the place.

In 1838, surveyors camped where the city would be built. "We saw no indication of any former settlement at this place," wrote Z. N. Morrell ("Flowers and Fruits in the Wilderness") "but were informed by an Irishman accompanying the surveyors that this was the point at which the (Irish) colony of San Patricio procured its supplies."

So the old Indian trading grounds were still being used as a place to land goods. While traders and surveyors found no village here, Mary Sutherland ("The Story of Corpus Christi") wrote that a shipwreck survivor in 1824 found villagers living where Corpus Christi is today. She wrote that the villagers were killed in an Indian attack and the survivors carried into captivity. There is no evidence to support the story, but the pre-Kinney record is very thin.

The Kinney record began in September of 1839. Henry Kinney, a merchant from Pennsylvania via Illinois, moved from Live Oak Point to the old Indian trading grounds and built a trading post on the bluff commanding a view of the bay. For two years, it was called Kinney's Rancho.

Under the Republic, Kinney's Rancho had its troubles. It was the capital of no man's land, the territory between the Nueces and Rio Grande claimed by the Republic of Texas and Mexico. Kinney, between two fires, kept his options open. He would write Mirabeau Lamar, president of the Republic of Texas, then write Gen. Mariano Arista in Matamoros. A British consul at Galveston, William Kennedy, wrote a dispatch *(Southwestern Historical Quarterly)* saying that Corpus Christi was important as a Texas trading post, "which Mexican contrabandists resort to for the purpose of smuggling goods across the Rio Grande." Though Corpus Christi was claimed by Texas, that didn't stop Mexican cavalry from operating around the settlement. Texas was at pains to counter that. The new Republic was

Henry Kinney's fortified trading post was located on the bluff next to the Blucher Arroyo, where the Southwest Telephone building is located today.

broke, without an army, so the government authorized volunteer "spy companies" to keep an eye on Mexican forces. Members of the spy companies, who were not paid, took their authority as a license to plunder, to continue the war by attacking peaceful traders from Mexico.

One spy company of 40 men under John Yerby operated out of Corpus Christi. Kinney in a letter to President Lamar called Yerby's men "robber Texians" and urged Lamar to take steps to stop them from preying on peaceful traders.

"Having arrived home two days back," Kinney wrote Lamar on Aug. 15, 1841, "we find as expected a gang of desperadoes on our frontier perfectly regardless of the rights of anyone, robbing indiscriminately . . . if this state of things continue, we shall be compelled to give all up for lost at this place."

In one attack, eight merchants from Mexico were killed for their goods and in an argument over dividing the spoils, Yerby's band split up, with most of the men leaving with

23

James Ornsby (also spelled Ormsby). A force of 200 Mexicans (Kinney called them "rancheros") ambushed the remnant of Yerby's company below Corpus Christi at La Parra and nine of the band, including Yerby, were killed. The men who went with Ornsby disbanded and some were hired as gunmen by Kinney (the Lamar Papers).

Another renegade spy company riding out of San Patricio was led by W. J. Cairns (also spelled Karnes). This outfit attacked a caravan of Mexican traders that left Kinney's Rancho on Christmas Day, 1841. A Mexican patrol caught up with Cairns, killing him and four others in his band.

Four years later, Corpus Christi in 1845 became a major military outpost with the concentration of half the U.S. Army under the command of Zachary Taylor. Even on the eve of war, traders still came over from Mexico, bringing horses, mules, Mexican blankets, and silver bars molded in sand. The town almost ceased to exist during the war with Mexico, but after the war, Corpus Christi, site of the old Indian trading grounds, fell back on the original purpose for which it was founded, trade with Mexico.

LOST YEARS

The "lost years" of Corpus Christi lasted from 1846, when Zachary Taylor's army left, until 1848 when the war with Mexico ended. In those two years the town was nearly deserted; it almost ceased to exist when most of the men left to follow the army or, really, to follow the excitement.

Half the soldiers of the U.S. Army were encamped at Corpus Christi from August 1845 until March 8, 1846. The first unit to leave marched away to the tune of "The Girl I Left Behind Me." One officer looked back to where the army had spent seven months and wrote: "The fields of white canvas were no longer visible and the campground looked like desolation itself, but the bright waters of the bay looked as sweet as ever."

Marching orders in the *Corpus Christi Gazette* warned: "As the army marches south, the commanding general wishes it distinctly understood that no person not properly attached to it will be permitted to accompany the troops."

Despite orders, grog-shop purveyors packed up — lock, stock, and barrels of whisky — and followed the army. On the way, at Santa Gertrudis Creek, some were sent back in irons and their liquor poured out, but other whisky drummers, gamblers and prostitutes traveled south, like troopers themselves. There was no reason for them to stay in Corpus Christi, without 4,000 soldiers getting regular wages to spend on whisky and other vices. They followed the money.

A Houston paper, *The Telegraph*, noted the town's downfall. "Since the removal of the U.S. Army from Corpus Christi, the town has fallen almost as rapidly as it rose. The population has dwindled from nearly 2,000 souls to a few hundred. The 200 grog shops that were the glory of the citizens a few weeks since, the faro banks, the roulette tables . . . have disappeared. A few stores . . . are about all that is left of the late flourishing town of Corpus Christi.''

Even the town's founder, Henry Kinney, left with the army. He was appointed to the staff of Gov. J. Pinckney Henderson, in command of Texas troops, and Kinney's partner, William Aubrey, went south with a wagonload of Dicky Jones brandy, Madeira wine, and Monongahela whisky. When Taylor occupied Matamoros, grog shop owners who had been at Corpus Christi were in business again.

Later that year, in October, a young soldier from Kentucky, William McClintock, passed through Corpus Christi on his way to join the army in Mexico. He wrote in his diary that he thought it was a town living on borrowed time. "The town is situated on a low beach containing some 30 houses, and on the hill are 15 or 20 Mexican huts now deserted. Corpus Christi was a poor insignificant place until the army took up its quarters there. I think its existence will be an ephemeral one."

Samuel Bangs, editor of *The Corpus Christi Gazette*, joined the exodus. He packed up his type trays to get closer to the "seat of conflict." He was soon printing *The American Flag* in Matamoros, but he kept up with the news from Corpus Christi. On July 17, 1846, *The Flag* printed a report from a correspondent, most likely Kinney, who was able to visit the town regularly while he was with the army. Kinney, a good many things in his time, was always the town's top promoter.

Corpus Christi as it appeared in 1846 before the U.S. Army marched south to the Rio Grande at the start of the war with Mexico.

"According to promise," the correspondent (Kinney?) wrote, "I write you what information I have been able to gather since my return to Corpus Christi. I found the old inhabitants of the place, almost to a man, had departed for the Rio Grande, and not only the men, but the women too. Corpus Christi is indeed deserted. But think not that those who have departed, under excitement, will have left us forever. When they have 'seen the elephant' and find that his haunts afford no resting place so lovely and calmly beautiful as this delightful village, they will return . . ."

The American Flag reported a rumor that a Comanche raiding party had attacked Corpus Christi and forced the citizens to "retire for safety to St. Joseph's Island." The paper said the rumor was unfounded, but noted that the town was badly exposed. "Nearly all the male population of the place are now in Matamoros or upon the Rio Grande and there are no ranging companies nearer than San Antonio."

27

Rumors of the attack led to orders returning a company of Texas volunteers from Corpus Christi, under the command of "Mustang" Gray, to be sent back to protect the town. McClintock met Gray when he passed through Corpus Christi. "Last night I was introduced to Capt. Gray, commandant of the company of Texan rangers stationed near this town," McClintock wrote. "Gray is a fair specimen of the ranger, at all times ready to engage in a fight, foray, amour, dance or drinking bout." Gray's company spent several months at Corpus Christi in the fall of 1846 before they were ordered back to Camargo to protect Taylor's supply lines.

When the war ended in February 1848, things began to look up. In the next two years, many soldiers who had "seen the elephant" were ready to settle down in Corpus Christi. They included some of the most prominent names in the coming history of the city: Norwick Gussett, Forbes Britton, Cornelius Cahill, and Matthew Dunn, among others.

Corpus Christi began to prosper again. Kinney bought surplus army wagons and sold them to 49'ers on their way to California. He bought a dredging machine to cut a channel through the mudflats and the town again had a newspaper, *The Corpus Christi Star*. Even the army returned when Corpus Christi was made headquarters for the Eighth Military District.

ROSALIE'S STORY – 1

She was baptized Bridget Hart in County Wexford, Ireland in 1825, but her confirmed name was Rosalie, which stuck. Her father Thomas Hart was appointed to the lighthouse at Cork. The Harts lived in a stone house with a view of the bay in one direction and in the other a view of farms in the green fold of hills.

Her father sold his commission and they moved to a farm near Wexford, though her father, Rosalie said, knew no more about farming than a baby. Rosalie went to school near Ballygarrett. She would go to the baker's across the street to buy a penny's worth of caraway seeds and a bit of sugar.

In 1833, James Power, who had lived in Mexico for 20 years, returned to Ireland to encourage people to move to Texas. His contract with the Mexican government allowed him and his partner, Dr. James Hewetson, to settle 400 Irish Catholic colonists. Power and Hewetson were two of four Irishmen (with James McGloin and John McMullen) authorized to establish colonies in South Texas.

Power talked up Texas at the house of his sister and people came to hear of the wonders of that frontier land. Rosalie said he described Texas as one of the richest countries in the world, with a delightful climate. Rosalie's father decided to sell everything and go to Texas. He put up $30 per adult for passage and bought seed corn, farm tools, and food to last a year. He wrote out a contract with Power on the back of his marriage certificate. They sailed to Liverpool, where they spent Christmas 1833, then early in 1834 some 350 colonists, with families, goods and supplies, boarded the *Prudence* and *Heroine* for New Orleans; the ships were too large for Texas ports.

They hit a storm in the Bay of Biscay and the captain ordered everyone below. Rosalie, a lighthouse girl who was not afraid of the storm, hid so she could watch "the play of the elements." On the way over, her five-year-old sister Elizabeth, a favorite of the captain, suffered a sunstroke and died. She was buried at sea.

In April 1834, a dark pallor hung over New Orleans, stricken with cholera, as pots filled with pitch were burned to ward off noxious air. So many died they were buried in trenches. In May 1834, the Power colonists sailed for Texas on two schooners. Both ran aground trying to thread through the sandbars and mudflats that clogged the Aransas Pass channel, then cholera broke out and many died. Rosalie's father took the body of a child to bury it in the sand of St. Joseph's Island.

The colonists were landed at the port of El Copano where a customs house stood by the bay. Rosalie's father came down with fever; he was so ill he had to be put ashore on a feather bed. On the beach, Mrs. Hart put up pitchforks to use as tent poles to make a shade of bedclothes. The sun was so hot the ground burned their feet. Thomas Hart told his wife he was going to die and begged her to keep the children from bad company. "I was sick and lying on the pallet with him when he died," Rosalie wrote. "I thought at first he was only sleeping, but when I tried to awaken him I found he was dead." They buried him, wrapped in a blanket, in the sand.

"We were in a strange country, thousands of miles from friends and relations, on a sand beach exposed to the burning heat." Compared to the green fold of hills of Ireland,

Rosalie B. Hart Priour came to Texas from Wexford, Ireland with her immigrant parents.

this must have looked like the end of the world. A company of Mexican soldiers stationed at the Copano customs house refused to let them move inland for fear of spreading the cholera. After two weeks, they were allowed to travel by oxcart to the old mission at Refugio. There were about four crude houses in the settlement. The abandoned church was being used as a warehouse, filled with corn, for a Mexican cavalry unit.

Mrs. Hart piled their belongings to make a lean-to next to the mission walls. "It was not very comfortable, but it was the best we could do." Some came down with fever and Mrs. Hart nursed the sick; Rosalie, age 9, did the cooking and taking care of her little sister. Many died; because there was no wood for coffins, they were buried in blankets. "It was dreadful to look at them after death; their eyes were wide open and clear as crystal."

In 1835, her mother married John James, a prominent widower with two young sons, then came the Revolution and James joined Capt. Philip Dimmitt's company at the fortress of La Bahia (Rosalie calls it "Labardee") at Goliad. A third of Dimmitt's 92 men were Irish, from San Patricio or Refugio. This is where the first flag of the revolution was flown. Nicholas Fagan, also from Wexford, cut a sycamore pole to hoist a flag with a severed hand holding a sword, meaning: "I would rather cut off my arm than bow to the orders of a dictator."

This was the beginning of the Runaway Scrape: flight and fight. Men with oxcarts came to take women and children to Victoria to safety. They took food for two days, a coffee pot, frying pan and change of clothing. The women put feather beds on the wagons for the sick. "It was a sorrowful sight to see so many women and children driven from their homes."

Rosalie's stepfather at Goliad was one of the signers of the first declaration of independence. On March 27, 1836, he was massacred with Fannin's men, along with some 400 Texas prisoners, an example to the rest. As Rosalie learned later, when the men realized they were to be shot, some began to plead until Robert Fenner yelled, "Don't take on so, boys; if we have to die, let's die like men."

Rosalie learned of the massacre from a survivor. "One who escaped (William Hunter) told us he had seen my stepfather shot down with Fannin's men." After the massacre, the Harts went to Lavaca Bay, boarded a schooner and landed at Mobile. They were in Alabama while Texas independence was being decided on the battlefield at San Jacinto.

ROSALIE'S STORY — 2

Rosalie Hart saw the body of her younger sister sewn into a sail-canvas bag and buried at sea on the wide ocean. She saw her father Thomas Hart buried in the sand by Copano Bay, a cholera victim, with other Irish colonists bound for the Power-Hewetson colony at Refugio.

The confrontation with death was not over. In 1835, during the Texas Revolution, her mother's second husband was slain in the massacre at Goliad. Rosalie, her mother Elizabeth and younger sister evacuated to Mobile, Ala., while the issue of Texas independence was being decided. In Mobile, Rosalie's sister Mary Ann died of fever. Of what had been a large family, only Rosalie and her mother were left.

Rosalie went to boarding school at the Convent of the Visitation of the Blessed Virgin while Mrs. Hart traveled back to Texas. In 1844, Rosalie married Jean Marie Priour, a Breton who emigrated to Mobile, and they had three children in three years.

Mrs. Hart agreed to take a load of goods for sale in Texas on commission. She planned to open a store. Rosalie left in April 1848 to join her mother in Corpus Christi. Mrs. Hart's first store was in Zachary Taylor's old headquarters on Water Street, then she built her own shellcrete building nearby.

The day before Rosalie arrived at Corpus Christi, "The Indians killed a man named Long Scotty and a Mexican about nine miles from town . . . The town was a scene of excitement and terror, the inhabitants making preparations to take refuge in a large brick building surrounded by a brick wall known as the Mann warehouse."

Rosalie's husband (she called him Mr. Priour) moved to Corpus Christi and bought land near town at the Salt Lake. Her mother returned to Mobile for another supply of goods. On May 31, 1857, Elizabeth Hart was on the steamer *Louisiana* when the ship caught fire and burned. Thirty-five passengers were killed, but Mrs. Hart, who was 65, saved herself and others by launching a lifeboat.

The Civil War forced Mrs. Hart to close her store; the blockade made it impossible to get goods. She moved to her ranch on the Aransas River. In August 1862, Rosalie and children were at her mother's ranch when Lt. Kittredge sailed four Union warships into Corpus Christi Bay. Kittredge landed a shore party of sailors and marines; they were repulsed by Confederate forces, then Kittredge's ships began to shell the city.

Rosalie heard of the evacuation of the city from Mr. Priour, who had stayed behind. "You could see in every direction women and children running to the country loaded with chickens, wash tubs, pots, kettles and every imaginable article they could carry."

Rosalie, 25 miles away, could hear the bombardment, which sounded like thunder or heavy furniture being moved in a distant room. "We sat in a hollow near the river where we could hear every shot fired, as the river emptied into the bay and the sound followed the water."

This was a time of drought and misery and Rosalie's energy was focused on survival. At her mother's ranch, Rosalie taught school in return for whatever provisions the neighbors could supply. Her mother died on Dec. 20, 1863. There was no lumber to make a coffin. They tore off planks

Rosalie B. Hart Priour wrote about Civil War hardships in Corpus Christi in her memoirs.

from the house to use. They buried her under a large live oak by a field, a place she had picked herself.

Rosalie walked four miles to teach school. She became so exhausted from work and anxiety that she hardly had enough strength to ring the school bell. "When I could no longer stand to walk so far and teach, I had bedclothes taken to the schoolhouse and slept on benches. I kept the youngest of the children with me. We would go to the school every Monday morning and remain there until Friday evening."

After her mother's death that winter, Rosalie decided to take the children back to Corpus Christi. There was one ferry operating on the Nueces River, at San Patricio, and the roads were nearly impassable. It was cold and sleeting. They camped out in the elements, shivering in the dark, and Rosalie was so weighed down with grief and worry that "I longed to rest in my grave from all the troubles of life."

In Corpus Christi, Rosalie taught school in the building where her mother had kept her first store, while the family lived at the Salt Lake. Confederate soldiers drove cattle there to slaughter for meat. Mr. Priour would go to Caney (Matagorda Peninsula) for a load of corn or Austin for flour. When her oldest son Julian turned 18, he was conscripted into the local militia. And so the time of the war passed . . .

Rosalie Bridget Hart Priour died on Aug. 24, 1903. She was buried next to her mother on the ranch at Papalote. Rosalie left a large family, a contrast with her mother. All of Elizabeth's eight children except for Rosalie died young — of whooping cough, sunstroke, yellow fever. Only one of Rosalie's nine children died in infancy. Rosalie's oldest son Julian was a dairyman in Corpus Christi. Theodore became a rancher; Ambrose worked for a time as a newspaperman with Eli Merriman; Isadore became a rancher in Kerr County; Frances married James Hatch; Rose married Professor J. J. Charlier; Elizabeth married George Craven, a rancher in Bee County. The most famous was her second son, John M. Priour, a born naturalist with a vast knowledge of wildlife. A hunting trip with John Priour was the basis of the book "A Man From Corpus Christi" (reprinted by Copano Bay Press in 2008).

The story of the Hart family, the story of troubles and travails of the Irish who came to Texas with James Power, the story of Corpus Christi during Civil War times, are given poignant reality in the memoirs written by Rosalie Bridget Hart Priour, a young girl who left Wexford, Ireland for Texas in 1833, a survivor of her parents' dreams.

Information for these columns was taken in part from the autobiography of Rosalie B. Hart Priour, "The Adventures of a Family of Emmigrants Who Emmigrated to Texas in 1834" (her spelling). An account of this family, "Of Pride and Pioneers," written by Sally Robeau, and Hobart Huson's "Refugio" were instructive.

NORTHER

What is a norther? J. Frank Dobie wrote that weather forecasters never use the term, preferring cold wave or cold spell, but it is a term familiar to all Texans. Northers, said Dobie, blow the world inside out and freeze the lining, cold enough to freeze the horns off a brass billy goat. Another Texas writer from the 19th Century, Alex Sweet, said the thermometer falls rapidly during a norther, sometimes 40 degrees in an hour. A man in Austin, wrote Sweet, "saw the thermometer fall three feet in two seconds — off a nail."

Whether they are called cold waves, northers or blizzards, the worst to hit Texas, in the recorded memory of man, came in the middle of a Saturday night on Feb. 13-14, 1899. It swept down into Texas and within hours temperatures dropped to the lowest the state had ever seen. It was fiercely cold. The temperatures are hard to believe, but they were well-reported at the time. In the Panhandle, temperatures plunged to 31 degrees *BELOW* zero at Tulia. The temperatures dropped to 23 degrees *BELOW* at Abilene, 16 degrees below at Denison, 11 degrees below at Dallas, and four below at San Antonio. The oasis of warmth in the state was at Corpus Christi, which registered a balmy 11 degrees above zero.

It was stone cold around the country. Trains were stalled, causing "coal famines" in the frozen cities. "There is great suffering," the *Caller* reported, "especially among the poor in New York and other large cities where the cold is the

37

worst known in decades." Some people were found frozen to death while others were burned to death. Pot-bellied stoves, the main source of heat in many homes, were loaded up with coal, if the occupants had it, or wood. The fires were stoked until the stoves glowed red-hot. There were tragic accidents caused by people trying to get warm by crowding in too close. In Corsicana, a 10-year-old girl burned to death when she stood too close to a hot stove. In Alice, a woman was burned to death when her dress brushed against a stove and ignited. There were similar stories from all over.

The *Laredo Times* reported that many thousands of lambs and other livestock were frozen to death on the range. The *San Antonio Express* reported that "for the first time in human memory, the San Antonio River was turned into a cake of ice of sufficient thickness to hold human weight."

Capt. Andrew Anderson, who came to Corpus Christi with his parents in 1852, got caught in that terrible blizzard.

"We were 50 miles down Laguna Madre (when the storm hit). We were iced in. The Laguna had frozen over. It was snug and warm in the cabin (of the boat) all night, but in the morning we couldn't get the cabin door open. By chopping with a hatchet we were able to open it, and what a sight we beheld. There was snow and ice over the sails and rigging. It was impossible to move them. After much beating and shaking of the canvas, however, we were able to hoist the sails. Then we went to work on the anchor, and finally got that loose. It was so intensely cold we had to stop every little while and get a drink of hot coffee. Finally we started out with a head wind. We got up 25 or 30 miles, as the wind was rather favorable, and anchored at sundown. We had to climb the hoops around the masts to get the sails down that night . . . It was about noon when we reached the bay and the wind died down. We had to pole in from the beacon to the wharf.

"During this same terrible cold spell, a fellow in an open boat with vegetables from Ingleside landed in front of my house (on Water Street). There was so much steam from the water he couldn't see anything, and so he anchored. He was so cold he didn't see how he could live if he remained on the boat. So he jumped overboard, thinking he would just as soon freeze to death in the water as in the boat. After swimming a ways he was able to walk. Reaching shore, he asked me to go out to the boat and get another fellow off, who had remained behind. The bay was frozen out 30 or 40 feet from shore; my skiff was on top of the ice, and the oars were about six inches thick with the ice. We found the man on the boat nearly gone, just sitting huddled up, covered with canvas; he didn't respond when we called to him. We pulled him off the boat and tumbled him into the skiff and made for the shore in a hurry. He just lay there in the skiff, appearing to be dead. But on shore they put some whisky in him first, and then some coffee, and brought him to."

The *Caller* correspondent at Alice reported it was five degrees above zero. At Tarpon (Port Aransas), the boat harbor froze over and people walked on the ice between the boats. Thousands of frozen fish, stunned by the cold, lined the shore. At Corpus Christi, according to the *Caller*, the blizzard killed all the cabbage and garden truck around the city . . . It killed the city's oleanders . . . It froze meat in the market; saws had to be used to cut it . . . It froze vinegar in bottles, ink in ink stands, and bluing in the stores (breaking the bottles) . . . froze the combs off chickens and froze "a bunch of goats to death back of town". . . froze the river solid at Nuecestown (near Calallen); people could walk from bank to bank . . . froze Nueces Bay from shore to shore;

Snowball fight on Mesquite Street in 1897.

a man who delivered mail from Rockport to Corpus Christi by horseback rode his horse across a frozen Nueces Bay . . . . It froze Corpus Christi Bay out past the piers; fishing boats at the wharves were encased in ice; boys walked on the ice as far as the Central Wharf bathhouse (past where the L-Head is today) . . . It froze seagulls, which fell like stones. The bay-freezing blizzard of 1899 was surely the coldest weather Corpus Christi has ever shivered through.

ADAMS BROTHERS – 1

Robert and William Adams came to Corpus Christi in 1852, the children of English immigrants attracted to Texas by Henry Kinney's land promotions. The Adams brothers hauled cotton down the Cotton Road and became sheepmen and cattlemen in Nueces and Jim Wells counties.

Henry Kinney, founder of Corpus Christi, distributed handbills in Britain and Ireland offering 100 acres of land for one dollar an acre and, with the purchase of 100 acres, a horse, yoke of oxen, 10 cows and a lot in Nuecestown. Robert Adams Sr. put down money for 100 acres. He and wife Maria and four children, including William and Robert Jr., crossed the Atlantic on the *Essex*. At New Orleans they took the steamer *Mexico* to Galveston, then the mail boat for Corpus Christi and landed in November 1852 at Ohler's Wharf.

The handbills portrayed Corpus Christi as a major city, but "Corpus Christi was a little ordinary place," William said. "It extended only about as far up as Artesian Square. There may have been one or two houses up towards the hill, but not much was built up." Robert's recollection was similar. "There were three little stores. Old lady Hart had one on the beach . . . Old man Noessel had a small store on Chaparral Street; and Norris had a store on the hill. There was a meat pickling plant on North Beach, then called the Rincon."

41

Robert Sr., a former railway inspector, wanted to farm, but the land he put a down payment on was not farmland. He didn't take up the land and lost his down payment. Adams got a job as a hired hand and moved the family to a farm near Nueces Bay. As oxen plowed the fields, Robert Jr. would lead them, resting when the oxen were turned. Maria Adams, a former seamstress, brought her feather bed from England, a silk shawl, and two cherished dresses. She was homesick; to cheer her up, Robert took her to visit English families at Nuecestown.

In 1855, Robert Jr., who was 8, went to work for Samuel Colon, a freighter. "Quite a bit of Colon's freight went to San Patricio and to Rancho Grande (across the river)," Robert said. Robert's job was to handle the oxen that pulled Colon's wagons. "One time Colon broke my leg," Robert said. "There were five or six yoke of oxen hitched to the wagon and some of them weren't very gentle. Colon told me to unhitch them. I didn't go to do it, and he picked me up and threw me down on the floor so hard it broke my leg. I crawled away under the porch. They didn't set my leg, just bandaged it. After a while I would walk with one crutch and a cane, but my leg would break time and again."

Maria Adams died in 1861 and William, the oldest son, inherited her feather bed.

During the war, Robert and William, 16 and 17, hauled cotton to Brownsville. With ports blockaded, cotton was taken down the Cotton Road and sold at Matamoros, providing cash to buy war materiel for the Confederacy. Robert and William each had four yoke of oxen to handle. After Union forces captured Brownsville, the cotton was hauled to other points on the river. "I drove an ox wagon from Banquete to Rio Grande City in 1864 loaded with cotton," said William. "When the Yankees got to Rio Grande City, the cotton was diverted to Laredo; here they crossed the river with it and hauled it down the Mexican side by ox team to Brownsville. I drove wagons loaded with cotton from Laredo to Brownsville in 1864, receiving $10 (Confederate) a month."

Robert Sr. arranged for Robert Jr. and William to tend sheep for H. A. Gilpin and Frederick Belden on Penitas Creek. The brothers would get a share in the wool profits and half the increase in the flock. William went back to hauling cotton while Robert stayed with the sheep for three years. He said he didn't see a house for a year and was not inside one for two years. He did his own cooking and ate nothing but meat. He made buckskin britches and shirts out of sheepskin. He didn't have a needle or thread, using an awl to punch holes in the sheepskin and ran strings through the holes. He found the buckskin soft and warm, until wet, then he was in for a miserable time.

In the fall of 1866, the father, Robert Adams Sr., returned to England for a visit; he took the youngest son John with him. On the return voyage, the steamer *Raleigh* caught fire off the coast of South Carolina and Robert Sr. and John were lost at sea.

After four years tending sheep, Robert's share of the increase gave him 750 sheep. Robert married Lorene McWhorter and they moved into a *jacal* built of mesquite posts with a palmetto roof. William built his own jacal when he married Sarah Dodson. William brought his mother's most prized possession, her feather bed, to the jacal. Robert and William became prominent sheepmen in what then was the northwestern part of Nueces County. In the 1870s, the brothers had 15,000 sheep. When the sheep era came to an end, the brothers turned to cattle.

In 1891 William bought a ranch near Alice and the partnership ended two years later, with Robert keeping the Tecolote ranch. William served as a county commissioner in Nueces County for 16 years and played a role, with his brother, in establishing Jim Wells County. The high school

Robert Adams arrived in Corpus Christi
in 1852 when he was a young boy.

in Alice was named the William Adams High School in his honor. William was interviewed about the early times in Texas when he was 93; he died a month later. Robert was interviewed when he was 94, between 1938 and 1940; he died in 1944, at age 97. His younger sister, Mary Ann Adams, who married Henry Monroe Hinnant, lived to be 108. She was known at the end of her long life as the "Queen of the Brush Country." Robert Adams in his 1940 interview said, "I went through a lot of hardships the early part of my life . . . People don't know what hard times are; they think they do, but they don't."

ADAMS BROTHERS — 2

William Adams — pioneer rancher, sheepman and cattleman — died in Alice on Jan. 12, 1939. The month before he died, he sat down with an interviewer and talked about his English immigrant family coming to Texas in 1852 and how they struggled to build new lives.

William, the oldest son, was six when the family left Liverpool. His brother Robert was five. They crossed the Atlantic on the *Essex* bound for New Orleans. William said the captain gave the boys raisins. The voyage lasted seven weeks. At New Orleans, they took an old black steamer, the *Mexico*, to Galveston and boarded a stern-wheeler for Indianola, and from there a small mail boat schooner brought them to Corpus Christi.

They landed on a November day in 1852. Rube Holbein met them at Ohler's Wharf. Holbein's father was Kinney's land agent in London. It was a new and strange place. William remembered the big iron grillwork front going up on Conrad Meuly's house on Chaparral. Corpus Christi, he thought, was a small, ordinary place. It extended to Artesian Square, with one or two houses up towards the hill, and on the bluff Col. Kinney had a place near Forbes Britton's house.

The Ohlers, Edward, wife and two sons, had a house on the bluff and a two-story concrete building where the Nueces Hotel would be built. Ohler's Wharf was in front of the house. The first school William attended was in Ohler's building. George Noessel, one of the town's principal merchants, lived on Chaparral. Father Reilly was the priest. The schools, William thought, didn't amount to much. The first he attended was in a house owned by a Mrs. Murphy, in the Gussett (400) block of Chaparral. In the next block of Chaparral was the government mule yard. The Army maintained headquarters in Corpus Christi when the Adams family arrived. Army supplies were freighted from Corpus Christi to as far as El Paso by mule teams. The young English immigrant men got jobs with the government at $20 a month, and board, driving mule teams. Each six-mule team wagon, said William, had a wagon master and teamster. Three years after William and his family arrived, the Army moved the headquarters back to San Antonio.

There were two very prominent men in town then: Forbes Britton, who lived at Britton Mott in the country, and Judge Webb, who lived at Avery Point. The place should have been called Webb Point, William thought, for all the improvements Judge Webb made there. He built houses and barns and cultivated several fields, which were enclosed with fences made of ebony. William recalled that Webb had many slaves. The Adams family, farming in a small way, lived near the Webbs for several years.

It was beautiful country when they came to Texas. From the Oso Creek to Agua Dulce, William recalled, it was all rolling prairie, with no brush or timber except along the creeks, where hackberry and live oak could be found. The prairie continued nearly to San Diego. William said you would think nothing of saddling up a horse and wherever night found you, unsaddle and go to sleep. William said he slept out many nights using his saddle for a pillow.

Before the Yankees came to the mouth of the Rio Grande, in late 1863, Brownsville was the only outlet in Texas for many thousands of bales of cotton. After the Yankees captured Brownsville, William drove an ox wagon from

William Adams landed in Corpus Christi with his immigrant family in 1852.

Banquete to Rio Grande City and then, in 1864, from the other side of Laredo down the Mexican side to ships waiting at anchor off the port of Bagdad. On the return trip, he brought back Confederate supplies.

Two years after the Civil War, in 1867, William and Robert, his younger brother, formed a partnership on a sheep ranch on the Barbon Creek in what then was Nueces County. The partnership continued for 26 years. As the sheep era came to an end, the Adams brothers fenced their land and brought in purebred cattle and they soon knew as much about cattle as they did sheep. In 1892, William bought a ranch near Alice and, two years later, the partnership came to an end. He married Sarah Dodson in 1867 and after her death, after 30 years of marriage, he married Nina Young.

47

William once attributed his long life to the fact that he didn't smoke and got drunk only once. "My first wife Sally was out in the yard waiting for me when I came riding up. I thought I might as well tell her the truth, and I said, 'Sally, I'm drunk, but don't you worry about it. This is the first time and it's going to be the last.' "

William was a county commissioner in Nueces County for 16 years; people called him "Uncle Bill" and he once said he never asked a man to vote for him. He was a leading figure behind the creation of Jim Wells County in 1912, serving initially as an ex-officio county judge. It was said that he was very proud of an orange grove behind his house and the high school in Alice bearing his name. William Adams celebrated his 93rd birthday with an open house on Jan. 12, 1939. He died nine days later following a stroke.

ADAMS BROTHERS — 3

Robert Adams died in 1944 when he was 97. Like his brother William, Robert related recollections of coming to Texas with his hard-luck immigrant family in 1852. Their parents came seeking a better life; it eluded them and took decades before their children achieved the success their parents crossed an ocean to find.

Robert, born in Norfolk, England, came to Corpus Christi with his family when he was five. They arrived in Corpus Christi in November 1852 and soon moved into the country. They lived on a farm at Avery Point. When they arrived, Army headquarters were located in Corpus Christi; supplies were carried on mule trains to forts on the frontier. Army sentries patrolled the edge of town, on the lookout for hostile Indians; Robert's mother would hear coyotes howling and think the Indians were coming.

Mrs. Gravis, a widow, kept a hotel. B. F. Neal printed the paper (the *Nueces Valley*). The Ohlers lived on the hill; one day Robert saw them boiling soap in an iron pot. "It was yellow and was sold in the town." Old man Kinghorn was a wheelwright and Jim Barnard kept a saloon. D. S. Howard and Col. Moore were digging a canal in the mudflats . . . "I went through there once with my father; they were mudflats sure enough. Everything behind the boat was just loblolly, thick mud."

The schoolteacher, Mr. Craft, taught in a red brick building on Water Street. A couple named Holthaus (he was

German and she was French) owned a bakery on Chaparral. On his first Fourth of July in Texas, Robert went across the bay with his father in John Dix's schooner to get watermelons at the Hatch place at Ingleside. Old man Priour (Jean Marie Priour) lived at the Salt Lake west of town, where he grew vegetables to sell. His wife was the daughter of old lady Hart, who had a store.

"The country was beautiful, with grass three to four feet high," Robert said. "It was wild grass that made good hay. Chaparral Street used to be full of wagons; there was a good demand for this hay for the mules and horses."

When he was eight, his father arranged for him to work as an apprentice for a freighter, Samuel Colon. When he was living with Colon, Robert gathered salt at the Laguna Madre. "When the water came in high, it filled all the shallow lakes, and when it receded the salt could be gathered. It was in small grains, about the size of peas. You had to take it out of the water, which was about two inches deep. We would pile the salt on the bank and let it drain, and later put it into sacks or buckets. The wagons used for hauling salt were drawn by six yoke of oxen. We would go up the old salt road, which ran to Nuecestown. Here it was stored in a small house to be sold. Most of it was exchanged, not sold. All of North Texas came to Corpus to get salt (during the war) for home use and for stock."

Robert left Colon in 1862 to work at the Holthaus bakery. That winter, when he was 15, he was sent to Victoria to get a supply of yellow sugar used to make cookies. They took two oxcarts; a man named Long drove one and Robert drove the other. "The road wasn't very good, and we had to ford all the rivers. One of these was the Guadalupe at Victoria. It was all I could do to keep on my feet, the current was so swift. Of course I walked alongside the oxen to drive them across. You had to whip them."

Robert, Mary Ann (Hinnant) and William Adams

He left the bakery in 1863 and moved to Casa Blanca. His father made a deal for the brothers to take charge of Belden and Gilpin's sheep on shares. "William stayed only one year, when he quit and went off; that left it all on me. I stayed the three years out. One time I didn't have any clothes or shoes to wear. I dressed me some sheep skins and made me a pair of buckskin pants and some shoes. I made them with my hands . . . Buckskin is warm until it gets wet.

But if it gets wet, if a norther comes, you do get cold. I never saw a house for a year, and was not inside a house for over two years. The elements were my roof and the wilds were my house. I did most of my own cooking for four years, and had nothing to eat but meat. I had no bread and didn't know what a vegetable looked like."

Robert Jr. married Eliza Lorena McWhorter in 1867; they lived in a *jacal*, a hut, at the sheep camp. He and William went into a partnership in the sheep business; when the sheep era came to an end, they turned to cattle. The partnership was dissolved after William bought his own ranch near Alice. In 1939, Robert Adams celebrated his 92nd birthday with a chicken barbecue in a grove of elm trees, hung with moss, on his Tecolote Ranch, eight miles north of Alice. He died in on Aug. 26, 1944 when he was 97. Among those attending his funeral was his baby sister, Mary Ann Hinnant, who lived to be 108 before she died in 1964.

The Adams brothers and other pioneers have been gone a long time. The world they found, and the world they helped to shape, doesn't exist anymore. But the memories of that world, of the way things used to be, survive. That past has a strong pull on us, whether we know it or not.

COLT'S REVOLUTION

The tale differs with each teller, though some things are not in dispute. A 16-year-old sailor relieved the monotony on a voyage to Calcutta by whittling a wooden gun. This was in 1830 and the sailor was Samuel Colt. Six years later, he got a patent for a revolving pistol based on his wooden toy.

The gun was considered more a novelty than a real weapon. The U.S. Army rejected it as impractical. Army arms purchasers could see no need for a sidearm that could fire five times. They noted its flaws: It was light and had to be broken into three components for reloading. The Army figured it would be difficult to juggle three pieces under battlefield conditions.

Colt turned to the new Republic of Texas. In 1838, he sent a gift of a pair of dueling pistols to President Sam Houston. The next year, George Hockley, colonel of ordnance for the Texas Army, rejected Colt's weapons. He thought the barrel would become too hot to handle and "the whole formation seems to be too complicated for use in the field."

The Texas Army wasn't interested, but the Texas Navy was. A Washington hotel owner whose son was in the Texas Navy wrote Memucan Hunt, secretary of the Navy, praising Colt's repeating pistol. In 1839, Hunt ordered the purchase of 160 of the five-shot revolving pistols and the same number of the carbines ("Lone Star Navy," Jonathan

Jordan), but only 50 of each were bought and 30 of the pistols were stolen.

The Colt pistols bought for the Navy were turned over to John Coffee Hays' ranging company. One account says Hays met with President Sam Houston, who told him of the Navy's pistols ("Texas Ranger," James Kimmins Greer). What was left of the Texas Navy had no use for them and the surplus Colts were turned over to Hays' Rangers.

The Rangers found a use for them. Hays and 12 men stopped south of the Pedernales River on June 9, 1844. A Ranger climbing a bee tree after honey yelled, "Jerusalem, captain! Yonder comes a thousand Indians!" In the ensuing fight between the Rangers and 75 Comanche warriors led by Yellow Wolf, Hays ordered his Rangers to "Crowd them! Powder-burn them!" When the fight was over, 30 Indians were dead, one Ranger killed and three wounded, including Samuel Walker. Most accounts say this was the first fight in which Colt repeating pistols were used. It is variously called the battle of the Pedernales River, the battle of Walker's Creek, or the battle of the Pinta Trail Crossing. Newspaper accounts (*Telegraph and Texas Register*, and the *Morning Star*, both Houston papers) describe the battle as below the Pedernales on the Pinta trace.

A. J. Sowell ("Texas Indian Fighters") writes that the first use of Colt pistols against the Indians came in a fight near Corpus Christi. He quotes an entry in colonizer Henri Castro's diary which describes the battle, but Castro's account includes many of the same particulars of the Pedernales fight, except he places it near Corpus Christi. One explanation could be that Castro confused two engagements that happened at the same time. The day before Hays ran into Yellow Wolf, Indians attacked Corpus Christi. Henry Kinney and 11 other men chased the Indians west of town where a pitched battle ensued. Castro may have confused the two battles. The diary entry was certainly wrong because Hays and his company of Rangers were up near the Pedernales and nowhere near Corpus Christi in early June of 1844. If Hays' Rangers fought a band of Comanches near Corpus Christi earlier and used Colt pistols, the action did not get the attention of newspapers like that of the Pedernales battle.

The basic result was the same. The Colt revolvers caused a revolution on the Texas frontier. While Colt may have invented the five-shot and later six-shot repeating pistol, the Rangers discovered its utility and thereby ended the advantage Indians had with the bow and arrows. The accuracy, range and versatility of the bow and arrow surpassed that of flintlock and percussion cap rifles and pistols. An Indian on horseback could shoot any number of arrows, while it was almost impossible to fire the long rifles from the saddle and hit anything. Rangers had to dismount to fire and reload. Indians would retreat out of range, taunt the Rangers into firing, then charge when their guns were empty. It was a tactic used over and over. The Colt changed the equation. A Comanche in the Pedernales fight told an interpreter that the Rangers had a shot for every finger on the hand.

In the Mexican War, Texas Rangers attached to Gen. Zachary Taylor's army wanted Colt's repeating pistols. Taylor urged the War Department to buy all they could lay their hands on. There weren't many. Colt had shut down his factory in 1842. He didn't even have one of his own pistols; he had to go out and buy one to use as a model to begin production again.

One Ranger who knew what the Colts could do in a desperate fight was Sam Walker, who had been badly wounded with a lance in the Pedernales fight. When a new regiment, the Texas Mounted Riflemen, was organized in Mexico in 1846, Walker was chosen to lead the company. On a recruiting trip East, he visited Samuel Colt and

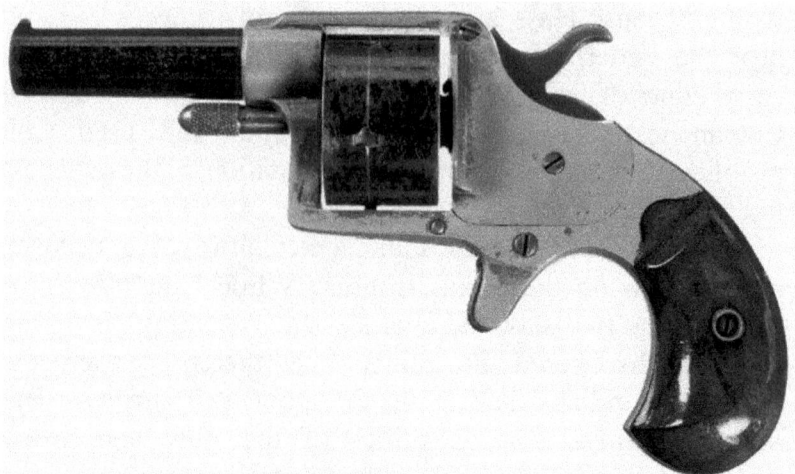

Colt 5-shot repeating pistol

suggested improvements to his five-shot repeating pistol. The result was a heavier gun, beautifully balanced, with a trigger guard and six cylinders. It was named the Walker Colt. They were in great demand by the Rangers in Mexico. Rip Ford ("Rip Ford's Texas") wrote that the men held a contest at Jalapa between the Mississippi rifle and the Colt six-shooter and the Colt threw a ball a greater distance than the rifle.

Not far from Jalapa, at the battle of Huamantla, Samuel Walker was mortally wounded. His last words were said to be, "I am gone, boys. Never surrender! Never surrender! Hand me my six-shooter."

HENRY KINNEY

Corpus Christi founder Henry Lawrence Kinney was a visionary and scoundrel. He was born on June 3, 1814, the third of six children of Simon and Phoebe Kinney at Sheshequin, Pa. He worked in his father's store until he was attacked by a man who accused him of seeing his wife. Kinney left for Illinois.

Kinney opened a store in Peru, Ill. In 1837, some accounts say Kinney proposed to Daniel Webster's daughter and was rejected, prompting him to leave Illinois. He had other problems. He took a contract to dig a canal to Lake Michigan; the project failed, Kinney went bankrupt and skipped, leaving canal workers unpaid.

Kinney arrived in Texas in 1838 and opened a store in Aransas City with William Aubrey, selling supplies to a Mexican federalist army at Lipantitlán and dealing in the Mexican trade. In 1839, Kinney moved his store to the bluff overlooking the old Indian trading grounds, which he called Kinney's Rancho, then Corpus Christi.

Kinney's trading post was inside a stockade. He hired a force of armed men and had three cannons for protection. Mexican traders came in with saddles, Mexican blankets, and crude silver bars; they carried away unbleached cloth, guns, ammunition, and tobacco.

In 1841, Texas created "spy companies" to counter incursions by Mexican forces. Kinney warned Austin that the companies were attacking trade caravans, killing merchants and stealing their goods. After Mexican forces killed the members of one band, others became hired guns for Kinney.

In May 1841, Philip Dimmitt opened a store at Flour Bluff to compete with Kinney. A Mexican cavalry unit raided Dimmitt's store and carried him to Mexico, where he was killed or committed suicide. Kinney and Aubrey, suspected of instigating the raid, were tried and found not guilty, though suspicion lingered that they were involved.

Kinney faced other troubles. The land he occupied was claimed by Enrique Villarreal, who had a grant for ten leagues of the Rincon del Oso. Villarreal showed up with a small army to reclaim his 400 square miles of land along Corpus Christi Bay. To avoid a battle, Kinney agreed to pay him $4,000 (two cents an acre).

In 1844, a riding contest was held at San Antonio between Jack Hays' Rangers, Comanche warriors, and Mexican vaqueros. First prize went to Ranger John McMullen, second prize went to Kinney and third prize went to a Comanche chief, Long Shirt. A man who knew Kinney said he could throw a silver dollar before him, with his horse in full stride, and pick it up leaning from the saddle. "There was nothing which could be accomplished in the saddle he could not do on his favorite horse, 'Old Charlie.' "

After the riding contest, Comanche warriors attacked Corpus Christi. Kinney and 11 other men chased the Indians 10 miles west of the settlement. The Comanche chief rode to the front, holding up his shield, daring them to shoot. They fired at him, but the bullets bounced off the tough rawhide. Before they could reload, the Indians charged. When it was over, many Indians had been killed and three Corpus Christi men. Kinney appealed to Austin for help and was authorized to raise a company of 40 men for protection.

Kinney, elected to the Senate, helped ratify annexation to the United States and helped defeat a bill to strip property rights from those who left Texas for Mexico during the revolution; Kinney argued it would deprive loyal citizens of Mexican descent of their homes and land.

With war looming over Texas joining the Union, Kinney promoted Corpus Christi as a place to concentrate U.S. forces. After Zachary Taylor's army landed in 1845, Kinney's spy "Chipito" Sandoval kept Taylor informed of the movements of Mexican forces. Corpus Christi thrived with 4,000 soldiers in camp. By the time the army left, Kinney was reputed to be one of the richest men in Texas. Kinney went south with the army, along with most of the men in Corpus Christi, and returned at war's end to a nearly deserted town.

Kinney had ideas. He started a slaughterhouse on North Beach, where mustangs were killed for their hides, and opened a beef packing house. When Brigham Young's Mormons were looking for a place to settle, Kinney tried to sell them land. Kinney bought surplus army wagons and advertised Corpus Christi as the best place to head for the California gold fields. The stream of 49'ers stopped when they learned that the Chihuahua route was very hazardous.

Kinney lobbied the Army to survey a road from Corpus Christi to the upper Rio Grande and, in 1852, he promoted the Lone Star Fair to help pay his debts. Kinney expected to attract some 20,000 visitors to the fair, hoping some would settle and buy his land, but only 2,000 attended. After the fair, creditors closed in.

Kinney tried to recoup his fortune by setting up his own empire in Nicaragua. He left for New York in 1854. He was jailed briefly on charges of violating the neutrality act but finally set sail on June 6, 1855. "I expect to make a million dollars," he wrote a friend. After landing, he wrote, "I am at last on Central American soil with 100 men. My force will be augmented in the course of three weeks to 2,000 men, when I shall move up country. I have a larger space to act in

Henry Lawrence Kinney in Washington about 1855. Photo by Matthew Brady from the Library of Congress.

than I had in Corpus Christi and the result of my undertakings in Central America can hardly be imagined." His supporters deserted him in favor of William Walker of Tennessee and Kinney barely escaped with his life. He returned to Corpus Christi in 1858.

In 1861, bankrupt and in bad health, Kinney wrote Abraham Lincoln, offering to be his foreign minister to Mexico. Lincoln didn't respond, so he made the offer to Jefferson Davis, who also turned him down.

Kinney and his wife divorced when he returned from Nicaragua; they had separated years before when she learned he had a mistress, Genoveva Perez, in Mexico. Early one morning in February 1862, he was shot to death in front of the house of his old flame, apparently by her new husband. From the amorous 18-year-old brawler in his father's store in Pennsylvania, to a midnight caller at the door of his former mistress in Matamoros, Henry Lawrence Kinney, in the end, had come full circle.

BASCULE BRIDGE

A mud slough separated Corpus Christi from North Beach. One day in the 1840s, wranglers hid and watched Comanche braves throw buffalo robes in the slough to keep their ponies from sinking in the mud. Later a wooden bridge was built over the slough, which was called Hall's Bayou. Where it emptied into the bay was a place where boys went crabbing and behind it to the west was a low flat salt marsh.

This all changed in the 1920s. The Rivers and Harbor Act in 1922 authorized dredging a channel 25 feet deep, 200-foot wide, from the Aransas Pass jetties to Corpus Christi, contingent on building a terminal, wharf and turning basin. Dredging the ship channel was completed in 1926. Constructing the wharf and transfer sheds was done by a Chicago firm, Summer-Sollitt, under the supervision of engineer Robert J. C. Cummings.

The big event came seven years to the day after the 1919 storm. The port was opened with a citywide celebration on Sept. 14, 1926. The port wasn't much then. There was the 25-foot channel across the bay, a turning basin, four transfer sheds, and the bascule bridge. The SS *Ogontz* was the first large commercial ship to dock at the port. The day after the celebration, the *Colonel Keith*, a seagoing barge, took on 100 bales of cotton for Beaumont.

While there was interest in the ships, the bascule bridge fascinated Corpus Christi. The town learned that bascule means "seesaw" in French, that the bridge was so finely balanced it took very little electrical power to raise and lower it. It was built by the Wisconsin Bridge and Iron Co. at a cost of $400,000. It was 121 feet long, 52 feet wide, and one end could be raised 141 feet in the air. It was painted black and covered with grease to protect it from the corrosive salt air. The U. S. Corps of Engineers opposed building it, arguing that a 97-foot-wide opening was too narrow, but the city was paying for the bridge and the bascule was the cheapest it could find.

The fascination turned to exasperation. When an approaching ship wanted the bridge raised, it would give three blasts on its whistle. When traffic on the bridge cleared and the barrier went down, the operator signaled with a siren for the ship to come on. If the bridge couldn't be raised, he would give four blasts, the danger signal. A locking device prevented the bridge from being raised if a train was crossing. Drivers fumed because the ships were way out in the bay, but the bridge had to be raised long before they drew near.

Nothing to do but wait. Children loved it; they could play by the cars and watch the ship. Adults hated it. Traffic would back up, sometimes 30 times a day. When it was raised, the bridge stayed up 10 minutes (or 20 minutes or more) for seagoing vessels and five to 10 minutes for coastal barges. It had to be raised more frequently as port traffic increased. It was raised 46 times in one day. In one year, 1950, it was raised 6,487 times. One bridge tender said the bridge became a ready excuse for wayward husbands who would say, "Honey, the bridge held me up."

For large ships, it was more than a nuisance. The 97-foot opening was a tight squeeze called "threading the needle." One accident closed the bridge for 10 days and part of the hull of the *USS Constitution* was scraped off when the ship smashed into the bascule in 1932. Ships brushed against the bridge fenders. It was such a tight maneuver for larger

The Bascule Bridge stands raised to allow the SS Ogontz to enter the turning basin on Port Opening Day, Sept. 14, 1926.

ships that some shipping companies refused to come here. A Dutch captain said "it scared the hell out of me." After several accidents, larger vessels were required to use tugs to thread the needle.

The bascule became inadequate as the volume of traffic grew, as the frequency of it being raised increased, as the size of ships grew. During the New Deal, the city tried to get federal funds to build a tunnel. In 1941, it pondered digging a toll tunnel, but the war put that on hold. One plan called for a high-level toll bridge, but the state said no. The argument in the 1950s was reduced to either a tunnel or a high bridge, with the town split between tunnelers and high bridgers.

Some wanted a tunnel like the Washburn Tunnel under the Houston Ship Channel. They were afraid that a high bridge would be a bigger, uglier version of the bascule, and argued that the bridge approaches would destroy historic homes. The city wrangled over the question for two years until the state highway department said it would spend $9 million for a high bridge, but not a penny for a tunnel. On March 24, 1954, the City Council voted to build a bridge. Mayor Albert Lichtenstein, leader of the tunnel faction, resigned in protest.

Construction of the high bridge began in June 1956. It took three years and four months to build. Four workers were killed in falls. One victim was a 16-year-old painter working beside his father when he lost his footing. His father watched helplessly as his son fell to his death. The sides of the cantilever truss bridge were joined on March 13, 1959. When the two met in the middle, the spans were off by a few inches, which was expected. One side was jacked up until the spans fell into line. The structure included 21 million pounds of steel, 134 million pounds of concrete, for a total weight of 155 million pounds. Harbor Bridge opened to traffic on Oct. 23, 1959, a big day for the city, like the port opening 33 years before.

Within two years, the bascule was sold for scrap and dynamite charges shattered its concrete foundation. Some hated to see the old bridge removed. It had been a symbol of the city for three decades. But for those who had spent too many hours waiting for a ship to creep across the bay to thread the needle, they were glad to see the greasy old thing go.

PADRE'S ISLAND

In 1804, a priest established a ranch on Isla de Corpus Christi. Padre Jose Nicolás Ballí obtained a grant from the Spanish crown for 51,000 acres, a third of the island, which cost him about $40. He got the price down from $50 by pointing out there was no fresh water on the island.

Padre Ballí's brother, Juan José Ballí, had land grants around San Salvador del Tule, the salt deposits that covered parts of what would later be Willacy, Hidalgo and Kenedy counties. Other Ballís had vast tracts along the Rio Grande.

Padre Ballí established Rancho de la Santa Cruz 27 miles north of the southern tip. Buildings and corrals were built of driftwood. Ballí stayed close to his parish in Matamoros and left running the ranch to his brother's son, Juan Jose Ballí II. The Ballís had 1,000 cattle on the island by 1811; the island began to be called Padre Ballí's island. After the padre died in 1829, his nephew ran the ranch for another 15 years, leaving after a hurricane hit on Aug. 4, 1844.

In 1847, John V. Singer shipwrecked on the island. Singer was the older brother of Merritt Singer, who invented the Singer Sewing Machine. John, his wife and two kids were sailing to the mouth of the Rio Grande on the *Alice Sadell* when they were caught in a storm and washed ashore on Padre Ballí's Island.

The Singers turned into a Robinson Crusoe family. They grew vegetables, ran cattle, and searched the beaches for salvage. The Singer homestead was on the site of Balli's old ranch. In 1851, Mrs. Singer (Johanna Shaw, of a wealthy Louisiana family) bought part of the island from Ballí heirs (the ownership of the island has long been in dispute). The Singers renamed the ranch Las Cruces.

Army Maj. William Chapman and wife Helen visited the Singers. Helen Chapman wrote ("Letters from Brownsville") that they went in a boat and "carried a table, dishes, meat, sugar and tea . . . We found Mr. Singer waiting with a little kind of handcart to which was harnessed a little old donkey . . . Their house had been built by joint labor of their hands and all their furniture consisted of wood thrown upon the shore. The children are beautiful and perfectly healthy. The wife is a great, strong, muscular looking, good humored woman; she helps him regularly with his outdoor work." John was much older than his wife; Helen Chapman noted he had already had one family and was starting another (John and Johanna would have six children on the island).

Singer had left the family home in New York to follow the sea. On a visit to New York City, he ran into his brother Merritt, who said he had an idea for making a sewing machine, but he needed $500; John gave him the money. John later got a shipment at Brownsville, a Singer Sewing Machine, perhaps the first to reach Texas. By 1860, Merritt's firm was selling sewing machines around the world. He informed John that he would get $150,000 in return for the $500 loan.

Not that John Singer needed it. The 1860 census showed him to be wealthy, with property valued at $110,000, a substantial sum then. With the outbreak of the Civil War, Texas officials invited Singer to move off the island. They considered him, a Yankee, a security risk living close to Brazos Santiago Pass.

Singer buried a cache of jewelry, gold and silver worth $60,000 to $80,000 in a stone jar, between two scrubby live oaks, on the ranch. The family moved to Flour Bluff, where other Union sympathizers were sitting out the war. Federal troops garrisoned on Mustang Island ranged down the islands, foraging for wood to build winter huts. They tore down the Singer ranch buildings and slaughtered Singer's cattle.

When the war ended, Singer went to reclaim his treasure, but storms had changed the landscape. After Johanna died in 1866 and another hurricane in 1867 covered the ranch with sand, John gave up and left for Honduras. He died in Mississippi at an advanced age.

About the time the Singers left, another family moved in. At the beginning of the war, a Baptist preacher from Alabama, Carey Curry, and family settled 17 miles below Corpus Christi Pass. Preacher Curry had two sons, Joe and Uriah ("Coot") and two daughters with husbands and families. Their place was called the Curry Settlement or "The Settlement."

The book "Padre Island" said Carey Curry was known for being resourceful: "Not a piece of machinery was in the Settlement, not a manufactured tool, yet Mr. Curry made flues, mixing the mortar of sand and lime, contrived home-made implements, and even made his own ox-carts." The family grew vegetables and found that the island often provided what was needed. After the war, a Yankee teacher named Lively taught school at the Settlement. One of the Curry children said, "Mr. Lively, I want to see your belly 'cause Grandpa says it's blue." Other families lived around the Settlement, including the Woods, Dinns, Griffins, Lynes, and Chapas.

In 1874, a beef packing house was built next to a channel at Corpus Christi Pass. This part of the pass became known as Packery Channel. Men at the Settlement worked at the packing house. After it closed and Pat Dunn began his

The Gulf shoreline of Padre Island in the 1930s, though the scene is timeless.

ranch, families at the Settlement drifted away. The Curry family held on until near the end of the 19th Century.

In 1931, a Brownsville man found a site 27 miles up from the lower end of Padre. Buried in sand were pieces of timber held together with ship hardware. He found a box stuffed with 1802 Spanish doubloons, Belgian coins, U.S. Army sword handles, bullets from muzzle-loading guns. It was supposed that this was the site of Padre Ballí's Santa Cruz Ranch and John Singer's Las Cruces Ranch. They called it the Lost City.

ARANSAS CITY

Before there was Port Aransas or Aransas Pass, there was Aransas City. It was on Live Oak Peninsula near the old Spanish fort of Aranzazu, at the south end of where Copano Bay Causeway is today. Aransas City looked to become an important port before politics got in the way.

Aransas City was James Power's town. The great impresario had a contract with Mexico to bring in 400 colonists from Mexico and Ireland. Mexico wanted Catholic families to move to Texas as a buffer against American encroachment. Power and James Hewetson would be granted vast tracts of land if they completed the colonization by 1834.

This became moot when Texas gained independence, except that Texas recognized existing land titles. Lands granted to Power and Hewetson covered the shores of Copano and Aransas bays, Live Oak, Lookout and St. Charles peninsulas, and Matagorda, St. Joseph's and Mustang islands. Between them, Power and Hewetson owned 250,000 acres.

Power was in New Orleans when a letter told him of the death of his wife Dolores, in childbirth, on Oct. 2, 1836. Power's sister-in-law, Tomasita Portilla, brought his two children to him in New Orleans. Soon afterward, on Aug. 19, 1836, Power married Tomasita and built a home and a store at Live Oak Point. The store was stocked with trade goods of the time. A wharf was built for ships to unload, and the Republic put up a customs house.

President Sam Houston asked his friend Power to sign a peace treaty, for the Republic, with Lipan Chief Castro. The chief and his retinue, in full ceremonial dress, arrived in January 1838 and the treaty was signed. That April, Power advertised the sale of town lots in the *Houston Telegraph & Register*, but two weeks later the paper said the sale was postponed "due to rumors circulating relative to the incursion of the Mexicans."

They were not rumors. A Mexican cavalry unit under the command of Antonio de los Santos arrived at Aransas City, one of many incursions by Mexican forces after independence. The store was plundered and Power taken to Matamoros at gunpoint, then paroled on the promise he wouldn't leave the city. After five months, he was freed.

Power returned to find a new town going up across the channel on Lookout Peninsula. He could see it from his porch. Adding insult to injury, it was on Power's "premium" lands granted him by Mexico. It was the work of one of Power's colonists, James Byrne, who called the town "Lamar" in honor of the new president of the Republic, Mirabeau Lamar, and Byrne built wharves and warehouses. Among the first settlers in the town was Seth Ballou, who ran a ferry between Lamar and Aransas City.

Political intrigue took a hand when Byrne asked President Lamar to move the customs house from Aransas City to Lamar. The struggle between the towns involved the great political rivals of the day, Lamar and Houston. Byrne was an ally of Lamar while Power supported Houston. Lamar, the new president, ordered the customs house moved. An angry meeting at Aransas City drew up a petition opposing the move, saying it ran contrary to the citizens' wishes, but President Lamar ignored it.

Still, in 1839 Aransas City looked to be a coming place. A man named Gideon Jaques ran a tavern. New merchants in town were Henry Kinney and partner William Aubrey. More troubling for Power, as events unfolded, was the arrival of land speculators and boiled-shirt lawyers, at a time when sharp lawyers and land grabbers searched for legal loopholes to claim rich lands. Power's vast holdings attracted interest.

Henry Smith, one of the lawyers, had been the provisional governor of Texas before he was impeached. Smith built a home at Aransas City and Power hired him to do legal work. Smith's son-in-law, George Ware Fulton, was made customs inspector and Smith's nephew, Joseph F. Smith, another sharp lawyer, showed up. The former governor and nephew acquired land certificates, which could be bought for next to nothing from soldiers or their heirs. The holders of such certificates could claim unclaimed lands in the public domain.

Smith's nephew concluded that Power's titles to the premium lands were invalid because he hadn't fulfilled his contract. If so, the rich lands of the coast were in the public domain and up for grabs by those holding unused land certificates. They only had to make a survey and stake their claim. The litigation that resulted continued for years.

Power used his influence with the Congress of the Republic to get the customs house back, but Aransas City began to decline and by 1847 it ceased to exist. Lamar, meanwhile, flourished. James Byrne built a church, the Stella Maris Chapel, which still stands, and he got the gunmakers, Samuel and James Colt, to invest in land on Lamar Peninsula, although the Colts never came to visit.

Henry Kinney left Aransas City in 1839 to found his own town of Corpus Christi. Benjamin F. Neal, who hung up his law shingle at Aransas City, became Corpus Christi's first

Live Oak Point is depicted in a painting in 1842. James Power's first town, Aransas City, was already in decline and within five years would be gone.

mayor. William Mann, a customs inspector at Aransas City, became Corpus Christi's wealthiest merchant. George Ware Fulton helped start the Coleman, Mathis, Fulton Cattle Co. and built a fine mansion, still standing, in the town bearing his name. Henry Smith, the impeached governor, joined the gold rush and died in 1851; Texas' first American governor lies under a sycamore in an unmarked grave in a canyon in California.

James Power moved to a new town, Copano, site of the old Mexican port on the western end of Copano Bay. He died on Aug. 15, 1852 with Tomasita at his side. He died before the land suit was decided in Joseph Smith's favor, clearing the way for the development of St. Mary's.

The town of Lamar eventually lost out to a new town called Rockport. Like Lamar, Aransas City, St. Mary's, Saluria, Fulton, Aransas Pass, Port Aransas and the village of Aransas Wharf on St. Joseph's Island, it, too, was located on what once were James Power's premium lands.

SHORT CENTURY

British historian Eric Hobsbaum calls the 19th Century the short century. He believes it began in 1914 with the start of World War I and ended with the fall of communism in 1991. By that measure, Corpus Christi really had a short 18th century, from its founding in 1839 to the collapse of the Ropes boom in 1893. In actual terms, that's little more than half a century, but a lot of history was packed into that "short century."

A short review. Henry Kinney built a trading post on the old Indian trading grounds in 1839. Kinney's Rancho was the capital of no man's land, claimed by Texas and Mexico. Kinney hired gunmen to protect the village from Indian attacks. In 1844, Comanche warriors raided the town and were chased by Kinney and 11 men west of town, where they dismounted for hand-to-hand fighting. Three Texans and seven Comanche warriors were killed in what, for its size, was called one of the bloodiest fights on the frontier.

As Texas moved toward statehood, war with Mexico threatened. The United States assembled an army in Louisiana. Kinney successfully lobbied Zachary Taylor to bring his command to Corpus Christi. The first units arrived on Aug. 1, 1845, their landing contested by rattlesnakes buzzing in the tall grass on North Beach. Thousands of canvas tents went up along the shore to shelter 4,000 soldiers, half the U.S. Army. After the army left in March 1846, Corpus Christi became a veritable ghost town.

After the war, after gold was found in California, Corpus Christi became a transit point for 49'ers going to California. Corpus Christi was made headquarters for the Eighth Military District and Kinney hosted the Lone Star Fair in 1852, hoping to attract 20,000 visitors. Some 2,000 showed up. The town was packed, wrote Maria von Blucher, with circus riders and German girls of low morals.

The blockade in the Civil War stopped trade; commerce in the town all but ceased. In the second year of the war, in February 1862, Kinney, the town's founder, was shot to death in Matamoros at the door of his former lover. For Corpus Christi, the war's big event was the battle between Union warships and a Confederate shore battery in August 1862. Residents fled to the country before the bombardment. After Union forces captured Fort Semmes on Mustang Island, Union soldiers raided Corpus Christi for lumber to build huts during a frigid winter. Much of the activity of the war related to the blockade, to efforts to disrupt the salt traffic from the Laguna Madre, and hauling cotton down the Cotton Road to Matamoros.

Corpus Christi suffered more than most Texas cities during the war. The city was in a ruinous state, the houses deserted, the streets full of mud and dead dogs. Food was scarce; many were on the verge of starvation. Confederate soldiers butchered cattle at the Salt Lake west of town. Thomas Noakes wrote in his diary, "War and famine and want is all we see, hear or talk about." In the spring of 1865, after one of the worst droughts ever, the land was green again and there was peace.

The city was beginning to recover when it suffered a yellow fever epidemic in 1867, which claimed one out of every 10 residents.

For Corpus Christi, the 1870s ushered in trade based on the sheep and cattle industry in the region. After the war, there were 1.2 million sheep in Nueces County and Corpus

Christi was a thriving wool market. In shearing season, the streets were crowded with big two-wheeled carts at the stores of wool merchants. And South Texas recovered from war with the sale of longhorns in Kansas. In the spring of 1871, the greatest cattle drives in history were made, with 700,000 head going up the trail. Then beef prices plummeted and cattle drives were not profitable. But huge profits could be made on the hides and tallow. Beef packing houses sprang up from Corpus Christi to Rockport. The wharfmaster at Corpus Christi reported the shipment in 1872 of 132,000 dry hides, 19,000 wet hides, and 1,225 barrels of tallow. Around the packeries were mountains of rotting meat.

This was a time of bandit raids and violence linked to the "Skinning War." After a drought and freezing winter in 1871, cattle died by the thousands. The skinning season began in the spring of 1872; ranch hands stripped dead cattle of their hides, which were worth more than the whole steer. Hide thieves worked the ranges, killing cattle and skinning them where they fell. Outrages during these violent times included the murders at the Swift Ranch near Refugio, the Morton store killings at Peñascal on Baffin Bay, the Nuecestown raid near Corpus Christi. The violence was reciprocated by vigilante riders who were not overly concerned about guilt or innocence. Harsh measures were meted out in harsh times. Capt. Leander McNelly's Rangers were dispatched to quell the violence.

Using Hobsbaum's method of measuring a century, Corpus Christi's "short century" ended with the end of the Ropes boom. A New Jersey tycoon, E. H. Ropes, arrived in 1888 and began to promote Corpus Christi as the next Chicago. He had access, he said, to unlimited capital. With borrowed money, he started the Aransas Cliffs development off Ocean Drive, built the Alta Vista Hotel, began dredging a pass across Mustang Island, and started laying track for a

A bird's–eye view of Corpus Christi in 1887 by Augustus Koch, a German-born mapmaker who applied his skills for the Union Army in the Civil War.

railroad. Ropes' activities set off a fever of speculation. Land that had sold for $8 an acre shot up to $1,000 an acre at the height of the boom.

Then Ropes' sources of capital dried up in a "money panic." People who paid stupendous prices for real estate saw their values drop to almost nothing. Ropes left town, his assets were sold for debt, and weeds grew on the grounds of the Alta Vista Hotel. Ropes died in New York in 1898, at 53; Corpus Christi hardly noted his passing. The town went into a period of economic stagnation that lasted 10 years, until about 1905, well into the new century. Which began, I guess, in 1893. This could get confusing.

THE ANDERSONS

John Anderson and sons were ship captains and bay pilots who lived by the bay and made their living from the bay. They had a good look at the unfolding of Corpus Christi's history, from the time of Zachary Taylor's encampment to building the seawall a century later.

In the 1840s, John Anderson, from Ystad, Sweden, ran a schooner between Mobile and New Orleans. When Zachary Taylor's troops pitched their tents along the shore in Corpus Christi, his ship carried supplies for the army. In 1852, Anderson married widow Hannah Bowen Yung and built a shellcrete house on Water Street, as close to the bay as he could get, for his wife, stepson, and son Andrew. In 1855, a second son, William, was born. The Andersons lived by the Ohlers. Andrew said Mrs. Ohler would sit on the porch and ring a bell for a slave to come. One slave, "Old Rachel," was caught stealing silver. She was taken to the jail whipping post. Andy peeked through the cracks as they lashed her, and "with each blow of the whip, she would give a big jerk."

Anderson built a flat-bottomed scow named the *Flour Bluff* to haul freight on the shallow bays and Laguna Madre. Young Andy went with Capt. John to Padre Island where John Singer, brother of the man who invented the sewing machine, lived. Singer was convinced oil was under the dunes and hired the *Flour Bluff* to deliver timber to build an oil derrick. The search for oil was interrupted by the start of the Civil War.

In August 1862, Lt. John Kittredge, commanding Union blockading forces, sailed his warships into Corpus Christi Bay to threaten Corpus Christi. The Andersons evacuated west of town. In the country, they could hear shells exploding. Afterwards, they returned home to find a hole in the roof and their old gray cat injured and missing an ear. The Andersons moved to Flour Bluff to sit out the war, staying in a salt warehouse at Anderson Point.

Young Andrew was at Flour Bluff when Kittredge came ashore. He gave the people bacon and coffee, knowing they were Union sympathizers. Andy said an old man came up on a horse, which Kittredge borrowed. "'I'm going to kill a deer,' he said. When he returned, he said, 'Boy, feed this horse good. I'll be back.' " The Confederates were tipped off. When Kittredge returned, he was captured and taken to Corpus Christi, which he had so recently attacked with shot and shell. People came out to see "that damned Yankee pirate." He was taken to San Antonio and given his parole.

In 1863, a French couple, anxious to get out of Corpus Christi, paid Capt. John Anderson $150 to take them down the Laguna Madre to Peñescal on Baffin Bay, from where they could walk to Brownsville and board a ship for New Orleans. They were intercepted by federal launches and captured. The French couple was sent to New Orleans while Anderson was held at the federal outpost on Mustang Island. He was freed and given provisions for his trouble.

When Capt. John Anderson returned with food given him by the Yankees, his loyalty was questioned. He was accused of aiding the enemy. His friend Bill Tinney overheard Confederates threatening to string up old man Anderson. Warned, Anderson escaped and went over to the other side, serving as a pilot for federal ships. At war's end, he was captain of a steamer that brought in three regiments of

African-American soldiers as occupying forces for Corpus Christi.

After the war, Andy Anderson was there when a mob lynched the killer Jim Garner. "A lot of us boys caught hold of the rope down near the end," he said. "He kicked and kicked. The crowd was quiet. Everybody left pretty quick."

Capt. John Anderson built a windmill next to his home on Water Street. He used four cannon balls from Kittredge's bombardment as ball bearings to turn the windmill. The windmill was used to saw wood brought up from the Nueces bottoms on the *Flour Bluff* or *Two Brothers* and to grind salt from the Laguna Madre salt flats.

Capt. John Anderson and his son Andy worked for Mifflin Kenedy, taking supplies by boat to the Laureles Ranch. They delivered hides and tallow from Kenedy's packing house at Flour Bluff to Rockport. After the storm of 1875, Capt. Andy carried relief supplies to the stricken city of Indianola. Will Anderson and his partner took over a former packing house on Padre Island. They killed birds for feathers to be sold in New York to decorate women's hats.

When the San Antonio and Aransas Pass Railroad, the SAAP, prepared to build a trestle bridge across Nueces Bay, Capt. Andy made soundings of the bottom. Because of bottomless mud, the bridge went up over the reef road. In 1880, when the jetty was built at the Aransas Pass, Capt. John Anderson's schooners ferried rocks for the project from Point of Rocks in Baffin Bay. Rocks from this place were used to build a breakwater in front of the Seaside Hotel.

Capt. Andy married Mary Grant on Mustang Island in 1890 and Capt. Will married Mary Wrather. Their father died on Aug. 19, 1898; he was buried in Old Bayview. He was survived by six children: Andrew Jackson, William, Charles, John James, Amanda Jane, and Lillie Hannah. Two years later, the Anderson windmill was pulled down. Capt.

Andy built what was called the finest yacht ever built in Texas, the *Lone Star Margaret*, launched by the Seaside Hotel with great fanfare in 1905. In 1913, Capt. Andy bought the pleasure boat *Japonica* and the *Gipsy* (his spelling). In retirement, Capt. Andy made sailboats and lived in a waterfront shack where he could smell salt air and watch ships slip into the new port. His company included two cats and a brown pelican named George William. The shack was torn down in 1938 to build the seawall. Capt. Andy died Oct. 10, 1949, three years shy of his 100th birthday. Tourists stroll along the bayfront today, down by Whataburger, where Capt. Andy and pelican George William spent their days gazing out to sea.

Captain John Anderson's windmill on Water Street was built in 1874. It was used to cut firewood and grind salt. The windmill was demolished in 1900.

The schooner Flour Bluff was built by Capt. John Anderson in 1860. It went down as a total loss in the 1919 storm.

The Japonica survived both the 1916 and 1919 hurricanes. She was finally scrapped in the 1930s.

Capt. Andrew Anderson built the yacht Lone Star Margaret for Maj. L. E. Campbell of Denver, Colo. The Margaret referred to Campbell's wife, Margaret Dent.

The Gipsy served as a tourist excursion boat on Corpus Christi Bay.

TEXAS CAMELS

When Jefferson Davis was Secretary of War in the 1850s, before he became president of the Confederacy, he had a novel idea to use camels to carry supplies to frontier forts in the Southwest, between Texas and California. Davis convinced Congress in 1855 to spend $30,000 to study using Arabian camels. Maj. Henry Wayne was sent to the Middle East to buy the camels. They were brought to Texas on the ship *Supply* commanded by Navy Lt. David Dixon Porter.

Wayne and Dixon made their way around the Middle East buying camels. They bought 34 one-humped and two-humped camels and hired five handlers to make the trip. After the animals were loaded, Lt. Porter wrote Washington that the camel deck was scrubbed daily and the whitewash brush kept going. The camels liked the salty taste of the whitewash.

They arrived at Indianola on Matagorda Bay on May 14, 1856. There were Arab handlers in flowing robes and 34 two-hump Bactrians, one-hump Arabians, and the cross-bred mule camels called "booghdee."

The people of Indianola turned out to see the exotic arrivals. It was as good as a circus. The camels had been on the ship for three months. When their hooves touched dry land, they went wild, jumping over each other's backs, crying out with joy. Mrs. Amelia Lewis (quoted in "Texas Camel Tales" by Chris Emmett) remembered the camels.

"They were decorated with red blankets. My sisters and I ran after them. On Sunday, everybody looked at the camels. A great sight."

Maj. Wayne demonstrated the animal's strength. A camel was made to kneel and two bales of hay were placed on his back. They weighed 600 pounds. People expected the camel to fall over, but then two more bales were strapped on the camel's back for a load of 1,200 pounds. To the crowd's amazement, the camel rose and trotted off.

"Lord almighty," said a man. "That would take two mules and a wagon, easy."

"Hell, four," said another.

Lt. Porter was sent back to the Middle East for a second shipment. Another contingent of 40 camels arrived the following year.

The first herd of camels left Indianola on June 4, 1856. Because the camel smell frightened horses, a rider was sent ahead warning that "the camels are coming." In reports to Washington, Wayne wrote that the camels had found good grazing and luxuriated in the Texas grasses. The caravan stopped near Victoria. A rancher's wife on the Indianola-Victoria Road, Mrs. Mary Shirkey, collected camel hair and used it to knit a pair of socks which she sent to President Franklin Pierce.

From Victoria, the camels went to San Antonio and finally reached Camp Verde, three miles from Bandera Pass, near Kerrville. From Camp Verde, the Army conducted experiments with the camels. In one experiment, 3,648 pounds were carried by six camels from San Antonio to Camp Verde. A load that size normally would have required two wagons pulled by six mule teams. Maj. Wayne was enthusiastic. He wrote Washington: "The camels thrive in this climate. Two full mule teams played out on the San Antonio test haul, but the camels sauntered ahead on schedule. Troopers are now accepting the camels (with less profanity). The mule is obsolete in the West."

In another experiment, camels were sent over mountainous terrain which wagons couldn't cross. Each camel carried 328 pounds and covered 60 miles in two days, with no sign of fatigue. The one experiment that caused the camels problems was in the Big Bend country where sharp flint rocks nicked the soft pads of their hooves. In June of 1857, a mission to survey routes to the West was ordered. The trip by camel covered 1,200 miles and lasted four months. These camels were kept afterwards in California and Arizona.

A Corpus Christi newspaper, *The Nueces Valley*, in January 1858 reported that, "The experiment of our government in introducing camels as beasts of burden has proved eminently successful . . . under every conceivable hardship, the camels remained sound in foot and body, and elicited admiration of their remarkable qualities."

After Texas took over Camp Verde in the Civil War, the Confederates used camels to haul salt and to carry cotton down the Cotton Road. Each camel could carry two bales of cotton. Col. John Salman "Rip" Ford, who acquired command of the camels, didn't have much use for them. Ford wrote in one report, "The camels have been sent to Guadalupe for corn. Two are reported to have died on the way. They can live best on grass; it is not certain they will live on corn."

After the war, the remaining 80 camels at Camp Verde were sold at auction. Most went to a man planning to run a mail and freight operation from Laredo to Mexico City. The Ringling Brothers Circus bought five. Eventually, many were turned loose to fend for themselves.

The lead camel driver who came over with the camels was a Syrian named Hadji Ali, which was shortened to "Hi

Jolly." He died in Arizona in 1903. There is a monument to him at Quartzsite, Ariz., that reads, "Hi Jolly: camel driver, packer, scout. Over 30 years a faithful aide to the U.S. Government." The last surviving descendant of Hadji Ali died in Rialto, Calif., in 1959.

It was said that the camels that were turned loose to live in the wild liked to feed on prickly pear leaves and mesquite beans, but they would eat anything, one man said, from a well-rope to a wheelbarrow. For years, wild camels were hunted for sport in South Texas. Hunting parties were organized to track them down and kill them. Dr. Oscar S. McMullen, a doctor in Victoria, quoted in "Texas Camel Tales," said, "About 1891, I was out near where Kingsville is now located, on the sand dunes, hunting burros. The cattlemen wanted the burros killed out as they were there in great numbers and depleting the grass. I was not a little surprised to find two old camels browsing around the sand dunes. Although I was there often after that, I never saw them again."

1883

In the first edition of the *Corpus Christi Caller*, published on Jan. 21, 1883, business ads did not list an address. It was a small town. People knew John Hall's tin shop was next to Mrs. Merriman's boarding house. Most of the town's 48 businesses were below the bluff.

Top firms in 1883 were bankers Doddridge and Davis, wool dealers Norwick Gussett and John Woessner, lumber dealer E. D. Sidbury, hardware merchant J. B. Mitchell, dry goods merchants Morris Lichtenstein and Julius Henry. Jose Acebo had a dry goods store on the bluff. A. A. Myers repaired carriages at a blacksmith shop on Antelope Street.

In a heavy rain, the town's dirt streets became almost impassable; big delivery wagons would bog down and caked-up wagon wheels had to be scraped. Prisoners were put to work digging ditches to drain streets into the bay.

Before the coming of electric lights, stores and homes were lit by candles and kerosene lanterns. Streets had kerosene lanterns, which the lamplighter lit at sundown and put out at sunrise. A city water system was 10 years away. People relied on cisterns to store rainwater. The cisterns often had a plank covering to keep out kids and dogs. In a drought, when cisterns were drawn down to the dregs, people bought water from water carriers called "barrileros." Volunteer firemen pumped saltwater from the bay. Fire wagons would roll out to stubby piers at the end of cross streets to lower their hose ends into the bay.

There were signs of progress in 1883. Western Union had arrived and the Tex-Mex Railroad was two years old. The town had a mule-drawn transit system.

Chaparral was called "Front Street." Mesquite was "Back Street." At the corner of William and Chaparral was the Berry boarding home. Mrs. Berry would send out a boy with a dinner bell on a pole to ring at meal times. Facing north, on the right side, was David Hirsch's wool office, with a Star of David, followed by the Crescent Hotel, with its famous Oyster Saloon. Next door was George Roberts' Favorite Saloon, with a billiard parlor and ten-pin alley. The Favorite advertised "choice liquors, fine cigars, and polite bartenders."

Between Lawrence and Schatzel, on the east side, was the Doddridge and Davis Bank. In this building was E. H. Wheeler's shoe store. Wheeler's sign was decorated with a big black horse; traders from Mexico called it "*casa del caballo prieto.*" The sign said "Boots and Shoes" and "*Botas and Zapatos.*" Next was Julius Henry's store, Friend and Cahn's Bank, Gradwhol's shoe store, Charles Parker's Orleans Barber Shop, Blumenthal and Jordt furniture store, and George Westervelt's ship chandlery.

On the corner of Lawrence was the St. James Hotel, run by William Biggio, a veteran of the Confederate Navy. The St. James had its own telegraph office and the mule trolley ran from the front of the hotel to the Tex-Mex Railroad Depot. From Schatzel to Peoples, east side, was Keller's Saddlery, with a white horse painted on the store. Then came E. Morris's drygoods and Norwick Gussett's store and wool warehouse. Gussett's place, sporting a rooster weathervane, was known to wool-sellers from Mexico as "*la tienda del gallo.*" Gussett, who had been wagon driver in Zachary Taylor's army, became a wealthy man with his own fleet of schooners.

On the west side was Max and Otto Dreyer's toy store and George Mew's ship chandlery. In the middle of the block stood a large mulberry tree that tempted boys to climb the fence to steal the fruit.

Between Peoples and Starr was Lichtenstein's first store. Up the street was Evans and Hickey grocery and commission house, the telegraph office, and John Woessner's wool warehouse (with a dance floor upstairs) and store. Across Starr Street was George French's wholesale and retail grocery.

Across from Lichtenstein's was DeRyee and Westervelt's drug store. In the middle of the block was John Hall's tin shop, which sold "Texas Girl" cast-iron stoves. Up the street was the Merriman boarding house and the Ranahan home, which was hit by a cannon ball during a bombardment by Union gunboats in 1862. Up the street was Artesian Square and Irishtown beyond.

At the southeast corner of William and Mesquite (often spelled "Mezquit"), Thayer's sold "Yankee notions," such as Montgolfier balloons. Next was John Fogg's Livery, where one could rent a hack or board a horse. In the next block was Uehlinger's bakery, which ran bread carts throughout the town. Between Schatzel and Peoples was Market Hall, with city offices and butcher stalls. Dances were held on the second floor and there was a watch tower and fire bell on top of Market Hall.

Facing Market Hall was Conrad Uehlinger's Saloon, with a hitching post for cowboy patrons. On the corner was a two-story building housing W. S. Rankin's grocery store and McCampbell and Givens' law firm.

From Peoples to Starr, east side, was R. G. Blossman's grocery, with a wagon yard in back. On the west side of the street, on the north corner, was Norwick Gussett's lumber yard. In the next block to the north was the Male and

In 1883, in the 600 block of Chaparral, on the east side, were John Woessner's wool warehouse and George French's grocery store.

Female Academy, followed by Royal Givens' home. On Taylor was the city's most imposing landmark in 1883, the Episcopal Church of the Good Shepherd with its tall steeple that could be seen far out into the bay.

Corpus Christi in 1883 was a small town, with 3,000 people, long before the population explosion, what William James called "the horrible numerosity of society." Almost nothing of this village remains, but the history is still there. The House of Rock is on Gussett's lumber yard; Sonja's Restaurant is where Headen's wool emporium stood; the Executive Surf Club is on the site of the Berry boarding house. The past is all around us, in the soil and subsoil, underneath the modern city.

COTTON ROAD

When Union warships bottled up Southern ports during the Civil War, the Confederacy opened a back door on the Rio Grande, which by treaty was an international waterway. Cotton was hauled by wagon, oxcart and mule cart down this road to Matamoros, the greatest cotton market in the world.

Wagons groaning with cotton from East Texas and Louisiana plantations converged at Samuel Miller's ferry on the Nueces. This was at Santa Margarita which for the last two years of the war was the seat of government for Nueces County.

The Cotton Road began at Alleyton, near today's Columbus, the terminus of the railroad from Houston, and ended at the Rio Grande, at the extreme end of the Confederacy. The Cotton Road ran 10 miles west of Corpus Christi along the old Matamoros Road. The cotton came down in a never-ending stream, with hundreds of wagons hauling thousands of bales, bringing back gold and war materiel on the back haul.

John Warren Hunter was 16 when he drove a cotton wagon to Brownsville, recounted in "Heel-Fly Time in Texas." He described Santa Margarita, with wagon trains loaded with cotton waiting to cross the river. On the other side were pack mules returning from Mexico loaded with medicine, guns and ammunition. "It was sundown when we rode into this vast encampment with its bright fires and incessant din of oxen and horse bells and shouts of herdsmen." The teamsters drank whisky, Hunter wrote, that would make a rabbit spit in a bulldog's eye and box his ears.

From Santa Margarita the road followed the route Zachary Taylor's army took when it left Corpus Christi in 1846. The next major stop was Banquete, where long trains of wagons and oxcarts passed day and night. Confederate troops camped on San Fernando Creek to guard this vital artery. The Cotton Road branched into several directions during the course of the war. For the first three years, the road ran south to Brownsville, then later turned west to Rio Grande City.

After Banquete, the next stop was King Ranch headquarters at Santa Gertrudis, a receiving depot for the Confederate government. Teamsters could replenish their water and buy supplies at the ranch commissary. Richard King was an organizer of the Cotton Road. Tom Lea in "King Ranch" wrote that from the ranch watchtower, King on any day could see hundreds of wagons loaded down with cotton moving south, the long trains stretching to the horizon and kicking up a tan ribbon of dust.

To the south came the Big Sands, known as the Desert of the Dead, *El Desierto de los Muertos*. For slow-moving wagon trains, getting through the sand belt was an ordeal of searing heat, with no shade and no good water. One freighter said it was "hell with bells attached."

Many of the teamsters were men and boys too old or too young for the army. Robert Adams and his brother William, 16 and 17, were conscripted and forced to take loads of cotton to Brownsville, for which they were paid $10 a month in Confederate currency. Each drove a wagon pulled by four yoke of oxen.

Sally Skull, a deadly gunfighter, was a freighter on the Cotton Road. Before the war, she made her living selling horses. With the war, she bought a fleet of wagons and hired Mexican teamsters to drive them. This was very profitable; cotton selling for 3 or 4 cents a pound in inland Texas sold for 50 cents or more a pound at Matamoros, paid for in gold. When Hunter saw Sally Skull at Rancho Las Animas, on the other side of the Big Sands, she was wearing a black dress and sunbonnet with a six-shooter hanging from her belt. She was sitting on a black horse as erect as a cavalry officer on parade.

This boom time in Mexico was known as *Los Algodones*, the cotton times. Matamoros was crowded with speculators, foreign agents, gringos buying and selling cotton.

From Matamoros, cotton was hauled 25 miles east to the fishing village of Bagdad, a shantytown filled with tent hotels and tarpaulin restaurants. Cotton was piled everywhere waiting to be lightered to foreign ships at the mouth of the Rio Grande. At times, as many as 300 ships rode at anchor waiting for cargoes of cotton.

A British military officer, Lt. Col. Arthur James Lyon Fremantle was on his way to join Robert E. Lee's army as an observer; he eventually watched the battle at Gettysburg from the forks of a tree. Fremantle landed at Bagdad on April 2, 1863. He wrote in his journal that for an immense distance endless bales of cotton could be seen.

After spending some time around Brownsville and Matamoros, he traveled up the Cotton Road with two mule drivers "much addicted to liquor." Fremantle saw many wagons loaded with cotton. "Generally there were 10 oxen or six mules to a wagon carrying ten bales, but in deep sand more animals are necessary. They journey very slowly towards Brownsville, from places in the interior of Texas at least 500 miles distant. Want of water and other causes make the drivers and animals undergo much hardship. We are continually passing cotton trains going to Brownsville, also government wagons with stores for the interior."

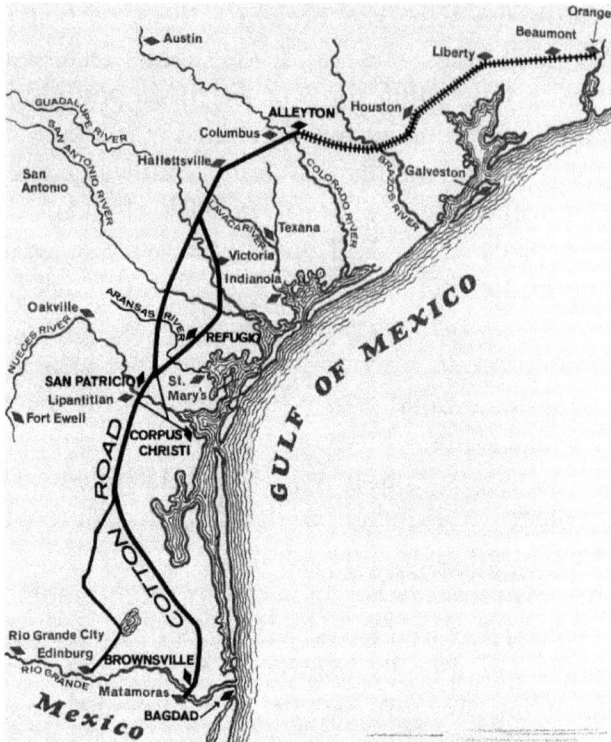

The Cotton Road began at Alleyton, near Columbus, where the railroad line ended. The route crossed the Nueces River and traveled west of Corpus Christi through Banquete and the King Ranch and on to Matamoros. Later in the war, the road shifted west.

After the Union army captured Brownsville in late 1863, the Cotton Road shifted upriver to Rio Grande City, where it crossed the river and made its way south along an old road running parallel to the river.

Throughout the war, a river of cotton flowed down the Cotton Road to be sold in Mexico for gold, which bought military supplies for the Confederacy. The end of the war spelled the end of *Los Algodones*. It was said that for years the route of the Cotton Road could be seen by sprigs of cotton that had snagged on the brush.

April 7, 2010

TRAMMELL MURDER TRIAL

J. M. "Scotty" Jetton, an oil-lease gatekeeper on King Ranch property on the Laguna Madre at Flour Bluff, was shot to death on Feb. 28, 1941. His drinking buddy, a one-armed fence-rider for King Ranch, Phillip Trammell, was indicted for the crime.

Sheriff John B. Harney's officers found that in a gun fight, Trammell was shot in the shoulder by Jetton's shotgun while Jetton was killed by two shots from Trammell's rifle. Trammell told friends, "He got me but I got him." What sparked the fight was never revealed.

The trial began the day after the attack on Pearl Harbor. Judge George Westervelt called a recess so jurors could hear President Roosevelt's "day of infamy" speech. Two walls of Jetton's cabin were reconstructed in the courtroom to show what happened. On Dec. 13, 1941, jurors found Trammell guilty of murder. He was sentenced to 99 years. The conviction was overturned on appeal, but because many of those involved were in the military overseas it was not retried for six years.

In 1947, in the second trial, Rev. Lester Roloff arrived to protest Judge Cullen Briggs' decision to let jurors have a beer with their supper. Roloff told the judge that "after a person drinks one bottle of beer, you can put a needle in his big toe and find alcohol there." Judge Briggs wouldn't back down, but he told the bailiff to allow each juror only one bottle of beer. This time, Trammell was found not guilty.

The late Cecil Burney was an assistant prosecutor in the trial. He later wrote about it for the Nueces County Historical Commission Bulletin.

FLORESVILLE HANGING

In 1897, a farm worker, Maximo Martinez, killed three members of a family near Floresville with an ax. He was arrested in Duval County, returned to Floresville for trial, convicted and sentenced to be hanged. On hanging day, they gave the condemned man whisky in a tin cup and kept refilling the cup. From his jail cell, Martinez made speeches and sang songs.

W. L. Wright, who was deputy sheriff before he became a Texas Ranger, was there. He later told Bob McCracken of the *Caller*: "It was a gala day in Floresville when the murderer was hanged. Everybody turned out; there must have been 4,000 people there."

Salesmen worked the crowd. A gramophone salesman played records. A fire extinguisher salesman put up a small model house in the street, then set it afire so he could put it out with his extinguisher. Some people didn't know it was a demonstration and began to run. One man yelled, "Keep your seat; there ain't no fire!" Another ran by, shouting, "You're a damned liar!"

At the scaffold, Capt. W. L. Wright put a black cap on the condemned man's head and fixed the rope. Wright forgot to move away from the trapdoor. He managed to jump aside at the last second when it was sprung. Wright said it would have been like the two Rangers who hanged a man in Brownsville and forgot to get off the trap door. "When the trap was sprung, they went through it, too; fell six feet to the ground."

THE COLLECTORS

I collect books, but I am not a book collector. Yes, that makes sense. I am not a serious collector, though I share one thing with the serious collector, the love of books. If some cataclysm destroyed my house, I would hope my bookshelves would be left untouched. And as someone who loves books, I understand what motivates the serious collector. That is the desire to own, to hold in one's hand, a rare book, or letter, or original manuscript. There is no substitute for having the real thing, to touch it, to hold it, to own it. We owe a lot to these collectors. It has been said that societies that forget their past have no future. Well, the serious collectors help make sure we do not forget the past.

A new book has been published by the Book Club of Texas titled "Collecting Texas," with essays on Texana collectors and the creation of research libraries. The book was edited by Thomas Kreneck, Associate Director for Special Collections & Archives at Texas A&M University-Corpus Christi, and Gerald Saxon, Dean of the Library at the University of Texas at Arlington.

"Texana," the authors write, covers all material dealing with Texas history. "No place on earth," they write, "has a more intriguing past," which explains why Texana has had such a lure for serious collectors, such as Swante Palm, the Swedish immigrant who gave most of his 12,000 volumes to the University of Texas at Austin.

Another great collector was Earl Vandale, the subject of a book by J. Evetts Haley, "Earl Vandale on the Trail of Texas Books." Another was Thomas W. Streeter, who sold his Texana collection to Yale for $275,000. That collection includes Alvar Nuñez Cabeza de Vaca's *La Relacion y Commentarios*," published in Spain in 1555.

The book has two chapters of particular interest. One is by Al Lowman, one of the state's top book collectors, who

The late Dan Kilgore (left) began collecting in 1947. Book collector Al Lowman grew up in Nueces County.

grew up on a farm in Nueces County in the 1930s. Lowman said the two big events in his childhood were the coming of electricity and the arrival of the county bookmobile.

Another chapter is about the late Dan Kilgore, public accountant, historian and collector of all things Texana. At an auction in 1947, Kilgore acquired several volumes on local history, including Mrs. S. G. Miller's "Sixty Years in the Nueces Valley" and he was hooked on collecting and on South Texas history.

Kilgore's collection, assembled over 35 years, amounted to 10,000 printed items and 45 linear feet of manuscript files. It was valued at $385,000. Today it comprises the Kilgore Collection at Texas A&M University-Corpus Christi, a valuable resource which students and historians will draw on for their researches.

The authors note in the introduction that private collectors like Dan Kilgore have been crucial to the creation of the holdings of research libraries, so vital to the preservation of history. The single-minded pursuit by the serious collectors may be a form of gentle madness, but it helps ensure we do not forget the past, that the record is preserved, that the memory bank is filled.

BANKS' INVASION

After Vicksburg fell on July 4, 1863, a Union army, suddenly without a job, was given the task of invading Texas to close the Confederacy's back door on the Rio Grande.

Cotton went through that back door to be sold for gold, which helped sustain the Confederacy. Another reason to invade was the possibility that French forces in Mexico might make common cause with the Confederacy. A Union presence would discourage any such alliance. In command of the invasion was Gen. Nathaniel P. Banks, whose orders made it clear the expedition had political purposes: "There are important reasons why our flag should be restored in some part of Texas with the least possible delay."

Banks' first move at Sabine Pass ended in defeat, so he turned to the back door on the Rio Grande. He brought up a 7,500-man force made up of veterans from the Vicksburg campaign. Units included the 13th and 15th Maine, 94th Illinois, 20th Wisconsin, 19th and 20th Iowa.

The 13th Maine marched to the levee in a pouring rain. Units boarded 13 transports, escorted by gunboats, on Oct. 23, 1863. On board the *Clinton* there was not enough room for all to lie down; some slept sitting up. A storm scattered the fleet, but on Nov. 2 they landed on Brazos Santiago without opposition. Soldiers of the 15th Maine raised a U.S. flag and Banks sent a message to Abraham Lincoln: "The flag of the Union floated over Texas today at meridian precisely."

Lt. Col. Frank Hesseltine of the 13th Maine ordered his men to strip and wade the Laguna Madre; their guns were ferried over by boat. As the naked men carried their clothes in their hands, razor sharp oyster shells cut up their feet. As they prepared to attack Brownsville, Confederate Gen. Hamilton P. Bee abandoned the city and retreated toward Corpus Christi. At Brownsville, Union soldiers slept in a cotton warehouse then moved into Fort Brown, Zachary Taylor's old Mexican War fort.

They were not able to shut off the flow of cotton; Confederates moved the Cotton Road upstream and over to the Mexican side, and Union warships dared not interfere with French and British vessels loading cotton in international waters.

With Brownsville in Union hands, the 13th and 15th Maine and 20th Iowa embarked on ships for their next objective: Fort Semmes, a Confederate strongpoint on Mustang Island. They landed at Corpus Christi Pass at sundown Nov. 16 and began the 18-mile march to the fort, each man carrying 100 rounds of ammunition, gun, knapsack, and food for three days. They were also dragging two heavy siege guns through the sand dunes on the island.

In sight of Fort Semmes at daybreak, they shot at Confederate sentries, driving them back. When a Union gunboat shelled the fort, the defenders raised a white flag. A man came out, waving in a friendly gesture, but he was shot; his arm had to be amputated. They captured three cannon, 140 horses, nine officers, 89 men, and a Confederate flag that had been presented to Lt. William Maltby on the steps of the Nueces County Courthouse at the beginning of the war.

Corpus Christi residents could hear gunfire. They worried about Corpus Christi defenders at the fort. Gen. Bee, riding in from Banquete, sent Lt. Walter Mann under a flag of truce to find out what happened. Mann was taken prisoner. Bee retreated north of the Nueces River.

The 20th Iowa, composed of farm boys from around Marion, Iowa, was assigned to garrison the renamed Fort Semmes to Post Aransas. It may have been punishment because Maj. William Thompson, commander of the regiment, complained too forcefully about having to drag the cannon through the sand. But Thompson wrote his wife that the 20th was given the duty as a mark of respect for the fine job they had done.

Thompson's men were industrious in getting wood to build winter huts. They tore down the Singer ranch house (Las Cruces) for lumber and made forays in Corpus Christi, pulling down houses for planks and stealing furniture.

The invasion force prepared to move on. A norther hit on Nov. 19 as troops were ferried across the pass to St. Joseph's Island. They reached Cedar Bayou, separating St. Joseph's from Matagorda, four days later. Confederate Maj. Charles Hill raised a white flag across Cedar Bayou. He wanted to know what happened to the men at Fort Semmes. A sergeant from the 15th Maine swam across to talk. After angry words, the major shot the sergeant and Union troops fired on and hit the major; his body was found in the dunes. (The Confederate account claimed he was executed without provocation under a flag of truce.) The Union troops crossed Cedar Bayou on flatboats brought up on wagons.

On Nov. 27 they reached their objective: Fort Esperanza. The massive earthworks on Matagorda near the town of Saluria were built early in the war by some 500 slaves. The walls were 12 feet high and 15 feet thick. The fort was armed with eight 24-pound cannons and one 124-pound "Columbiad" to guard Pass Cavallo.

Union troops fired on Confederate pickets, driving them inside the walls. They dug rifle pits and prepared for a siege.

*Gen. Nathaniel P. Banks commanded
the Union invasion of Texas in 1863.*

Cannon fire was exchanged on Nov. 29. A Union soldier foolishly stuck out his foot to stop a spent cannonball rolling along; his leg snapped like a matchstick and had to be amputated.

Confederates spiked their guns, burned powder magazines, and evacuated before the escape route was closed. It was bitterly cold as Union forces settled into camps. They had little to eat except beef by butchering cattle on the island. They had no tents. They dug holes in the sand and covered them with hides of slaughtered cattle.

In February, they were ordered back to New Orleans. Garrisons were left on Matagorda and Mustang to guard the passes, but they were pulled out two months later. The Confederates moved back into Fort Esperanza. Both sides must have realized that Banks' invasion was a sideshow and the war was reaching a critical stage where victory or defeat would be decided on the great battlefields of Virginia.

ISLAND SKIRMISH

It was December of 1862. Corpus Christi had not had much good news. Three months before, after the Union blockading fleet bombarded the town, many people moved inland to Goliad and Refugio. The feared Lt. J. W. Kittredge, who commanded the blockade, kept the coast in a frenzy with raiding sorties and cutting-out expeditions. He had been caught and gave his parole. Kittredge was gone, but the offensive striking power was still with the Union fleet off Aransas Pass and Pass Cavallo.

Confederate forces were thin on the ground that December. They seemed powerless against "Abe's abolition fleet." The Confederates hunkered down in earthwork forts on Mustang and Matagorda islands — Fort Semmes and Fort Esperanza — and in the port cities of Corpus Christi, Saluria and Indianola. The clashes between Union and Confederate forces mostly occurred around the passes connecting the Gulf to the inner bays.

On Dec. 5, 1862, Confederate Capt. H. Willke and Capt. John Ireland (who was later elected governor of Texas) took a sloop, the *Queen of the Bay*, to sound the depth of water at Corpus Christi Pass. Willke was the senior officer. They took seven soldiers from Ireland's infantry company, a captain of the sloop, Jack Sands, and three sailors. They measured the depth on the bar on the Gulf side of the pass (where Packery Channel is today) at 5½ feet and on the bay side at 3½ feet. Due to contrary winds, they spent the next two days in the pass.

On Dec. 7, they were chased by two launches manned by 22 sailors from the Union blockade ship, the USS Bark *Arthur*. The *Queen of the Bay* tried to escape, with the launches in pursuit, using sails and oars. The Confederates ran their ship ashore on Padre Island. The men of Ireland's company, crack shots from Seguin, clambered to the top of sand hills and opened fire on the Union men in open boats. They tried to escape by beaching their boats on Mustang Island, across the pass, and running for cover in the dunes. They fired back at the Confederates, who returned fire, killing one of the sailors.

As shots were fired, the wind blew the launches away from shore. Capt. Ireland secured one of the boats, in which he found a dead man, another wounded, heavy coats, arms and ammunition. The other launch, drifting toward the Gulf, was secured by Capt. Sands.

On Mustang Island, the Union man in charge of the two launches, Acting Ensign Alfred Reynolds, had been shot twice. Reynolds and another wounded sailor began the slow march up Mustang Island toward Aransas Bay to join the federal fleet.

The Confederates recovered the body of the man killed in the dunes. Capt. Willke's command returned to Corpus Christi without the loss of a man. One wounded man they brought back had been helping guide the Union launches. He was a civilian from Corpus Christi named Peter Baxter, an immigrant from Scotland.

Andrew Anderson was a teenager then. He had a different version of the story. He said the Union launches arrived at Corpus Christi Pass by mistake, that after the shooting started they tried to surrender. "As the launches entered the pass," Anderson said, "the Confederates on the big hill some 40 or 50 feet high could look down into the boats and shoot the soldiers. There must have been much bitterness by the Confederates because the federals were helpless and made every effort to make them understand that they would surrender; but little attention was given this and a number of federals were killed and the others captured."

Anderson remembered that the wounded civilian, Peter Baxter, had a great ring on his finger. "He said they had wanted to surrender but were not allowed to; he died from his wounds and was buried somewhere in Corpus Christi, probably in Bayview." The launches full of bullet holes lay on the beach near the Anderson home on Water Street.

Maria von Blucher, whose husband, Felix, was a Confederate officer in charge of coastal defenses at Corpus Christi and Saluria, wrote her parents about the skirmish. "The other day eight of our soldiers took two boats from the Yankees in Corpus Christi Bay and killed three Yankees, who were buried here. Captain Ireland and Captain Willke were our leaders. They were in a small boat reconnoitering Corpus Christi Pass. Realizing they were being pursued by two launches (the Yankee blockade warship was near the mouth of the pass), they landed and lay in ambush until the 25 Yankees were near. Then they fired, killed three, wounded the officer, put the soldiers to flight, and returned to Corpus Christi, safe and sound, with the Yankee boats, three dead, and a great number of excellent arms and provisions."

The following May, there was another skirmish on St. Joseph's Island (across from today's Port Aransas). Confederate Capt. Edwin Hobby, with 28 men, hid in the sand dunes and attacked three Union launches carrying 40 men who came to load a cargo of cotton from a beached blockade runner. When Union sailors came in for the cotton on the morning of May 3, 1863, the Confederates, hidden behind the dunes, opened fire. Capt. Hobby in his report said, "We could distinctly see the men in the launches drop

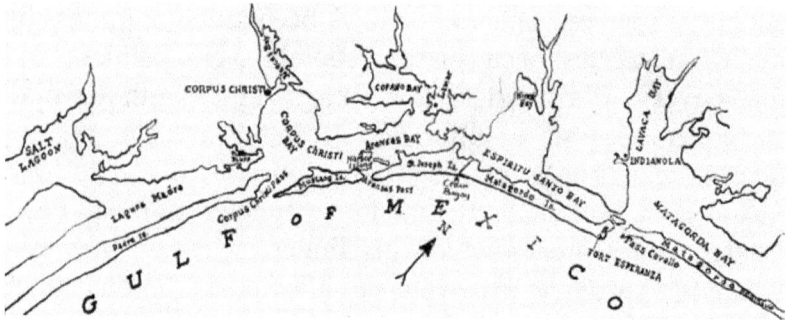

Union map of the South Texas coast shows the Salt Lagoon (Baffin Bay), Corpus Christi Pass, Aransas Pass and Fort Esperanza at Pass Cavallo.

their oars and fall as we fired. Several bodies were floating in the water . . . I do not think I am mistaken in estimating the loss of the enemy as 20 in killed, wounded and prisoners."

The action on the islands toward the end of 1862 and in early 1863 were "affairs" in the military parlance of the time, but for the people of Corpus Christi, who had suffered because of the Union blockade and the bombardment the previous August, the skirmishes showed there were limits to Yankee impertinence; they seemed to turn up exactly where you didn't want them to be. But Yankee "impertinence" was not at an end, not with Gen. Banks' invasion of the Texas coast coming that fall and the capture of Fort Semmes and Fort Esperanza, giving the Union control of Texas' barrier islands.

RANCH HOUSES

Richard King bought 15,500 acres of the Santa Gertrudis grant, for two cents an acre, and in 1854 he brought his bride Henrietta (Chamberlain) to reside in a primitive jacal at a cow camp on the Santa Gertrudis. They traveled back and forth from the cow camp to their home in Brownsville.

In 1857, King built a house on a hill between the Santa Gertrudis and San Fernando Creeks. Legend holds that King's friend Robert E. Lee picked the site. It was a low rambling house with that frontier essential, a porch gallery. It was enlarged to provide space for a growing family. The house burned on the morning of Jan. 4, 1912. The fire was believed set by a disgruntled gardener. The new ranch house was patterned after a Mexican hacienda and met Henrietta King's stipulation that the house should be elegant, yet comfortable for a man in boots. It was called the Big House.

A porch gallery was also the dominant feature on Martin Culver's house at Rancho Perdido. Culver was a free-range cattleman, who owned very little land and ran his cattle on the open range. After the Civil War, he bought Rancho Perdido (Lost Ranch) 12 miles northwest of San Patricio. Culver bought only 600 acres, but thousands of head of cattle carried his brand and he drove huge herds to Kansas.

Culver's ranch house near Penitas Creek was built by a former sailor, who was given a free hand to design the house. It included nine rooms and that long front gallery.

While it was called the lost ranch, the sailor-builder made sure the house wasn't lost, having it painted London purple with white trim. The old house reportedly still stands in a run-down condition.

John Howland Wood built his ranch headquarters at Black Point. When he brought his bride to the place, she said, "What a bonnie view," which became the name of the ranch, the Bonnie View Ranch. Wood was one of the first cattle kings of Texas. He founded his ranch a decade before King Ranch was established. The Bonnie View Ranch stretched from Copano Bay to the present town of Woodsboro.

Wood built a three-story Greek Revival house in 1875. The mansion included an observation deck so Wood could watch ranch activities. The restored house is still standing at Bayside.

Thomas M. Coleman teamed up with George W. Fulton, a wealthy meat packer, to found one of the great ranches, the Coleman-Fulton Pasture Co., which covered 115,000 acres in Refugio, San Patricio and Aransas counties. Coleman and Fulton became fierce rivals for control of the company, and they were rivals in house-building.

After Fulton built his mansion, he held a housewarming party one night in 1877. Among the guests were Coleman and his wife. On the way home, Mrs. Coleman reportedly told her husband, "If she (Mrs. Fulton) can have one, I want one twice as big." Work began on the Coleman Mansion on Chiltipin Creek. When finished, it looked like the Fulton Mansion, only grander. The Second Empire mansion, with its Mansard roof, in the heart of the brush country was surrounded by 25 acres of imported magnolias. After Coleman died in 1896, it stood vacant for years before it was demolished in 1930.

After Mifflin Kenedy and Richard King divided their ranch holdings in 1867, Kenedy bought the Laureles Ranch, sold that, then bought 400,000 acres of a new ranch, which he called La Parra (Grapevine). In 1882, Kenedy built a pier on Baffin Bay to bring in lumber to build a ranch house. The result was a two-story, clapboard house vaguely resembling a steamboat. In 1919, the ranch house was placed on rollers and with the help of 200 mules moved a few thousand yards to make way for a new, Spanish-style hacienda that is still used today.

D. C. Rachal bought land at White Point, across Nueces Bay, and built a house in 1867. When the yellow fever hit, he took planks from his new house to make coffins for fever victims, members of the White family that gave White Point its name. In 1883, Rachal and his wife Julia enlarged the one-story house for a growing family. The big house was built of Louisiana cypress. Tables, benches and chairs with rawhide bottoms were made by hand on the ranch. The house had a great view of Nueces Bay. The old mansion was razed in 1956.

Josiah "Si" Elliff ran away from home in Tennessee and made his way to Banquete, where he went to work on Martha Rabb's ranch, eventually becoming ranch foreman. After his marriage to Lois Alsup, Elliff started his own ranch, which became the 50,000 acre "44 Ranch." In 1888, he built a 10-room house at Banquete. It was remodeled in 1908; a third floor was added, along with 10 murals painted on the walls by a young Swede, A. E. Christofferson, depicting Texas scenes, one of a cowboy driving cattle in a blizzard. After the murals were finished, it was said, Christofferson tied heavy weights to his legs, jumped off the Central Wharf, and drowned. The Elliff home was torn down in 1955. The lumber was salvaged to build a house near Corpus Christi.

La Quinta, Spanish for "country house," was one of the most spectacular of the area ranch houses, built in 1907 overlooking Corpus Christi Bay. It was headquarters of the

120,000-acre Taft Ranch, the former Coleman-Fulton Pasture Co., and the home of Joseph F. Green, manager of the ranch. La Quinta's most famous guest was President William Howard Taft, who visited his half-brother Charles Taft in 1909. La Quinta served as ranch headquarters for 20 years. It was sold in 1928, after the death of Joseph Green. The house burned in January 1938.

The early ranch houses exemplified by Martin Culver's house were built for simplicity and function, with no hint of grandeur. But with the wealth that came from cattle drives to Kansas, with the improved economic situation after Reconstruction, the cattlemen began building great baronial mansions to show off their power and prosperity, mansions built not to blend in but to dominate the space around them, to make a statement, as shown by Coleman's and Fulton's mansions, and, later, by La Quinta, perhaps the grandest of them all. Virtually all the grand old cattle baron mansions are gone, which makes those few remaining all the more valuable as legacies of the past.

Rancho Perdido, the ranch house of Martin Culver.

Santa Gertrudis, the King Ranch house before the 1912 fire.

What became known as the Big House on the King Ranch house was built after a fire destroyed the older house.

Bonnie View, the Bayside home of John Howland Wood.

La Parra (Grapevine), the ranch house of Mifflin Kenedy.

D.C. Rachal ranch house at White Point.

The Banquete ranch house of Josiah "Si" Elliff.

Thomas M. Coleman Mansion on Chiltipin Creek.

La Quinta, the Taft Ranch house of Joseph F. Green, burned in 1938.

NOAKES' DIARY

Thomas J. Noakes left England when he was 16, came to Texas in 1845 and got a job on Kinney's ranch at Corpus Christi. His diaries that have survived (early ones were lost) tell us much about the terrible times during the last two years of the Civil War when drought, hunger, and hard times prevailed.

Noakes lived outside Nuecestown (near today's Calallen) with his wife Marie (Ludwig) and a young son (the first of seven children). Because his right lung was useless and he suffered from consumption, he was given a certificate of disability by Confederate military authorities, which allowed him to stay with his family.

These were desperate times. The Union blockade shut off supplies, causing acute shortages of food and necessities. Clothing, shoes, flour, sugar and coffee were scarce, very expensive, or not available at all. People had to improvise and adapt. They made clothes. They gathered oak bark and wild indigo to dye homespun cloth. Noakes, who was skilled with his hands, showed a genius for improvisation. He burned ashes from cow dung to make lye soap and used cow hides to make what he called square buckets and leather sacks. Everything had to be made by hand and it was all but impossible to buy tools. He made saddles for extra income and made his own shot to kill small game by beating lead into thin sheets and cutting it into small squares, which he found "answers very well."

The bad times brought on by war turned even worse with a severe drought in 1863, as if some Biblical affliction plunged them into a deeper misery. Death and destruction spread across the land like a stain spreads across a map. There had been no rain "worth mentioning" since July of 1863. Cattle and sheep were dying along the dried-up creeks and rivers.

Noakes wrote that dead animals met one's gaze in every direction. He counted 163 head of cattle and three horses dead in the mud at one watering place. They bogged down in the mud by creeks and rivers, the last place where grass could be found, and then they were too weak to pull themselves out; they died by the thousands mired in the mud. Noakes saw a team of work steers yoked together, one dead and the other standing quietly by its side.

"Go which way you will go," he wrote, "you see dead horses, cattle and sheep. All the creeks stink with them." Across the desolate countryside, denuded of grass cover, wind blew dust and sand, filling the sky with a haze that limited visibility. What you could see was parched and brown: "There is not a green thing to be seen."

The land was dry and hungry. Noakes had to travel far in an exhausting hunt for corn and flour. Because there was little to no grass, his horses wandered off seeking forage. He would spend days trying to find his cart horses. Then he would travel to the Salt Lagoon (Baffin Bay) 50 miles away to get a load of salt to trade for corn, sweet potatoes and other foodstuffs. These were hard trips for Noakes, with one lung, who was often spitting up blood and running a fever.

In March 1864, on the way to Goliad, he and a neighbor, Ned Taylor, cut down trees so their horses could eat the moss from out-of-reach limbs.

"As soon as we began cutting down the trees, crowds of cattle came running up and only with great difficulty could we get any moss for our horses, as the starved cattle fairly took it by storm. We could not drive them away. Very sad. They ate the moss and leaves and then the branches, eating everything under 1½ inches in diameter."

On his trips, Noakes found houses empty, yards overgrown with weeds, and ranches that were semi-derelict because of a shortage of manpower. On a trip down Banquete Creek, out of 12 or 14 houses, "I only saw one or two that were occupied, the rest having been abandoned; everything has fled east." He found Corpus Christi "in a state of desolation, everything gone to ruin and hardly a living soul to be seen." Noakes thought that Goliad, where he went to trade salt for corn, had "a substantial look about it. Unlike most Texas towns, a good many houses were built of stone and in very good taste."

Beeville was "a poor, deserted-looking place, nearly every house standing on the bare prairie without a fence and having the general appearance of so many wooden boxes standing about at intervals." Helena was also a "tumbled-down-looking affair," with the men gone to war and farms abandoned. He liked Seguin and noted that if it were not for war time, "it would have been a lovely and interesting neighborhood. There are some very nice-looking houses and the fine school house is a tasteful building."

He was surprised to find New Braunfels so big. "The principle street must be three quarters of a mile long with some very fine buildings." The streets were lined with chinaberry trees and the houses were all clean, with nice, shady gardens. Noakes walked all over New Braunfels trying to trade his salt for flour. He found the prices "ridiculously high. We had to pay 15 cents for a small glass of beer and everything else in proportion."

Noakes' diary gives us a glimpse of life on the home front in South Texas at the end of the Civil War. Near the end of his diary for 1864, he wrote, "I was working on my saddle tree and killed two large rattlesnakes, taking their fat, but

A self-portrait by Thomas J. Noakes. He came to Texas from England when he was 16 and settled at Nuecestown.

having nothing to put it in, I had to skin one of the snakes without ripping the skin and of that I made a bag in which I brought home the fat, by tying a knot at each end." In an entry on Oct. 28, 1864, Noakes showed his keen sense of humor: "I took a ride up the river, giving myself a Texas holiday, which consists in riding a broken-down horse all day, in search of game that you never find, and having nothing to eat."

May 12, 2010

FIRST STREETCARS

One hundred years ago, Daniel Hewitt started the city's first electric streetcar line, the Corpus Christi Street and Interurban Railway. Tracks were laid on wooden blocks on unpaved streets, with copper wires strung haphazardly above. The line had four cars. Hewitt bought electric power from the Peoples Light Co. The inaugural run was made on March 28, 1910.

A year later, Hewitt sold out to the Heinley brothers of Denver, who built their own power plant and added three cars. The Heinleys sold out to a Philadelphia syndicate in 1914.

The new owners added eight cars and the name was changed to the Corpus Christi Railway and Light Co. They installed coin boxes and introduced the "Pay As You Enter" system, eliminating the job of conductor. The car barn was north of the old Nueces County Courthouse.

One line ran from the City Drug Store at Mesquite and Starr to North Beach. The South Bluff line terminated at Third and Booty. Another ran to the Segrest area, one to Paul Court, one to Hillcrest and Nueces Bay Heights.

The system lost money until the Army opened Camp Scurry in 1916. With thousands of soldiers at the camp on the south end of town, the trolley business took off. Between 1916 and 1917, the number of riders exceeded one million. Open-air "summer cars" were used on the popular

One of City's First Street Cars

V. S. Heinley (Vincent Sweet) and his brother Earl bought the Corpus Christi Street and Interurban Railway in 1911.

runs to North Beach. In the summer, the cars were often packed with people going fishing or swimming.

The 1919 storm almost destroyed the streetcar line. When the system was put back into operation on Nov. 19, 1919, the newspaper said the city seemed to be getting back to old times. But old times were gone forever. Central Power & Light Company bought the power plant and streetcar line in 1925. The streetcar line lost money every year after 1919. On Jan. 31, 1931, the trolley cars made their last run. Most of the cars were sold to Laredo.

After CPL shut down the streetcar line, it ran a bus line for two years. For a very brief time, in 1930, it had some competition from the J. P. Medina Bus Line, which ran down Agnes Street. CPL in 1933 sold its buses to the Ekstrom brothers, who had started the company that became Greyhound. They renamed the line here the Nueces Transportation Company (fare 5 cents) with shop and office buildings on Sam Rankin.

The Nueces Transportation Company carried more than 18 million riders during its peak year of 1945. A fleet of buses ran out to the Naval Air Station, where the Naval

Base Bus Terminal was a busy place. The city bought the bus company in 1966.

During World War II, the city wanted to give 325 tons of streetcar rails to the War Production Board, on condition that the streets would be patched over and put in good condition after the rails were dug up. But the effort proved too costly. The old streetcar rails are still buried under the pavement of downtown streets.

MARKET HALL

In 1871, the city agreed to a public-private partnership that allowed two businessmen to build a structure to house city offices and to rent out stalls to meat and vegetable vendors. They built a two-story building on Market Square, between Schatzell and Peoples on Mesquite Street, at a cost of $10,000. Taxpayers didn't pay a nickel.

The agreement allowed the builders to rent stalls for 12 years, after which the building became city property. To sweeten the deal, the city made it illegal to sell fresh meats and vegetables inside the city except at Market Hall. When it was finished, the lower floor was divided into stalls, supervised by the "boss butcher." The upper floor had city offices, an auditorium, and a dance hall.

One tenant was the Pioneer Fire Company Number One. A bell tower housed the fire bell, which was rung to signal the beginning of the work day, lunch hour, quitting time, and of course when fires broke out.

Market Hall was torn down in 1911. A new brick City Hall was built on Market Square. The city in 1952 moved into a new City Hall on Shoreline, designed by Richard Colley, part of the Colley-designed complex that included the Memorial Coliseum. That City Hall lasted until 1988 when a new one was built on the bluff.

Market Hall, built in 1871, housed the Pioneer Fire Company and the city's butchers and vegetable vendors.

Market Hall lasted 40 years. The brick City Hall on Market Square lasted 41 years. The Colley City Hall on Shoreline lasted 36 years. The current City Hall is 22 years old. We're approaching the time to start thinking about building a new one. One thing is sure: We will never get another bargain like the city got with Market Hall.

CAPTURED

In 1845, John Jacob Thomas (Americanized from Thommen), an immigrant from Switzerland, got a job as a teamster with Zachary Taylor's army at Corpus Christi. His wife and five children were brought to St. Joseph's Island. After the war, Thomas returned to St. Joseph's until he bought his own place on Salt Creek on the Lamar Peninsula, a few miles inland from where it empties into St. Charles Bay.

On Oct. 19, 1850, a Comanche war party raided Thomas' ranch and captured two daughters, Sarah and Eve, 10 and 11 years old. The girls were out bringing in the milk cows. They were captured in sight of their parents. Thomas raised his gun and took aim at an Indian, but his wife Verna begged him not to shoot for fear the Indians would take their revenge on the girls.

That night, while they camped by the San Antonio River, Eve tried to escape. The Indians cut off her hair with their knives, stabbed her with knives and lances, and left her for dead. The Comanches were heading for their camping grounds on the San Saba, 190 miles to the northwest. They tied Sarah to her horse to prevent her from escaping. She slept on the ground in a slip; they took her clothes when she was captured. She ate what the Comanches ate, horseflesh and pecans. Weeks later, an Indian agent swapped an Indian boy and some blankets for her. She returned home. Her sister Eve, left for dead, was found by a search party, which included her brother John Thomas. She recovered from her wounds, severe as they were.

Eve married Henry Kroeger, who ran a hotel at Lamar. Sarah later married Anthony Strauch, who lived near the Thomas place on Salt Creek; they had five children and became a prominent family in Refugio. Sarah lived to an old age, known to all as "Grandma" Strauch, one of two little girls who were captured by Comanches and lived to tell about it.

"COMANCHE" RANGER

Warren Lyons also survived being captured by Comanches. In 1837, Warren and his father, DeWitt Lyons, were in a cow lot at their home in Lavaca County. Comanche raiders killed and scalped the father and captured Warren, who was 11. The boy lived with Comanches for 10 years; the man who killed his father adopted him.

In 1847, a surveyor visiting a Comanche camp saw a white man. He asked him if his name was Lyons. Warren said it was. The surveyor told him his mother was still alive, living at the old place.

Warren was able to escape from the Indians. When he went home and rushed to embrace his mother, she collapsed from shock. She had given up ever seeing him again. Warren found his old home had grown into a village called Lyonsville.

Warren told about his life with Comanches. He explained why his hair was cut short on one side of the head and left long on the other side. It was a mark of disgrace because he had run in a fight with Mexicans. He was torn between two worlds, yearning to return to his life with Comanches, and his two Comanche wives. But he settled down, married Lucy Boatwright, and joined Capt. J. S. Sutton's Rangers, though he retained the mannerisms and dress of a Comanche.

J. Williamson Moses, an old Ranger, said his friend John Duval liked to watch Lyons eat pecans. Duval said, "I wish I had a bushel of pecans so I could watch Lyons chew them." Moses wrote that Lyons made a good Ranger, first-rate scout and a valuable interpreter who knew and understood Comanches.

"Rip" Ford described Lyons in one fight with Comanches. "Warren Lyons, the guide and interpreter, had been raised among Comanches. He came at his old companeros in true Indian style: jumping, stooping down, changing position in several ways. He wished his boots off; they were too heavy. He told [the Rangers] what the Indians were saying."

OLD RIP

When John Salmon Ford came to Texas, he missed the battle of San Jacinto by a month, but he didn't miss much else in the next 50 years of Texas history.

Ford was trained in Tennessee as a doctor. In Texas, he practiced medicine, did surveying work, taught Sunday school, wrote for newspapers, and became a lawyer. Elected to the Ninth Congress of the Republic, Ford wrote the legislation that prepared the way for Texas to join the United States. When war broke out with Mexico, he joined Jack Hays' regiment of Rangers fighting in Mexico. One of Ford's duties as adjutant was to send out death notices. He would scrawl "R.I.P" at the bottom, which led to his nickname, "Old Rip."

After the war, Ford commanded a company of Rangers in the vicinity of Corpus Christi, and for the next decade chased border bandits and Comanche raiding parties. In one fight with Comanches near Fort Merrill on the Nueces, Ford yelled to a Ranger:

"Level, what is the matter?"

"Damn them, they shot my horse."

Gen. John Salmon Ford commanded the Cavalry of the West in the last battle of the Civil War.

"Oh, is that all?"

"No, damn them, they shot me, too."

When Texas seceded, Ford was given a desk job in charge of conscription, then he was given command of a make-shift regiment of Texas cavalry, which he called the Cavalry of the West. It patrolled the region between Corpus Christi and Brownsville. A month after Robert E. Lee surrendered, Ford's Cavalry of the West fought, and won, the last battle of the Civil War, at Palmito Ranch just east of Brownsville.

After many years of fighting Comanches, bandits, and Yankees, Ford died in bed, after a stroke, on Nov. 3, 1897, at the age of 82. He was a legendary frontier fighter, Ranger captain, soldier and statesman. It was said few men ever served Texas so long, in so many different capacities, or so well, as John Salman "Rip" Ford.

UP THE TRAIL

At the end of the Civil War, Confederate soldiers came home to find the ranges overrun with longhorns that had never felt a hot iron. They were chased out of the brush, branded, and walked to market. Driving herds to railhead towns in Kansas began in earnest in the late 1860s.

A Corpus Christi paper reported that James Bryden, King Ranch trail boss, "starts off with the first drove of cattle for the Kansas market, his herd consisting of 4,120 head from Nueces County." In 1869, some 600,000 cattle went up. In 1871, 700,000 went north. "Quite a number of our young men are starting for Kansas with cattle," said the *Nueces Valley*. "Among the number are Rufus Glover, John Merriman from the *Valley* office, Henry Parker and Frank Gregory of this city."

Trailing cattle began much earlier. In 1779, a herd was driven to New Orleans to feed the army of Bernardo de Galvez. Victoria's Martin de Leon took a herd to New Orleans before the Texas Revolution. In the 1850s, cattle were driven to Chicago, St. Louis, and California. During the war, herds were trailed east to feed the Confederate Army. But the great cattle-driving era began after war.

Some ranchers made their own drives; others sold cattle to a drover, who would gather herds in the spring. The drive took about four months; they wanted to get them to market before cold weather set in. The cattle were fattened on the way, except for those who would hurry them along and

127

fatten them in Kansas. In 1873, a steer worth $8 in Corpus Christi would bring $23 in Abilene, Kansas.

For about 1,000 head, there were 10 or more cowboys, called "waddies" or "screws." They were paid $30 to $40 a month. There was a trail boss, horse wrangler, cook, called a biscuit-shooter or coozie. Some drives had a scout to find bedding ground and river fords. The chuck wagon carried bedding, yellow slickers and provisions, such as beans, flour, sugar, bacon, lard, and coffee beans, Arbuckle's, which put a peppermint stick in every bag; this usually went to the one who volunteered to grind the coffee.

The two top hands rode point. Near the front were swing riders, then flank riders, and at the rear were drag riders eating the dust. In the early going, cattle were driven hard to break them to the trail and hurry them away from their home range. After it was trail-broken, a typical herd walked 10 to 15 miles a day. Trail-driving was said to be pleasant when skies were clear and there was grass and water. With a herd idling along, cowboys dozed in the saddle. They went up the Texas, Western and Chisholm trails. Where these trails ran has been a subject of endless dispute. The trails out of South Texas joined up to form the Chisholm Trail. One trail, the McCoy Trail, was said to begin at Corpus Christi.

Many trail hands were Hispanic and black cowboys. Cattleman Charles Goodnight wrote a tombstone inscription after the death of Bose Ikard, one of his black cowboys: "Served with me four years on the Goodnight-Loving Trail, never shirked duty or disobeyed an order, rode with me in many stampedes, participated in three engagements with Comanches, splendid behavior."

One woman who went up the trail to Kansas was Mrs. Amanda Burks of Banquete. She went up with her husband in 1871. She rode in a buggy and slept in a tent. She thought the drive was pleasant until they ran into "the worst

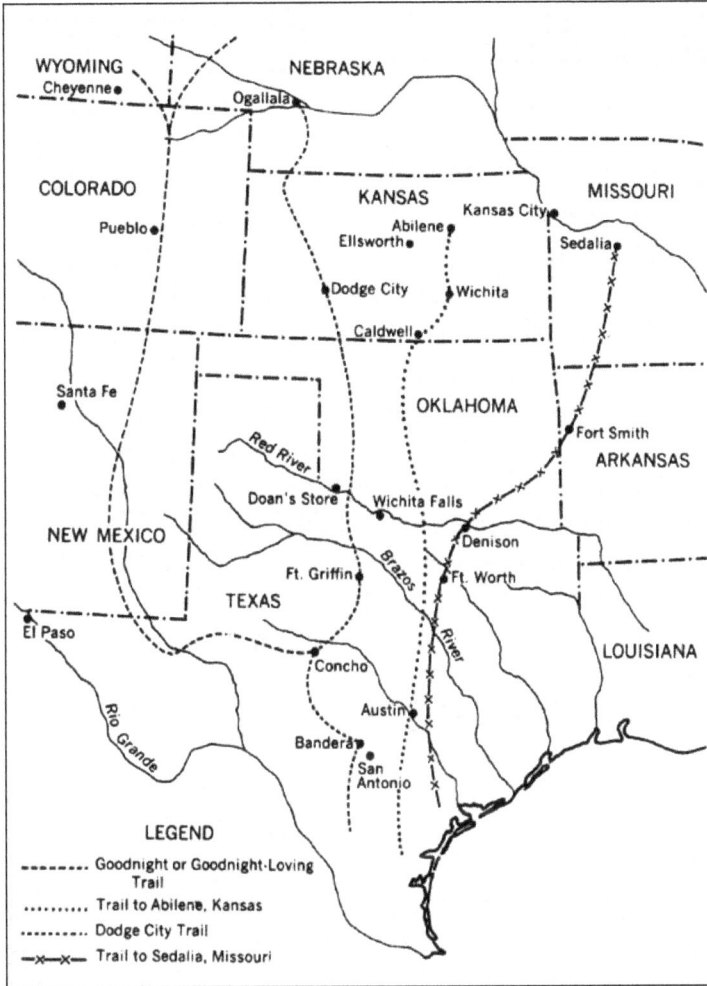

Map shows cattle trails leading from Texas to Sedalia, Mo., to Abilene and Dodge City, Kansas, and Ogallala, Neb. and through New Mexico and Colorado to Wyoming.

electrical and hailstorms I ever witnessed. The lightning seemed to settle on the ground and creep along like something alive." After the herd was sold, the Burks went by rail to New Orleans then took passage on a ship to Corpus Christi. "I arrived home in much better health than when I left it nine months before."

Cowboys worked long hours, ate beans and (a rare treat) fried beefsteak, drank Arbuckle's coffee strong enough to float a horseshoe, and liked a dried fruit dessert called son of a bitch in a sack. They played poker by the light of a bull's-eye lantern, told tales by the embers of a dying fire, and slept on a blanket with a saddle for a pillow, called a Tucson bed. It was dangerous when there were flooded rivers to cross or when a herd "pulled a big show."

"We took the river route," one wrote in disgust, "since we must have crossed every damned river in the country, and every one was wet." Worse than crossing a swollen river was a stampede, from the Spanish "*estampida*." J. Frank Dobie says the old Texian word was "stompede." In one storm, a cowboy could see lightning skipping across the tips of his horse's ears. One was so sure he would be killed by lightning he wrote his epitaph: "George Knight, struck and killed by lightning, 20 miles south of Ogallala on July 20, 1879." Some died on the trail, by lightning or drowning or some other mishap. They were wrapped in blankets and buried in shallow graves. One wrote that the saddest sight he had ever seen was a mound of fresh earth topped with a pair of boots, the last resting place of some unfortunate cowboy.

On the way home, cowboys nursed hangovers and memories, sometimes riding over the same trail, arriving in South Texas in the fall, often broke, having spent their wages on saloon women, fancy clothes and presents for the folks back home. One returning waddy said he was so tired of excitement he wouldn't give a nickel to see an earthquake. But many would wait for spring and be ready for another trip up the trail, repeating the cycle. One cowboy said after a drive he would never forget the feel of the saddle, the weight of the six-gun pulling on his belt, or what a blessing on a rainy night was the yellow slicker called fish. We will not see their like again.

CATTLE BARONS' MANSIONS

The bluff was where the city began. It was where Henry Kinney built his trading post in 1839, where Forbes Britton built his mansion in 1850 (still standing), where Martha Rabb, the "Cattle Queen of Texas," built her Magnolia Mansion in 1875. It was where Mifflin Kenedy and Henrietta King, the widow of rancher Richard King, built their own great houses in town, within reach of whatever social events Corpus Christi had to offer and perhaps to relieve the rural monotony of ranch life.

Martha Rabb's, Mifflin Kenedy's, and Henrietta King's magnificent mansions were built in the golden age of the cattle barons. Their homes stood on the east side of the bluff, on Upper Broadway, the best address in town, with a fine view of the city below and the bay beyond.

When John and Martha Rabb first moved to town from their ranch at Banquete, they lived at the south end of the bluff in a house they bought. This was about 1857. During the Civil War, while the family was at the ranch and while Rabb was serving as an officer in a Confederate cavalry unit, the house was used as a hospital by Dr. E. T. Merriman. (The house, in Heritage Park, is known as the Merriman-Bobys House.)

After John Rabb's death in 1872, Martha built a huge new place on the bluff called the Magnolia Mansion. After she married a preacher, the Rev. C. M. Rogers, she sold the Magnolia Mansion to David Hirsch, who sold it to Mifflin

Kenedy. The rancher bought it for his son John G. Kenedy. The house was used as a temporary hospital following the hurricane of 1919.

Mifflin Kenedy, Richard King's ranching and steamboat partner, built his own comfortable base in the city next to the Magnolia Mansion, at Upper Broadway and Lipan, in 1885. Kenedy's house was an Italian–style villa painted in three shades of olive green. It had a tower that soared 65 feet above the roof line. It was designed by an English architect, Alfred Giles, with alternating projections and recesses of porches and bay windows to reflect patterns of light and shadow at different times of the day. The interior was finished with walnut, oak, mahogany, cherry and cypress. The trim on the grand stairway was polished mesquite that came from the Kenedy ranch, La Parra. Acetylene gas was produced in a small building in the back for the 200 gas lights in the mansion. The *Caller* in an article on March 8, 1885, describing the house, said, "The residence is one of most complete in the state, and is furnished with all the modern improvements that can make a home comfortable."

The house was completed only three weeks before Mifflin's wife Petra died in March 1885. She moved into the house on Feb. 26, 1885 and died on March 16. After her death, Mifflin Kenedy's adopted daughter, Carmen Morell Kenedy, the daughter of a Monterrey merchant, moved into the mansion and kept house for him. Almost to the day, ten years after his wife's death, Kenedy died in the mansion following a heart attack on March 14, 1895. Kenedy's daughter, Sarah Josephine, and her husband, Dr. Arthur Spohn, moved into the house after Carmen Morell Kenedy died, in 1899. Dr. Spohn had the trees on the grounds wrapped in barbed wire to protect them from animals running loose.

The month after Petra Kenedy died in her new mansion on the bluff, Richard King, the greatest cattleman of the West, died in San Antonio, on April 14, 1885. He died of stomach cancer. Eight years after his death, his widow, Henrietta Chamberlain King, whom he had called "Etta," built a mansion north of Martha Rabb's remodeled and enlarged Magnolia Mansion.

The turreted and castle-like King home was designed by architect J. Riely Gordon and built by contractor Dan Reid, who later became mayor of the city. The home was built on the site of the old William Mann house, built in the 1850s. In front of the mansion, across Upper Broadway, were wooden steps with a hand railing that led down the bluff. The stables in the rear burned in March 1896, but the mansion itself was undamaged. When President William Howard Taft visited Corpus Christi in 1909, Henrietta King had a dinner for him. Knowing Taft's reputation as a man who enjoyed a good meal, she had a 60-pound turkey sent from Cuero for the main course.

Living with Mrs. King in the mansion were her daughter and her husband, Robert J. Kleberg Sr., and their five children. One of the reasons (among others) for building the house and moving from the ranch was so Mrs. King's grandchildren, the five Kleberg kids, could attend school in town. Another grandson, Richard King, moved into the house with Mrs. King after his own place on North Beach was destroyed in the 1919 hurricane. Henrietta King died in 1925.

What happened to the cattle barons' mansions on the bluff, the show places of the city? The Magnolia Mansion, John G. Kenedy's home, was moved across Lipan in 1939 to make way for the new Cathedral, then dismantled in 1952 and the timbers used to build the chapel for the Holy Family Parish. Mifflin Kenedy's mansion was torn down in 1938

The mansions of the cattle barons overlooked the Beach Section of Corpus Christi. On the bluff, from the left are the homes of John G. Kenedy and Henrietta King.

and the materials taken to La Parra at Sarita and used in building a church. Henrietta King's mansion (also known as the King-Kleberg house) was torn down in 1945. The materials were used to construct four small duplexes, three of them on UpRiver Road.

Martha Rabb, Mifflin Kenedy, Richard and Henrietta King and the Klebergs helped make history. Their mansions on the bluff added character and style to the city. They were all demolished during a time of transition when Corpus Christi was evolving into the modern city we know today. It took a generation from the town's founding until the cattle baron mansions were built. It took another generation before the mansions were demolished for what we call progress.

Martha Rabb's Greek Revival home, which she called the Magnolia Mansion, was built on the bluff in 1875.

The Magnolia Mansion was purchased by Mifflin Kenedy and remodeled to become the home of his son, John G. Kenedy. It was considered the most beautiful residence in Corpus Christi.

135

Mifflin Kenedy's Italianate mansion, designed by Alfred Giles, was completed in 1885. His wife Petra died soon after they moved in.

Henrietta King's castle-like mansion on the bluff was designed by architect J. Riely Gordon.

136

MORRIS & CUMMINGS CUT

There was good news for Corpus Christi in 1874. The Morris & Cummings Cut was completed and the town became a significant port for the first time in its history, marking the beginning of an era of bustling activity on the city's formerly sleepy waterfront.

This climaxed a 30-year effort to make Corpus Christi a port city. Until 1874, mudflats between Corpus Christi Bay and the Gulf prevented most sea-going ships from docking at Corpus Christi. The city was at a disadvantage in competition with Rockport and Indianola for Gulf commerce. Henry Kinney started the work when he bought a steam dredge in 1848. The work languished. In 1854 the city issued $50,000 in bonds to dredge a channel. There were setbacks and in 1858 the city voided the original $50,000 in bonds and issued new bonds to the D. S. Howard Co., of New York, to dredge a channel. These were revenue bonds to be paid when the work was finished by collecting a toll on the ships that used the channel. Howard hired Col. John M. Moore to supervise the work.

"I knew of D. S. Howard and Col. Moore, who were interested in a canal down there in what they called the mudflats, where they come out of Aransas Bay to Corpus Christi Bay," said Robert Adams, who came to Corpus Christi from England with his family in 1852. "They had a dredge to dig the canal with. I went through there once with my father; they were mudflats sure enough. Everything behind the boat was just loblolly, thick mud."

The dredging progressed slowly. There was little money. The man in charge of the dredge boat, Capt. J. C. Riddle, complained of "not having a cent," of having to borrow bacon, of being out of wood to fuel the boiler, of not having the funds to pay his workers. The dredging stopped when the Civil War broke out and Capt. Riddle's dredge boat was abandoned on the waterfront. The boiler was visible for years but the boat gradually disappeared as people dismantled it for firewood.

The dredging resumed in 1872 when the city signed a contract with Augustus T. Morris of Bloomfield, N. J., and James Cummings of New York City to gouge out an eight-foot-deep channel. The city agreed to pay $500,000 for the work, with the contractors authorized to collect a toll on every vessel using the channel.

When the Morris and Cummings Cut was completed in 1874, some of the larger ships did not have to wait outside the bar at the Aransas Pass channel to be "lightered," a cumbersome process of shifting cargo to smaller-draft vessels. They could sail or steam across the bay and dock at the Central Wharf, which reached into the bay from Water Street at William and Laguna (now Sartain).

The *Gussie*, a Morgan Line steamship drawing eight feet of water, arrived on May 31, 1874. This set off a big celebration at the Central Wharf. The *Corpus Christi Gazette* noted "the triumphant entry of the Morgan ship, *Gussie*, to our bay. For upwards of 20 years we have waited in anxious expectation to chronicle uninterrupted communication with the outside world. Notwithstanding the croaking of numerous people to the contrary, the indomitable working of the present contractors has brought the labor to a successful issue."

Behind this celebration, however, was a fierce controversy that split the town. The year before, in anticipation of the completion of the channel, several businessmen bought the Central Wharf. The prime mover was Uriah Lott, of later fame as a railroad builder. Lott was a shipping agent, wool and hide dealer, and part owner of a bank. Among his partners in the Central Wharf corporation were rancher Richard King and merchant W. N. Staples. Lott's business partner, Perry Doddridge, the town's mayor, was in on the deal.

Lott appeared before the City Council and proposed giving the city $1,000 a month, or one-fifth of the gross receipts of the Central Wharf, if the city would give the owners monopoly control for 30 years. The city agreed. The old wharf, built in 1853, was strengthened, a cattle chute added, and a new 20-foot-wide extension added, making a T-Head at the end. One man who didn't like this sweetheart deal was Norwick Gussett, and he had the money to challenge it.

Gussett came to Corpus Christi in 1845 as a sergeant with Zachary Taylor's army. He returned after the war, founded a town called Gussettville, and started a bank, mercantile store, and hide-and-wool business in Corpus Christi. He owned his own fleet of schooners plying between Corpus Christi and New York. Gussett opposed paying higher wharf fees to the monopoly owners of the Central Wharf. He led the anti-monopoly group that raised questions about the insider deal between Lott, Doddridge and the city. Gussett built his own wharf off North Beach, which was outside city limits and outside the council's control. (His wharf and warehouse were located where the Breakers Hotel would be built later.) Gussett's wharf did a big business, effectively ending the Central Wharf's monopoly. The syndicate quit paying the city $1,000 a month.

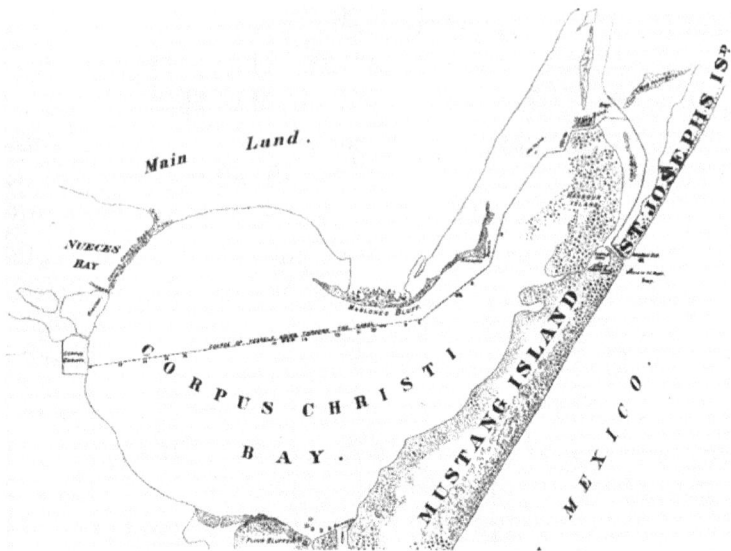

The Morris & Cummings Cut led from Aransas Bay to Corpus Christi

This was a time of growth and prosperity for Corpus Christi. Much of the commerce of South Texas flowed past Water Street. The bay was crowded with schooners, side-wheelers, steamships. Morgan Line ships became a common sight at the T-Head on the end of the Central Wharf. Exports from Corpus Christi included wool, hides, tallow, and cattle on the hoof. But wool was the major export.

On March 28, 1875, shipping tycoon Charles Morgan, owner of 100 vessels in the Morgan Line, arrived on his side-wheeler, *The City of Norfolk*, a floating palace. Mayor Perry Doddridge took Morgan on a tour of the city. Morgan later had a ship built for the Corpus Christi trade, named *Aransas*, specially designed for the shallow approaches to Rockport and Corpus Christi. Even with the Morris & Cummings Cut that gave the city an eight-foot-deep channel, Corpus Christi was still a long way from deep water. That wouldn't be realized until the port was opened in 1926.

SHOOTOUTS AND MURDERS

On Oct. 14, 1922, a Saturday afternoon, Fred Roberts was shot to death by the sheriff and a deputy. Roberts was an influential real-estate dealer who owned a farm near Bishop.

It was a strange story. Sheriff Frank Robinson and Deputy Joe Acebo entered a grocery store on Railroad Avenue at Staples owned by Mr. and Mrs. G. E. Warren. The sheriff asked Warren how business was going. Warren said it was slow. "That's how it is with you Ku Kluxers," Robinson said. "You are a Ku Kluxer, aren't you, Warren? By God, you know you are." The sheriff slapped Warren, then the sheriff and deputy left the store and crossed the street to Blake's Drug Store, where they stood lounging.

Mrs. Dove Warren called police. Police Chief Monroe Fox said the sheriff was minding his own business, that he could do nothing unless the Warrens signed a complaint. Warren called Fred Roberts, who came to the store, talked to the Warrens, then went to his car. He started the engine and Sheriff Robinson walked over, reached in, turned off the ignition and fired three shots at Roberts, all in the chest, killing him. Acebo fired one.

The *Caller* next day urged people to stay calm. The governor dispatched Ranger Capt. Frank Hamer and four other Rangers. Hamer's biography claims the sheriff and a gang of allies had barricaded themselves in the courthouse and Hamer kicked in the doors and, saying, "I'm Frank Hamer, Texas Ranger. I have warrants for the arrest of those involved in the murder of Fred Roberts. The rest of you put up those guns and get the hell out of there." Local accounts don't support that story.

Robinson, Acebo and two others were indicted for murder. The sheriff, deputy and a constable resigned. The trial was moved to Laredo. In his testimony, the former sheriff said he shot Roberts because "I thought he was going after a gun." The jury brought back a verdict on Jan. 13, 1923, finding all four not guilty. It was said that Robinson feared Klan retaliation. After the trial, he fled to Mexico where he lived for a decade.

SHOOTOUT ON SAM RANKIN

Another deadly shootout involved law officers. On Sunday, July 5, 1925, three men left Bessie Miller's, a house of prostitution on Sam Rankin Street. One was Paul McAllister, a game warden, another was George Ryder of San Diego, a third was Rufus McMurray of Three Rivers.

As McAllister and Ryder were getting into a car, Constable C. M. Bisbee and Deputy Constable R. R. Bledsoe drove up. Angry words passed, shots were fired until five men were down. Four men were killed: Bisbee, Bledsoe, McAllister, and Ryder. A fifth man was wounded but survived. An investigation concluded that Deputy Bledsoe started it when he shot Ryder. Then it became a general shootout. For weeks, people drove down Sam Rankin to point out the site of the bloody Sunday shootout.

SKELETON AT THE TRIAL

The 1930s had its own unusual murders. On Sept. 1, 1931, a body was found on the Oso. The skeleton had a hole in the skull. Near the body, deputies found an envelope addressed to the Sinclair Metal Works in Corpus Christi. They learned that the dead man was Alfred Steinbach, who shared a room with V. Don Carlis, a mechanic at Binz Service Station. The evidence pointed to Carlis.

Hair and bloodstains were found on one of his tools, a hammer, which fit the hole in Steinbach's skull. Carlis was indicted for murder.

During the trial, undertaker Maxwell P. Dunne wheeled a gurney with the skeleton on it into the courtroom. District Attorney D. S. Purl said Steinbach was there to tell of his fate. "Here, see this round hole in my skull, that's where the murderer hit me with a ball-peen hammer."

The jury found Carlis guilty and he was sentenced to 99 years, but the case was overturned. Appellate judges ruled that bringing the skeleton into the courtroom prejudiced the jury. In a second trial, there was no skeleton and Carlis, though found guilty, was sentenced to eight years in prison.

FLAT IRON MURDER

Another 1935 case involved a body found on a remote ranch. The body of a young woman, about 20, was found in the brush on the Gallagher Ranch south of Sandia. She was wearing a silk dress, but there was no identification. Her skull had been crushed by a blunt instrument.

Nueces County Sheriff William Shely investigated. People went to the funeral home to view the body, but no identification was made. Finally, a woman who ran a tourist camp on North Beach identified the body as that of Annabelle Evans, who had lived at her camp.

As the sheriff unraveled the story, he learned she was from Kansas, had been married with two children, but in the hard times of the Great Depression ended up in Corpus

Christi. She turned to prostitution, visiting oil-field workers on payday. She was killed by a blow to the head with a flat iron; it became the "Flat Iron Murder." H. T. Whitaker, convicted of the murder, was given a 25-year sentence. "While I bear Whitaker no grudge," the sheriff said, "I feel that 25 years is scarcely enough time in which to atone for the life of a woman whom fate had treated so shabbily as it had Annabelle Evans."

JOE BALL

In 1938, Joe Ball, a beer joint owner in Elmendorf killed a waitress and buried her body near Ingleside. He killed another waitress and stuffed the corpse in a barrel behind his bar, Joe's Place. After customers complained about the odor, he buried the body parts.

When these were found, police arrived to question Ball. He pulled a pistol and shot himself in the heart. Officers learned that Ball had killed another waitress and fed her to alligators. A schoolteacher infatuated with Ball had disappeared. Several women disappeared, but how many were killed by Joe Ball was never confirmed. Only one of his victims was buried in a sand dune near Ingleside. That was Minnie Gerhardt, shot in the head.

WAR YEARS

Corpus Christi learned in 1939 that a naval air station would be built at Flour Bluff. Sand dunes were leveled as the new base took shape. With an influx of thousands of workers, the city was booming. Hotels were packed. The Nueces Hotel put beds in its famous Sun Room. People seeking jobs lived in shacks on North Beach.

Corpus Christi's population had doubled in 10 years, to 57,301. The bayfront was being transformed by the seawall. The 20-story Robert Driscoll Hotel soon began to rise on the bluff. Buccaneer Stadium was being built, streets were torn up to expand water and sewer lines, and suburbs were springing up almost overnight to consume cotton fields.

Old license plates were collected in a "Bundles for Britain" drive. We were neutral, but neutral on Britain's side. Hills of scrap aluminum rose near the port as housewives donated pots and pans to a national aluminum drive. Men grumbled when barbers raised the price of a haircut from 50 to 65 cents. At "Papa" Shoop's Grill, hamburgers cost 20 cents and steak sandwiches 35 cents.

As war in Europe raged, Americans were split between isolationists and internationalists. Then came the surprise attack that ended debate. On a quiet December afternoon, people heard on radio the stunning news that Japanese planes had attacked the U.S. military bases at Pearl Harbor. That Monday, sailors and civilian workers at the base listened to President Roosevelt's war message: "Yesterday,

December the seventh, nineteen forty-one, a date which will live in infamy, the United States of America was suddenly and deliberately attacked by naval and air forces of the Empire of Japan." Roosevelt summarized the acts of war like a prosecutor reading an indictment. When he finished, it was said, people looked at each other, every face reflecting unasked questions.

Men were raring to fight. They crowded recruiting offices at the federal courthouse on Starr Street the day after the attack. Most of them were turned down because of age or physical condition. The city learned about its first casualties, "Billy Jack" Brownlee killed in the bombing of Hickam Field at Pearl Harbor and Warren Joseph Sherrill killed on the USS Arizona.

The war introduced rationing. Unless you were a doctor or had a defense job, you put a white "A" sticker on a black background on the car windshield that limited you to four gallons of gasoline a week. Civilians were allowed two pairs of shoes a year. Sugar registration was held in the schools. Housewives saved cooking fat to augment the national grease supply. Butcher shops were grease collection points. One shop had a sign reading: "Ladies, Put Your Fat Cans Down Here."

The Navy opened a radar training school on Ward Island. People had no idea what the secret about Ward Island was until after the war. Security measures were tight. Fishing boats were searched for cameras. Parts of Padre Island were reserved for bombing practice. A blackout drill was held on Jan. 19, 1942. Ten days later, the blackout was no drill. It was prompted by a U-boat sighting near Port Aransas. To prevent ships from being silhouetted against city lights, a dusk-to-dawn blackout was ordered. Bars were closed. Babies were conceived.

On April 21, 1943, President Roosevelt and Mexico's President Avila Camacho made a surprise visit to NAS.

FDR had been in the area before; he went tarpon fishing off Port Aransas in 1937. Where the NAS rail spur joined the Tex-Mex, at Port and Agnes, people got a glimpse of Roosevelt behind half-closed railway curtains. They thought he looked tired. One man said, as the train pulled out, "Well, I've seen the president, even if he didn't see me."

At the time of Roosevelt's visit, 20,000 civilians worked at the Naval Air Station, many of them women. Young women in coveralls were a common sight in Corpus Christi. Aviators trained here played a major role in the war in the Pacific. Gerald F. Child was in the first class of cadets who received their wings a month before Pearl Harbor. At the Battle of Midway, Child's PBY located the Japanese fleet and kept visual contact with the Japanese carriers to guide the dive bombers to their targets. Before the war was over, 35,000 aviators were trained at NAS and Rodd, Cabaniss, Cuddihy, Waldron, Beeville, and Kingsville.

In 1944, two German POWs escaped from a camp at Mexia and fled south. While a manhunt was in full cry, two Russians here to study refinery operations were arrested because they were "talking foreign." A man reported he had spotted the escapees on Port Avenue; he knew they were Germans by the way they walked. The escapees were captured at a tourist court on North Beach. They demanded that their interrogators call them "sir."

German POWs were housed at a POW compound at the Naval Air Station from Aug. 2, 1945 until March 16, 1946. They worked at manual labor jobs for 80 cents a day. In one chore, they dug up hackberry trees on the banks of the Nueces and planted them around the Naval Air Station.

Great events came in rapid succession. Roosevelt died on April 12, 1945. People cried in the streets. Stores closed. Students at George Evans Elementary sang two of the president's favorite sons, "Home on the Range" and "Abide With Me." Berlin fell to Russian soldiers. Adolf Hitler

In October 1941, Lt. E. W. Allen presented "wings" to the first cadets to solo in flight training at Naval Air Station Corpus Christi. More than 35,000 naval aviators were trained at the base, which played a major role in winning the war in the Pacific.

committed suicide and Germany surrendered. An atomic bomb destroyed Hiroshima and three days later another leveled Nagasaki. Victory over Japan came on Aug. 15, 1945. With news that the most terrible war in history was over, a celebration erupted along Chaparral. Thousands of cars filled with shouting, singing, kissing, drinking passengers drove up and down, moving among pedestrians milling the streets.

Returning veterans would find a larger changed city. The Dragon Grill on North Beach had burned. The night spot El Rancho had been turned into an apartment house. "Saddest of all the changes," the *Caller* reported, "will be those missing faces among the old corner gangs, the boys who used to gather at the drug stores and never took life seriously until their country was in danger. Many are gone and many who return will never be the same." They were part of the great machine of war and those returning faced the uncertainty of peace. The floodgates of eloquence were loosened in a sign asking a question: "What the hell now?"

MAT NOLAN

Irish orphans, a sister and two brothers, joined the Army after their parents died. Mary Nolan became a laundress and Matthew and Thomas, 11 and 9, enlisted as bugle boys in the 2nd Dragoons. They landed in Corpus Christi with Zachary Taylor's army in 1845. Mary married a soldier and after he died became a nurse. Mat and Tom were at the battles of Palo Alto and Resaca de la Palma and the campaign in Mexico.

After the war, they returned to Corpus Christi. Mary remarried and Mat, 16, and Tom, 14, joined the Texas Rangers. Ranger Capt. Rip Ford cited Mat in a fight with Comanches near Fort Merrill on May 26, 1850. When the Indians tried to steal their horses, Mat ran barefoot through prickly pear to get a shot as they rode away.

When the Rangers were disbanded, Mat and Tom returned to Corpus Christi. In 1858, Mat, 24, was elected sheriff of Nueces County. He hired Tom as a deputy. The Nolans joined Ranger expeditions against Comanches, but they were back in Corpus Christi on Aug. 4, 1860 when a drunken butcher stabbed a saloon-keeper. The Nolans found the suspect, John Warren, who pointed a gun and warned, "Stand back or I'll shoot!" When Tom reached for the gun, he was shot in the head. Warren was shot to death by Mat and citizens who joined the chase. Tom died 11 days later and was buried in Old Bayview.

When the Civil War broke out, Mat served in the command of Rip Ford, his old Ranger captain. In the second year of the war, he returned to Corpus Christi to marry Margaret J. McMahon. Nolan's company took part in the recapture of Galveston. He was promoted to major and recalled to Corpus Christi to deal with Cecilio Balerio (also spelled Valerio), who commanded an irregular Union cavalry outfit that rustled cattle on King Ranch to feed Union troops in Brownsville and attacked wagon trains hauling cotton on the Cotton Road.

In March 1864, Balerio's son, Jose, was captured when he visited his girlfriend in Corpus Christi. He was tried before a military court and sentenced to be executed. Nolan told Balerio he would let him go if he told them where his father's camp was located. Balerio refused but he broke down when they led him before a firing squad. His father's outfit, he said, was camped in the brush near the present town of Falfurrias. After a long ride, Nolan's forces surrounded the camp, waiting for daylight. At the last minute, Jose yelled a warning to his father — *"Cuidado!"* Five of Balerio's men were killed in the gunfight, but, in the confusion, father and son escaped. They stayed in Mexico for the rest of the war. (In 1870, Reconstruction Gov. Edmund J. Davis awarded Balerio's heirs a quarter-section of land for his services to the United States during the war.)

Nolan's company at Banquete played a cat-and-mouse game with Union forces on Mustang Island. Union soldiers would come in one day, to steal lumber and furniture, and Confederate soldiers the next, until federal forces were pulled back to New Orleans. In August of 1864, Nolan was re-elected sheriff, but he was still a Confederate officer. Ford ordered him to arrest Union sympathizers. On Nolan's list was the name of H. W. Berry, a former mayor of Corpus Christi and the first sheriff of Nueces County. The order to arrest Berry and other "perfidious renegades" could have led

Mat Nolan, an Irish orphan and bugle boy in the Mexican War, was elected sheriff of Nueces County and became a major in the Confederate Army.

to their executions as traitors. Berry was on the list because he had been seen loading cotton on a federal ship off Padre Island. In a report to Ford, on March 6, 1864, Nolan wrote, "On the night of Thursday under the command of Captains Gray and Doolittle, with 45 men, the enemy returned in their boats, landing with them a number of Corpus Renegades, among whom was H. W. Berry."

On Dec. 22, 1864, at sunset, Nolan was talking to a horse trader across the street from his house on Mesquite. Berry's stepsons, Frank and Charles Gravis, walked up, passed a few words, and shot Nolan with a shotgun. The horse-trader was chased down and killed with a pistol, left lying on the

151

street with a neat hole by the left ear. The wounded Nolan was taken to Dr. D. H. Lawrence, who told him the wound was fatal. Nolan said the Gravis boys were the shooters and that he knew why they did it, that they had their reasons, but he died before he could say more. Nolan was probably killed because of his intent to arrest Berry and other local citizens for treason. As a soldier, he could expect that death might come at any moment, but he probably didn't expect it to happen on a peaceful street in front of his own home.

The life and death of Mat Nolan could be summarized as: Irish orphan, Army bugle boy, Mexican War veteran, Indian fighter and Texas Ranger, sheriff and Confederate officer. He was buried in Old Bayview next to his brother. The headstone says nothing about his Confederate rank, but tells of his earlier days as a bugle boy in the Mexican War. It reads: "Matthew Nolan, Co. G, 2nd U.S. Dragoons."

A Confederate grand jury indicted Frank and Charles Gravis for murder. But nothing was done about the indictments in 1865 as the war wound down. When Union occupiers took power in 1865, Berry was appointed sheriff and stepson Charles Gravis was hired as a deputy. The indictments for the killing of Mat Nolan were relegated to a dark corner of the city's Confederate past.

SHERIFF JOHN B. HARNEY

Irish settler Edward Harney bought 100 acres at Nuecestown in 1852. His land fronted the Nueces River at a shallow ford; he charged a toll for cattle driven across his land to cross the river.

Harney married Margaret Riley in 1862 and enlisted in B. F. Neal's company of Confederate militia. He was captured in 1863 when Union forces attacked Fort Semmes and was held a prisoner of war until he was exchanged. He fought in the last battle of the Civil War at Palmito Ranch. After the war, Harney opened the Ruby Saloon in Corpus Christi and ran a butcher shop on Market Square. The couple had one son, John, born in 1863. John B. Harney spent his years on the family farm at Nuecestown. He married Julia Ball and they had four children, among whom was John B. Harney Jr., born on March 26, 1900.

John B. Harney (he dropped the "Jr." after his father's death) became inspector of brands for Nueces County in 1930 and held that post until the Legislature abolished the position in 1934. Harney was elected sheriff in 1938 and was re-elected two years later. Some thought Harney was the quintessential picture of a Texas sheriff. He was a towering man at 6-3 and weighed 280 pounds. He was gruff and wide as a bear. He wore broad-brimmed Stetsons, gray or black, wore cowboy boots, carried a six-gun, and had a badge decorated with diamonds.

The late Juliet Knight Wenger in her book "News To Me" wrote that Harney was a bully. He would persuade a small weak friend to get in an argument with a man who annoyed Harney and invite the man outside to fight. "When the man went outside, ready to beat up a weakling, he found Harney waiting and took the beating himself." She told of Harney's arrest, by city police, for DWI and leaving the scene of an accident. The arrest record at the Corpus Christi police station disappeared, no doubt a gesture of professional courtesy. As a reporter, she called Harney and asked him if he got arrested. "Hell yes," he said, "but I wasn't drunk. I only had 10 or 11 highballs." Harney said he was working a cattle-rustling case, was tired and sleepy, and didn't see the red light or the car he ran into.

When the DWI case went to the grand jury, Harney's deputies joked about the "cattle-rustling case." No one could remember when there had been such a case in Nueces County. He was not indicted. But bigger trouble was looming. In 1942, a suit was filed in the 94th district court by the Texas Attorney General's Office seeking Harney's removal from office for official misconduct and gross carelessness involving false arrest, false imprisonment and the beating and torture of prisoners. Alleged.

The case against Harney centered on the arrest and death of William Henry King, 33, a man from West Virginia. He was arrested on Feb. 1, 1941, without a warrant, held for seven days in the county jail, then taken out and shot by Harney, the state contended. Harney claimed he was taking the man out to look for stolen property, out on the Shell Road, when he shot the prisoner in a scuffle over a gun. Harney had already been tried for the murder of King in district court and found not guilty. Other allegations raised by the state involved beating prisoners with a rubber hose, forcing prisoners to stand for hours balancing on a tin can, and beating them if they fell off, until they confessed. A prisoner being interrogated was said to be "on the cans." The state claimed there were 57 causes that justified Harney's ouster.

Harney's attorneys argued that raising the King matter amounted to double jeopardy, since he had already been acquitted for that matter, and they questioned whether the Attorney General's Office had a constitutional right to come into Nueces County and prosecute a case against the elected sheriff of the county.

While the jury was out, Harney tried on the hat of former County Judge Walter Timon, slashed the air with Timon's cane, wielded as a sword, and joked with courtroom spectators. After deliberating 22 hours, the jury exonerated Harney on all counts. To make the victory complete, the Fourth Court of Civil Appeals in San Antonio ruled that the state had no constitutional authority to seek Harney's removal from office. The gist was that such an action would have to start with the district attorney's office.

Harney kept his badge and was re-elected to another term. He was not chastened by the experience. During World War II, Hispanic street gangs called "*pachucos*" kept their hair long, roamed in packs, and picked fights with military personnel from the Naval Air Station. Harney fought his own war against *pachuco-ism*. He would find some pretext to arrest *pachucos* and turn them over to the jail barber for a haircut. They would run like the dickens when they saw him coming.

In February 1944, two German prisoners of war escaped from a POW camp at Mexia and made their way to Corpus Christi, where they were arrested at a tourist camp on North Beach. The prisoners were taken to the county jail. Harney sat in when the FBI questioned them. One of the POWs, looking at Harney, said he was just like the Texas sheriffs he had seen in Western movies when he was a boy in Germany. Harney was not flattered. He didn't bat an eye, a

John B. Harney was sheriff of Nueces County from 1939 to 1953. Here, he holds the school bell of the Nuecestown School. He said he hated the bell so much that he stole it from a teacher, a Miss Blanchard, on his next to last day at school.

story said, and told them to get on with answering the questions.

Throughout the 1940s, John B. Harney was a political power in Nueces County. It was said he was one of the few who could stand up to the Parr dynasty in Duval County. Harney's power began to ebb and in 1952 he was defeated for re-election. He tried to reclaim the office two years later, but lost again. For Harney, it was true, as once was said, that every political career ends in failure. The good-old-boy era he represented, as a tough sheriff who made his own rules, was over. He died of a heart attack at his house on Louise Drive on Sept. 23, 1959. He was 59.

LOST HERITAGE

The cattle industry, Walter Prescott Webb wrote, began in a diamond-shaped area between San Antonio and Brownsville, Laredo and Corpus Christi. This was where the great cattle barons started ranching, learning from Spanish rancheros who came long before them. It was where the first cowboys learned to handle half-wild longhorns from Spanish vaqueros. If this region was the birthplace of the cattle industry, you could stretch a point and say it was the birthplace of the Old West.

Richard King, who wanted to own whatever ground he was standing on and the land next to it, began his ranch after visiting Corpus Christi in 1852. Other great cattlemen to come were Mifflin Kenedy and Shanghai Pierce. One of the better books of the era, "A Texas Cowboy," is by Charlie Siringo, who grew up on Matagorda Island. Some say one of the cattle trails, the McCoy Trail, began at Corpus Christi. A popular saddle on trail drives was the Apple Horn Saddle, made in Corpus Christi.

If the cattle baron, cowboy and trail-drive era represents an epic chapter in the history of Corpus Christi, why is this chapter virtually ignored? Dallas has a statue of a longhorn steer and Fort Worth calls itself "cowtown," though they were little more than way stations where trail bosses stopped to buy supplies before they crossed into Indian Territory. Corpus Christi has a closer connection to the legendary Old West than Dallas or Fort Worth. But those cities have been able to capitalize on their slim connection to this historic period.

Why has Corpus Christi ignored its heritage? I think that with the opening of the port in 1926, followed by building the seawall in 1939, Corpus Christi in effect turned its back on its cattle and ranching history in an effort to redefine itself as a seaport and nautical town. Without much thought, it turned away from the land and toward the sea. The loss, though, is a great part of the city's colorful heritage. The Old West began here, in the city's backyard, but visitors and tourists wouldn't know it. There are no monuments or visual reminders to tell them it was so.

ROPE'S END

In frontier times, riders found a simple way to picket horses on the open prairie. While Army cavalrymen carried picket pins to stake mounts, Rangers and Indian-fighters learned a simple method from vaquerors. When caught on the open prairie at sundown, they would "hole" their horses.

This was done by digging a slit-like hole in the ground with a knife. A big knot was tied at the end of a stake rope. The knotted end of the rope was buried deep in the hole, the dirt stomped down to close the hole. A hard pull straight up would yank out the rope, but horses tugged horizontally along the ground as they grazed. The knotted rope would hold. Rangers could sleep, spurred and booted, and their horses would be there at the end of the rope ready to saddle and ride. This was a safer method than hobbling a horse, which could cause injuries.

The fact that the knotted-rope technique was useful tells us how wide-open the country once was, when South Texas was open prairie, with hardly any trees or brush to speak of, except along the creeks. J. Williamson Moses, a mustanger in the 1850s, said the prairie was as pretty as a lawn with yard flowers, before mesquite and varieties of brush migrated up from Mexico.

The change began, from what I've read, after severe droughts in the 1860s and 1870s denuded the land, making it vulnerable to the brush invaders. Naturalist Roy Bedichek wrote that when the land was covered with a mat of grass, it was protected from mesquite beans, which mustangs and longhorn cattle ate. When the seeds fell to this thick grass mat, there was no opening to the soil for them to germinate. When droughts weakened that protective mat, brush migrants took root and took over.

Ranchers once set fires to burn off encroaching brush. But after they built fences, range burning stopped. Then the mesquite, chaparral and prickly pear spread over what was once open prairie covered with grass, buffalo clover and wildflowers. As the brush spread over the land in the 19th Century, so did asphalt in the 20th.

WAKING UP THE SHERIFF

Looking for a new book? Well, how about an old one? Andy Adams' "Log of a Cowboy" is filled with sharp observations that only someone who had lived the experience could have written. It was published in 1903.

It is a novel, not an account of a real drive, but it is a novel based on Adams' experience as a trail-hand in the 1880s. The protagonist in the book is cowboy Thomas Moore Quirk who could play the fiddle and thought nothing of riding 30 miles to a dance. He signed on for a drive to move 3,000 Circle Dot cattle from Brownsville to Montana.

They traveled up along the Laguna Madre. It took them a week to cross the Kenedy and King ranches. They passed west of San Antonio and took the Old Western Trail.

Pointing north, the herd is strung out like a mythical serpent. The cattle walk and graze, taking their time. The

Art in Harper's Weekly shows cowboys painting the town red.

narrative is pushed along like the cattle, at a natural pace. The Circle Dot cowboys deal with thieves, stampedes, cattle bogged in quicksand. When they reach Dodge City, they're warned about shooting up the town. An old hand tells them: "Don't get the impression you can ride your horses into a saloon, or shoot out the lights in Dodge; it may go somewhere else, but it don't go here."

Of course they didn't heed the advice. What's the point of having a gun if you can't shoot up the town? They had a few drinks at the Long Branch, until their heads swelled up bigger than their hats; they lost money playing faro; and after an encounter with a rude bouncer at the Lone Star Dance Hall, they shot out the lights and for good measure shot up the town as they rode out of Dodge. Cowboys called this "waking up the sheriff."

J. Frank Dobie wrote that if all the other trail-driving books were destroyed, you could get an authentic picture of trail men and cow country from Andy Adams' "Log of a Cowboy." I recommend it.

FIRST SCHOOLS – 1

Corpus Christi's first school was private enterprise schooling, the teacher paid by parents, with no government involved. In 1846, Amanda Brooks taught students for $2 a month each in a store on Chaparral. After she married the storekeeper and moved away, Madame de Meza, a doctor's wife, took over but the school didn't last long.

Charles Lovenskiold, from Denmark, opened the Corpus Christi Academy in a red-brick building on Water Street in 1853. Lovenskiold, a lawyer, was superintendent; M. P. Craft was principal. It was a private school with public support. The tuition of students who couldn't pay was paid from the county's free school fund.

At Lovenskiold's, students lined up for inspection; those with improper clothes or dirty fingernails were sent home. One morning, two nearly grown brothers came in with six-guns, angry over some insult. Lovenskiold ordered them to put down their guns. After a moment's hesitation, they did, and he addressed them as if pleading a case before a jury. The brothers broke down and promised to do better.

One day, Willie Hoffman, son of grocer Prokop Hoffman, showed up with his brother. Willie was too young for school. Lovenskiold said, "Well, little boy, have you come to school too?" Seeing the book he was carrying, Lovenskiold said, "And you brought a book with you." He opened the book which showed his past-due account at Hoffman's Grocery.

Lovenskiold's academy closed at the outset of the Civil War. During the war, classes were conducted at the Hidalgo Seminary on the bluff under the leadership of Father John Gonnard. Boys were taught moral and spiritual lessons and academic subjects. A school for girls was operated in the Dix home on Water Street by Mary Eliza Hayes Dix, said to be a ringer for Queen Victoria. She taught black girls sewing in the morning and white girls the "3 Rs" in the afternoon. After Mrs. Dix became ill, teaching was taken over by Jane Marsh, who practiced the Blueback speller and cowhide whip theory of education.

A student named Annie was mortally afraid of the cowhide whip hanging on a nail which Mrs. Marsh used when girls didn't know their lessons. Annie was asked to spell 'scissors.' She spelled 'scisors.' Mrs. Marsh gave her 15 minutes to spell it correctly. Annie, terrified by the thought of her punishment, jumped from a second floor window. She was not hurt, but that ended her schooling with Mrs. Marsh.

Schools that opened and closed included Farley's and Whitley's Academy, Mr. and Mrs. J. B. Carpenter's school on the bluff, the Corpus Christi Eclectic School, Professor Meredith's Female College, among others. All were private or parochial.

That changed when so-called "Radical Republicans" took over during Reconstruction. Back in 1854, the Legislature created a public school system and set aside $2 million to fund it, but the money was diverted to build railroads and public education was neglected until the radical Republicans passed school acts in 1870 and 1871 that mandated a state public school system.

More radical for the time, the state required compulsory attendance for all children, black or white. The last thing Radical Republicans wanted was local control, dominated by former Confederates. A public school system controlled by the state shifted the concept of education as being the private responsibility of every parent to the state's responsibility for all. This was a farsighted effort to institute and centralize public education.

Corpus Christi got its first public school in 1871. The two teachers were paid $50 a month. Classes for white students were held in the Methodist Church and classes for black students were held in the old Mann red house on Water Street. The following year, two school houses were built on Carancahua, one building for white students and one for black students, with a fence separating the two.

Nueces County was divided into four school districts with a board of directors. The board met in June 1873 and agreed that public schools be operated in all four school districts: Corpus Christi, Nuecestown, San Diego, and Santa Gertrudis. The board agreed that the teachers would be examined once a month for competence.

The state paid for only four months of operations and teachers bore the burden of an under-funded system. They were often forced to sell their vouchers for half the value. With no money, schools closed in October 1873. Trustees pleaded with parents to pay "subscription" fees so the schools could reopen. The following year, after the Legislature revised the school laws, the city took over schools inside the city and City Council members ordered religious instruction to cease. After a public outcry, the council backed down.

Solomon Coles, a former slave, was appointed principal of the black school. He was paid $42.88 a month. Coles was known as a strict disciplinarian. One of his reports to the school board said, "None of the school property has been the least bit damaged by the pupils. Not a pane of glass, a window blind, or desk has been broken, and if there has been a pencil or chalk mark on our school building, I am not aware of it." Coles served as principal from 1879 to 1894.

Charles Lovenskiold, a lawyer from Denmark, opened the Corpus Christi Academy in 1853 in a building on Water Street.

Solomon Coles, a former slave, was appointed the first principal of the school for black children in Corpus Christi.

A crusade to improve the schools began in 1889 when C. W. Crossley was named principal and he instituted a high school program with academic and commercial tracks. Academic courses included algebra, history, philosophy, English and German literature. Commercial courses included bookkeeping, business arithmetic, commercial law, and political economy. The city's first high school was built in 1892, at a cost of $1,563, next to the elementary schools on the bluff.

Professor Moses Menger was lured from Austin to become principal of the high school. Corpus Christi High School, under Menger's guidance, became one of the few in Texas whose graduates were accepted without an entrance examination at the University of Texas. Graduation ceremonies for the first graduates were held at Market Hall in June 1893. Four graduates sang a Civil War-era song, "Upidee," followed by a piano recital of "The Waves of Corpus Christi."

FIRST SCHOOLS — 2

In 1896, a room was rented in a building on Leopard Street to use as a classroom to teach three grades of Mexican-American pupils. Rose Dunne (later Shaw) taught children enough English to attend the main Central school, where they would go after they completed the Fourth Ward School. As students moved up a grade, they would move across the room. A water cooler in the classroom cut down on trips to the water jar in the yard.

"I would tap a bell for just about everything," Rose Shaw once said. "One tap meant one thing, two taps meant something else." She would ask Cheston L. Heath for help when her students couldn't buy school materials. Heath and his father owned a Heath's Emporium on Market Square. The younger Heath, president of the school board, routinely bought books for poor students. In 1902, Rose Shaw went to the graduation ceremony to see Julia Pena become the first Mexican-American student to graduate from high school in Corpus Christi.

An act of the Legislature formed the Corpus Christi Independent School District in 1909. The district counted 1,600 students, 29 teachers (paid $2 a day), four elementary schools and one high school, the two-story structure built in 1892. One of the first acts of the school district was to build a new high school. While it was being built, an old frame building was moved to Staples and Park which students called the "chicken coop."

The new high school, completed in 1911, on Carancahua was called the Brick Palace. One of the old school buildings on the site was moved to the Salt Lake west of town. In 1913, the Salt Lake School had 78 pupils and one teacher, Rose Shaw's sister, Geraldine Dunne, who rode a horse to school from her home on South Chaparral. After one year, the building was moved to Carrizo to become the Mexican Central School. After Cheston L. Heath died in 1918, Rose Shaw convinced the school board to name the school after him.

Not long after Rose Shaw started teaching, Mary Carroll, raised in Mexico, was hired to teach Spanish; she was only 18 and had no formal education. She taught sixth through 11th grades for $50 a month. Spanish was compulsory then. Though she was innocent of any college training, Mary Carroll was appointed principal of the high school in 1921, then superintendent the following year. Ella Barnes was named high school principal.

After the Brick Palace was built, three elementary schools were constructed: David Hirsch, Edward Furman, and George Evans. When classes began in the Brick Palace, Ella B. Wheeler Carter (class of 1912) said, "We thought we were grown, to be permitted to move from room to room for our classes, and to meet for assembly for the first time in history." A popular high school hangout was the Alcove, a chili parlor on Peoples Street. When fire escapes were added at the school, officials conducted sliding drills, with the older boys stationed to help girls onto the slides. After a week of ruining shoes and snagging clothes, the thrill of the exercise wore off.

The senior class of 1919 took the day off on April 1. They went Loyd's Pier for dancing and to the Amusu Theater for a box lunch. A class in domestic science (cooking) was conducted in the basement of the Brick Palace. After the

1919 storm struck on Sept. 14, the domestic science lab was turned into a soup kitchen for storm victims.

The Brick Palace was not two decades old, in 1929, when a new high school was built out in the country at the end of Leopard. The new Corpus Christi High School was later renamed for Roy Miller. A brick structure was built for the Cheston L. Heath School and the old high school, the Brick Palace, was renamed Northside Junior High. In the 1930s, with families struggling in the Great Depression, Rose Shaw, principal at Cheston Heath, provided a "bean line" for students. Merchants donated bread, milk and beans. The beans were cooked in the school heating plant.

Despite building the new high school and Wynn Seale, the lack of classroom space became a big problem at the end of the 1930s. Schools were overflowing. When the new high school opened in 1929, the district had 5,000 students. In 1939, enrollment had nearly doubled, at 9,113. Before wartime shortages stopped construction, the district built the Beach School on North Beach, the Robert Driscoll Junior High, and three new elementary schools. The school district absorbed outlying schools: the Fairview school on UpRiver, the Kostoryz district, and the Sundeen district.

Schools were even more crowded in the 1940s with the growth that came with the Naval Air Station. Adding to the problem, the state switched from 11 to 12 grades. When efforts to build new schools failed, the district adopted half-day sessions with one group of children coming in for four hours in the morning and another for four hours in the afternoon. After the war, wooden barracks from the auxiliary air fields were converted into temporary classrooms that were used for many years.

For the next two decades, the district built schools at a furious pace. The $3.5 million W. B. Ray High School opened in 1950. Only the library was air-conditioned.

Corpus Christi High School, built in 1911 on Carancahua, was called the Brick Palace.

Besides Ray, the district built another high school, Mary Carroll, seven junior highs, 17 new elementary schools, plus additions to existing schools. Richard King High was completed in 1965 and Foy Moody opened in 1967. People were reminded of the great educators of the past in the names of the schools: Mary Carroll, Rose Shaw, Ella Barnes, C. W. Crossley, Moses Menger and Solomon Coles.

After the Supreme Court struck down segregated schools in *Brown v. Board of Education*, the Corpus Christi district adopted a "freedom of choice" plan, which brought court suits and years of legal wrangling. In the 1970s, lessons were being taught to more than school students, the very same lessons the so-called radical wing of the Republican Party in Texas tried to teach 100 years before.

ARTESIAN PARK

You might expect to see a statue of a general. Perhaps on a horse, perhaps tipping his hat like the statue of General Jackson in Jackson Square in New Orleans. But the monument to Zachary Taylor in Artesian Park is a plain block of tombstone granite with a simple inscription: General Zachary Taylor's Army Encamped Here In 1845-1846. Hardly inspiring. Nearby is a zero milestone, from which distances to Corpus Christi are supposed to be measured, and an historical marker.

It is a sad little park and a sad little monument. There should be something more. The time when Taylor's army landed on North Beach in 1845 represents an important part of Corpus Christi's history. It was more hamlet than town when some 4,000 soldiers — half the strength of the U.S. Army — concentrated here in the likelihood of war with Mexico. The Taylor encampment became the springboard for the Mexican War. Several famous Civil War generals were stationed here, as young officers, during those eight months in 1845 and early 1846.

The Taylor monument could have been almost anywhere. The first units of the army landed about where the Aquarium is today. The tents stretched for three miles along the shoreline. Taylor's headquarters was on Water Street. But Taylor's soldiers dug a well in what is now Artesian Park and that often makes it the focal point when talking of the Taylor encampment.

Eight years after the army marched to the Rio Grande and fought the first battles of the war, Henry Kinney, in 1854, gave the site of the well to the city for a park. In 1887, the old well was re-drilled but, as in Taylor's time, the water smelled of sulfur and was almost undrinkable. Still, it became prized as a health tonic. After the turn of the century, a bandstand was erected and Sunday evening concerts were performed in the park. Later, politicians — including LBJ and "Pappy" O'Daniel — made stump speeches in the park. A new well was drilled in 1935, but it was plugged on orders of the health department. In the 1930s and 1940s, the park became a favorite hangout for domino and shuffleboard players and, in World War II, the Naval Air Station band played on Friday nights. So much for a bird's-eye history of the city's oldest park.

In 1975, a proposal was pushed to change the name of Artesian Park to LULAC Park. The historical community was aghast. *Caller-Times* columnist Bill Walraven wrote that, "The Nueces County Historical Society has its dander up. For all the sites in the city, Artesian Park is probably the richest in history." The name change was shot down.

What happened next may have been payback. The later controversy is worth pondering, which is what Herb Canales, longtime director of the Corpus Christi Public Libraries, has done in a very fine paper in the fall issue of the *"Journal of South Texas."* The journal is published by the South Texas Historical Society based at Texas A&M University-Kingsville. Canales' article is titled: "A Tale of Two Cities — How Brownsville and Corpus Christi Have Approached Mexican War Historic Site Designation."

In Brownsville, the community enthusiastically supported the creation of a national park to commemorate the Palo Alto battle, the first engagement of the Mexican War. By contrast, Corpus Christi could not get over the opposition of a few individuals to create a memorial at Artesian Park.

Canales points out that in 2002 Jim Moloney, who was then executive director of the Coastal Bend Community Foundation, offered the city $1 million to commemorate the Zachary Taylor encampment at Corpus Christi. The site would be Artesian Park. The main donor behind this effort was Ed Harte, former publisher of the *Caller-Times*, whose office windows once looked out over the park. There was also a silent partner. Robert Rowling agreed to donate the other half block south of Artesian Park, which he owns. The design called for a grass-covered pyramid next to miniature pup tents to represent the encampment, a visual recreation of the famous Daniel P. Whiting lithograph of 1845.

The resulting criticism was that it would glorify an unjust war against Mexico, that this was an episode in our history best forgotten. A critic on the City Council, Jesse Noyola, said the history of the war "still arouses anger in some Hispanics. Pursuing the plan would only cause division in the community." Walraven wrote that, "Like it or not, we live with the results of that history. No persons and no country are demeaned by a respectful recognition of that fact." But the damage was done. Harte and the other donors, sensitive to the criticism, withdrew the offer. This is detailed in Canales' article.

I went down the other day to look at the Taylor monument. Nobody was around. Why should there be? There's not much there: a little green space and that lonesome block of granite. The park is not a place where the imagination is stirred. Do you think students in Corpus Christi schools know about the city's role in the Mexican War? The Taylor memorial at Artesian Park was a missed opportunity to capitalize on the city's history.

You don't keep the memory of the past alive, with its rights and wrongs, through some pact of silence. To tell about great men and stirring events may put you down on one side or the other, but history can be presented as lessons

The Zachary Taylor monument in Artesian Park looks more like a tombstone than a historical memorial.

learned, which is far better than the historical amnesia of, "We didn't like that war, so we won't talk about it." This is like an amputation, a self-mutilation of history and memory and imagination. We don't like slavery, but it would be a travesty to draw the curtain on that part of our history.

Too bad we couldn't overcome our divisions when there was a generous offer to convert a sad little park into a real attraction that would say: What happened here was real. It was our history. People talk about the need for a downtown revival. Well, that revival could begin by remembering the city's rich history. Unfortunately, Herb Canales' article is one more reminder that you can't accomplish anything if you have to fight over everything. And that defines the main difference between what happened in Brownsville with Palo Alto and what didn't happen in Corpus Christi with Artesian Park.

PIONEER UNDERTAKER

Peter Dunne of County Kildare, Ireland married Margaret Maxwell and they emigrated to Corpus Christi in 1852 to seek fame and fortune. They found neither, but their grandchildren did. Dunne, called Uncle Peter, was a master blacksmith who made branding irons for ranchers. The shop on Water Street was decorated with branding irons he hammered out from glowing iron over the years.

One of five children of Peter and Margaret was Lawrence Dunne. He married Josephine Alzada Stevens in 1874. Lawrence worked for Sidbury Lumber and built a home behind the lumber company at 309 S. Chaparral. Two children of Lawrence and Alzada became well known to Corpus Christi — Rose Dunne (later Rose Shaw) and Maxwell Peter Dunne. Rose became an outstanding teacher and educator; she married E. J. Shaw in 1900 and later was named principal of Cheston Heath School. Maxwell founded one of the town's leading funeral homes.

Maxwell was born on Sept. 6, 1881. As a boy, he delivered the *Caller* on horseback. When he was 18, he tried to volunteer for the Spanish-American War, but was a fraction of an inch too short. He got his brother to hit him on the head with a plank to raise a knot, but the blow missed and took the skin off the side of his head. He went to Houston in 1903 with 85 cents and vague plans to study dentistry. An undertaker hired him as an apprentice mortician. Dunne learned the business and gained his professional license. He married Agnes Nikel in 1906 and moved to Corpus Christi in 1908.

Dunne bought out the undertaking subsidiary of Pitts Livery on Mesquite. "Livery stables," he once explained, "ran an undertaking parlor on the side because they had plenty of hacks for funerals. Everyone enjoyed funerals in those days, especially the children, who dearly loved the hack rides."

The funeral business was in transition. Bodies were usually bathed and dressed at home, then taken to cemeteries for burial. Few undertakers practiced embalming. But that was beginning to change and Dunne gained a reputation as an expert in embalming. He moved his mortuary business to a building on Starr, across from where the federal courthouse was built, then moved again in 1916 to Mesquite. This became the city's first funeral chapel and parlor where bodies could be viewed until burial, a novel idea at the time.

Dunne once told about an old sexton at the Catholic cemetery whose pack of hounds were always getting in the way at graveside services. At one funeral, the dogs were running about and the sexton was trying to shoo them away, but they thought he was playing. While this was going on, the Irish priest was finishing the dust-to-dust stuff and launched into the Lord's Prayer: "Our Father, who art in heaven — leave the dogs alone — hallowed be thy name, thy kingdom come, thy will be done — if you don't stop kicking the dog, you'll foul the grave — on earth as it is in heaven."

Dunne became well known after the 1919 storm. He was named chairman of the Red Cross disaster committee and given the baleful responsibility of trying to identify the dead. With the help of volunteers, he was able to identify 286 victims, all but 63 of the bodies recovered. Many of the dead were buried in mass graves near where they were found, on the other side of Nueces Bay, from Portland to White Point to the Turner Ranch.

Descriptions of bodies, kept on index cards, read in part: White female, hair blonde, blue bathing suit with red border, no shoes, lower teeth gone . . . White male, about 55, two guitar picks in pockets . . . White female wearing ring with words "Jim to Eva." . . . Female, Mexican, bathing suit, front teeth exceptionally large and good . . . White male, 10 to 14, found in pocket a ticket to Amusu Theater, five nickels and 10 pennies . . . White female, two years old, rope tied to left arm . . . There were hundreds of such cards.

A month after the storm, the bodies in mass graves were dug up, stacked on barges and floated across Nueces Bay to be reburied in Rose Hill Cemetery. The men doing this gruesome task held handkerchiefs to their noses that had been soaked in camphor. Dunne worked night and day then, a daughter recalled. "I remember how his hands bled and were sore from all the chemical solutions he was using. It must have been two years before his hands healed. He cured them by washing in the sulfur water at Artesian Park."

In 1931, Dunne helped solve the Alfred Steinbach murder mystery, which led to the conviction of V. Don Carlis. Dunne helped prove that Steinbach was killed by a hammer blow to the head and the hammer belonged to Carlis. The district attorney had the skeleton brought into a shocked courtroom, which led to a quick conviction, but also a quick reversal on appeal.

During Prohibition, Dunne bought the excursion boat *Japonica* and operated it with several partners. The sheriff and deputies boarded the vessel and tried to arrest Dunne for serving beer. Dunne claimed the *Japonica* was a ship on the high seas and the officers were committing piracy. The case was dropped.

Dunne was an undertaker with a playful spirit and a keen sense of humor. It was said he could mimic any accent and

Maxwell P. Dunne's first undertaking parlor was located at Pitts Livery on Mesquite Street.

had a fund of stories to entertain any audience. In the 1930s, he was known for playing a prank, repeated several times, in which he would get into a heated argument, pull out a gun and shoot a man. The dead man would get up and wipe the ketchup off his shirt, like the scene in "The Sting." It was all acting.

Maxwell P. Dunne, grandson of blacksmith Peter Dunne, died on Jan. 26, 1948. As an undertaker who knew how to tell a good story, Dunne would appreciate that death, as the point of final departure, provides a convenient ending to any story.

BUMPY PROGRESS

A century and a half ago in Corpus Christi a hot topic was not the prospect of a war that would soon swallow them all but the condition of the streets, a perennial topic then and now. The complaints of 150 years ago sound familiar today.

The town's newspaper, the *Ranchero*, wrote on Aug. 25, 1860 that the streets were scandalous. "The effect of the recent heavy rains has demonstrated to many an unfortunate pedestrian that, although we have reason to be thankful to the clerk of the weather, we have a good right to complain of the miserable condition of our public highways. What are the mayor and aldermen so engaged in that they cannot find time to make such improvements as our people demand? It seems to us that when public officials are insufficient and slack, it is high time to remind them of their shortcomings."

The *Ranchero* hit a nerve. A week later, the editor wrote that "our mayor and aldermen have gone to work in earnest and are now making some long needed street improvements."

With the outbreak of the Civil War, there were no more complaints about street conditions. During the last two years of the war, there was a lapse of government oversight, with no city government functioning and county government at Santa Margarita on the Nueces. After the war, county government was moved back to Corpus Christi and reorganized; there was no city government until 1866.

At war's end, the town's streets were covered with mud and littered with dead animals. To correct the situation, John Dix, the chief justice (today's county judge) ordered the town divided into five road precincts and all able-bodied men living in the precincts were designated as "road hands." They were conscripted to work repairing the streets without pay. It was an unpopular and unwelcome task.

In the 1870s, city streets still brought complaints. After a heavy rain, the clay streets became almost impassable with glutinous mud. In the wet season, the bottom dropped out. Chaparral and other downtown streets were damaged by heavy wagons and ox-carts loaded with wool and hides. They created huge potholes. Street work consisted of dumping shell in the deep holes. After a heavy downpour, gullies washed out on the bluff and the runoff carried mud onto streets and sidewalks below. They were made passable by placing wooden planks across them.

The Nueces Valley reported that Doddridge, Lott and Company "have had that mud pond" in the street in front of their office filled with shell at their own expense. "Our streets need more attention from the city fathers," the paper complained. "Corpus Christi should not lie in a lake at every good rain." Mayor John B. Murphy put prisoners to work digging drainage ditches to the bay. Those who refused to dig were fed bread and water only.

In 1894, the city paid the Fishermen's Union for 24 loads of oyster shell to spread on the streets. Four years later, the city paid John Burdette $35 a month to keep the downtown streets sprinkled on dusty summer days.

In 1902, the *Corpus Christi Crony* explained that "street improvement is a Latin term meaning to befoozle the public. This is done by 30 men with 16 wagons and mule teams. The 30 men get themselves with their wagons into the midst of the highway, where they can stop vehicles. When they have stood there for four hours, listening to leaves growing, they move forward three or four feet and block traffic some more. After three days, they become exhausted and desist, whereupon the foreman comes with a spade and searches until he finds a place where the street is smooth. There he digs a large hole, into which each of the 30 men drops a gravel. The 16 mule teams are allowed to paw the gravel until it is scattered, after which they all go draw their pay. Sometimes, where the street is very good to travel upon, it is improved with a plow, so that no one can ever pass that way again. But this is arduous labor, and for it the 30 men must have extra pay and two holidays."

The *Crony* editor wrote that, "The street you live on is easily remembered; the street you live on is Mud."

Mrs. A. R. Yeargen, who ran a grocery store on King Street, said when she arrived in 1911 the city had only two blocks of paved streets, on Chaparral. "The other streets were mud. From our store, I could see horses bogging down in mud when it rained."

During the Clark Pease administration in 1912, voters passed a $150,000 bond issue to pave streets. Property owners fronting the streets were obliged to pay three-fourths of the cost and the city one-fourth. There was a heated debate over which type of paving to use. Some favored wooden blocks, like ones used on some streets in Dallas. Those who won the argument wanted the streets paved with a new hot mix asphalt called bitulithic.

Plans were made in 1913 to pave Belden, Twigg, Taylor, Mann, Lawrence, Schatzell, Peoples, William, Aubrey, Laguna, Upper Broadway, and to finish paving Chaparral, Mesquite and Water. Part of the bond program was devoted to building the bluff balustrade. The *Caller* later tried to start a contest to name the bluff, noting that Rome has Seven Hills, San Francisco has Nob Hill and Chattanooga has Missionary Ridge. "It is regrettable that 'the bluff' has gone down almost indelibly in the city's history" and said it

Dirt streets such as Chaparral could turn into quagmires when it rained.

was high time steps were taken to rename the city's most dominant feature.

By 1926, most of the downtown area was paved and by 1930 the city had 35 miles of paved streets. The city is 10 times larger today and some of the names have changed. Laguna is now Sartain. Last Street is Alameda. Dump Road is Staples and Alta Vista Road is Santa Fe. But the routine complaints continue to be over pot-holed, poorly paved and badly maintained city streets. Things have changed greatly in 150 years, but some things haven't changed at all.

DARKNESS AND SLOTH

Between 1880 and 1900, Corpus Christi was always on the brink of something big — railroads, public transit, electric lights, telephones, resort hotels.

Uriah Lott's Tex-Mex Railroad made its first run in 1881. Lott went broke and sold the line to a syndicate, but the new owners turned it over to Lott's investors for a grand excursion to Laredo. Ranchers Richard King and Mifflin Kenedy and friends rode in a private car named "Malinche," drinking spiked punch. They reached Laredo in fine spirits. With the Tex-Mex in operation, a machine shop on Railroad Avenue began making boxcars, turning out one a day.

Two years later, in 1883, Corpus Christi got a transit system, which consisted of mules pulling coaches called "herdics." The name came from inventor Peter Herdic, a Pennsylvania lumber tycoon. The herdics ran from the St. James Hotel to the Tex-Mex Depot.

Corpus Christi got its second rail line in 1886 when the San Antonio and Aransas Pass Railroad (SAAP) built a trestle bridge across Nueces Bay. To celebrate, Corpus Christi held a beach party that featured baked oysters and fish chowder.

Another sign of progress was electric lighting. Before electric lights, streets had coal oil lanterns, lit by a lamplighter at sundown and put out at sunrise. Some opposed electric street lighting, arguing that it was a wasteful expense: "We have moonlight most of the time."

In 1890, the city gave a street-lighting contract to the Corpus Christi Electric Light Company owned by Dr. A. G. Heaney, T. P. Rivera and John Stayton. Light poles started going up in February and lights were on by April. The city, said the *Caller,* was "emerging from darkness and sloth."

The electric company also operated the telephone exchange, although there were few people to call. Dr. Heaney, the founding partner, got telephone number 1; his son got number 2; there were 15 other numbers. It was deemed OK for the operator to pass on gossip, but flirting on the line would get her fired.

New Jersey developer Elihu Ropes arrived in 1888 and quickly raised the speculative fever all over town. He bought land on Ocean Drive for the Aransas Cliffs development. He had a dredge boat digging a pass — Ropes Pass — across Mustang Island. He built the Alta Vista Hotel and laid rails for a streetcar line to the hotel at Three-Mile Point. In 1890, a visitor noted all the activity. "Went to town. A street railway is all the talk there now. Everybody talking railroads, electric lights, and street railway." Ropes' streetcar line began at the Courthouse, ran south on Chaparral and out Alta Vista Road (Santa Fe today). The tracks reached the hotel in October 1890. The coaches were pulled by a steam-dummy locomotive.

Another fancy resort hotel, the Miramar, was built by local investors on North Beach. It was the pride of Corpus Christi. It opened on June 1, 1891, and had registered 4,000 guests in three months, before it burned in a spectacular fire on Sept. 11, 1891. The fire began in an upstairs room at 3 a.m. on Sunday. Twenty-eight people escaped with their lives, some jumping from the second floor to mattresses spread on the ground as, the *Caller* wrote, "the fiery-tongued destroyer sprang from room to room."

Near midnight on July 14, 1892, fire broke out in a home on Chaparral and leaped to nearby buildings. Firemen raced to fill water wagons from box wells on the bay, but the raging conflagration burned an entire block before it was extinguished. The fire led to the establishment of a city water system, with water piped in from the Nueces. The *Caller* whooped, "Waterworks are a grand success. Hydrants are opened and water gushes out with tremendous force. The city is safe against fire."

The Ropes' bubble burst in 1893. Ropes' properties were sold for debt; he died a shattered man. The city was still sleeping off the effects of the Ropes' collapse when it got a boost in 1895. Famous prizefighter Bob Fitzsimmons came to North Beach to train for a fight with Jim Corbett. The publicity prompted F. E. Ring to build the first tourist courts on the beach. In September 1895, the *Caller* received an "astonishing" number of telegrams asking about Fitzsimmons and what he thought about fighting Corbett.

This attention, with the new tourist courts, perhaps marked the beginning of the tourism industry in Corpus Christi. Wealthy Texas families came to the seaside to enjoy the breezes off the bay. While Rockport was more popular, Corpus Christi was beginning to attract tourists. The *Caller* observed that Corpus Christi was losing thousands of dollars in the competition for tourists by not clearing up the beach in front of the town and building a first class hotel.

Farmers also were starting to arrive. After several bad droughts, large ranches, like the Taft and Driscoll ranches, made tracts of land available to land promoters to sell to farmers. This set off the homeseeker era. Thousands of Midwest farmers arrived to buy farm plots and move their families to South Texas. It also marked the beginning of the area's cabbage economy. In March 1896, the *Caller* noted: "Wagon after wagon loaded with cabbage continues to arrive from nearby fields . . . The SAAP depot was the busiest place in town. Men were making crates and loading

Farmers gather their cabbage harvest on a farm outside Corpus Christi.

cabbage into cars for shipment . . . Farmers with loaded wagons are making Mesquite a busy thoroughfare; without them, Corpus Christi would certainly look quiet."

Cabbage grown on the coast, truck farmers believed, was better than cabbage grown anywhere else. In those years, it was claimed that more cabbage was shipped from Corpus Christi than any other city in the world. The SAAP ran special cabbage trains from Corpus Christi. There were also large shipments of beets, beans and cucumbers, amounting, in one year, to 200 boxcar loads. Severe, punishing winters killed the cabbage era. All those fields around Corpus Christi where rows of cabbages once grew are covered with houses, malls, cars, parking lots, suburbia. And we have a long way to go. Some farm fields are still left unpaved.

THE ALTA VISTA

Elihu Harrison Ropes, a developer from New Jersey, built an elegant resort hotel at Three-Mile Point, where the S-Curve on Ocean Drive is today. (Three-Mile Point is three miles south of Artesian Park. The name was later changed to Airheart Point.)

Ropes arrived in 1888 and decided that Corpus Christi would be the next Chicago, with his help. He had grandiose ideas and access to capital backing. He began dredging a channel across Mustang Island, which he bought for $25,000; Ropes Pass was between Corpus Christi Pass and Aransas Pass. When the cut was completed, Ropes invited a party to celebrate. They took shovels to dig out the last few feet of sand. The guests shoveled until water trickled through. Trickle was all; there was no flow. The dredge "*Josephine*" started back across, to deepen the channel.

Ropes hired a contractor to build a railroad from Corpus Christi to Brownsville, which he projected would reach South America. Grading started at the end of South Staples (Dump Road then) on the way to Brownsville. Ropes bought 20 blocks of land on the shore south and began selling lots for a development called "The Cliffs." He planned Ocean Park that would extend five miles on the bayfront along a street to be called Ocean Drive.

Ropes' enterprises included the Corpus Christi and South America Railroad, a deepwater port at Ropes Pass, and "The Cliffs." But the pride and centerpiece was the Alta

Vista, a four-story resort hotel, with 106 bedrooms, which cost $50,000 (Ropes said $100,000). Since it was out in the country, to get the guests from the railroad depot, Ropes built a street railway that ran down Chaparral out to the Alta Vista, then to the Aberdeen community and "Farmer" Clark's. The railway line stretched 6.2 miles.

The coaches were pulled by a steam locomotive, called a "steam-dummy," with the streetcar built over it. When the street railway was finished in October, there were so many passengers, the *Caller* reported, "it was simply impossible to accommodate everybody, so large and unexpected was the rush."

In the Ropes' boom, land values soared. People who wanted in on a sure thing invested in property and bought stock in Ropes' companies. Land in Flour Bluff that sold for $8 an acre, before Ropes, soared to $1,000 an acre. In one incident, two elderly men fought over who would get to buy a lot near the Alta Vista selling for $900, a lot that had been on the market for $10.

But Ropes' sources of capital were drying up. He managed to get enough money to hold a gala opening on Aug. 15, 1891 at the Alta Vista, even though it was unfinished. Some guests took the street railway out to the hotel while others "hired hacks, with Negro drivers, and rode out to the hotel in style." The hotel had a bar and billiard parlor on the first floor. The dining room and ballroom were on the third floor. The guests dined and danced with a great view of the bay. One of the marvels of the hotel was the grand staircase, arching over the lobby office. It was constructed of polished mahogany. The mahogany had been salvaged by J. E. Curry, one of "Preacher" Curry's sons at the Curry settlement on Padre Island.

Then the bubble burst. A depression turned into the financial panic of 1893. Ropes was broke. He couldn't pay the taxes on his holdings. A Boston paper described Ropes as a confidence man and trickster. In Corpus Christi, the bottom fell out and real estate values crashed. Some local people lost their personal fortunes. Matt Dunn, an old Texas Ranger who lost money investing in Ropes' schemes, attacked Ropes and beat him with a walking stick. One of Ropes last acts before he left town in August 1893 was to file a $20,000 suit against Dunn. It was later dismissed.

The Alta Vista stood empty. Weeds grew along the streetcar tracks. The dredge silted in on Mustang Island and the dredge operator, M. A. Griffin, left for a job in Mexico. Ropes' assets were sold for debt and Corpus Christi underwent a flood of bankruptcies. One who saw an opportunity was rancher Nicholas Bluntzer, who bought downtown property and the unfinished Alta Vista Hotel. Norwick Gussett bought the street railway.

At the Curry settlement, it became a family joke about the money due for the mahogany logs used for the Alta Vista staircase. Ropes had promised to pay well for J. E. Curry's work. The Curry kids joked about all the things they were going to buy "When Colonel Ropes pays us for the logs."

Ropes never paid for the logs. He never returned to Corpus Christi. He died on Staten Island in 1897, at age 53, a shattered man. After Ropes, a skeptical Corpus Christi would not be easily swayed by a developer with grandiose ideas. Perhaps that skepticism became part of the city's mental makeup.

The Alta Vista story didn't end with Ropes. In 1905, J. J. Copley bought the hotel from Bluntzer and added a bathhouse, pavilion and pier in the bay. Within five years, Copley went broke. The summer of 1911 the hotel was leased by the Peacock Naval College of San Antonio. The pier built by Copley was used to dock six cutters on loan to the school from the U.S. Navy. Then the old hotel, symbol of a failed dream, again stood vacant.

E. H. Ropes' resort hotel, the Alta Vista, was built at Three-Mile Point, south of Corpus Christi, in 1891. It sat vacant for years before it burned in 1927.

Theodore Fuller wrote in his memoirs, "When the Century and I Were Young," that he went inside the old hotel in 1921. "The dust of decades, quarter of an inch deep, formed a habitat for an infinity of fleas. Heaven knows what they lived on." And there the place stood, with falling plaster and dust covering the hardwood floors until the afternoon of June 9, 1927 when it burned in a spectacular fire. The *Caller* reported that several hundred automobile loads of people went out to watch the grand old building burn.

The Alta Vista, the symbol of the Ropes' era, was gone. But for years, those who knew where to look could find Ropes' old dredge, the "Josephine," buried deep in the sand in the middle of Ropes Pass.

TEXAS DEMOCRACY

Anyone who does not believe in old-fashioned democracy, I was once told, should be taken out and shot. Funny. I thought about that before I voted yesterday. I also thought about how old-fashioned democracy worked in South Texas, how those in power manipulated the system to stay in power.

Until after the Civil War, only white males could vote. After Reconstruction, to dilute the voting power of freed slaves, Texas allowed non-citizens to vote. In border towns like Brownsville, Mexican nationals were ferried across the river and paid to vote. Turnouts could exceed 100 percent of registered voters. The much-maligned poll tax was a reform measure intended to prevent the importation of voters from across the border and to restore the integrity of elections.

Elections took longer. In 1870, polls opened on Monday and closed on Thursday, which gave the political powers time to count and recount votes until they came out right. Election judges would hide a pencil and use it to double-mark a ballot, thus invalidating it. "See, he voted for both candidates; we can't count this ballot."

In 1895, only males 21 or older were eligible to vote. It would be another 25 years before women could vote. This was the age of "machine" politics, meaning Democratic machine. Election outcomes were determined by heavy-handed tactics of powerful Democratic political bosses such as James B. Wells in Cameron County, Archer Parr in

Duval County, Manuel Guerra in Starr County and to a lesser extent Walter Timon in Nueces County.

How did they use their power, besides maintaining themselves in office? Property taxes could be assessed to favor supporters and punish opponents. County jobs were awarded as political plums. They could block prosecution of political allies. Incumbent sheriffs were not unknown for jailing opposing candidates on trumped-up charges. Deputies were stationed at polling places to intimidate voters. The full scope of the skullduggery will never be known.

In an interview in the *Caller* in 1936, an unnamed "old-timer" told how politics operated in Corpus Christi. "Back in '95 our political machinery started grinding two months before the election. There wasn't any messing around, once it got started. Every precinct had its chairman and committee and they didn't lag around when it came to digging up votes.

"By the night before the election both sides knew how many votes they would get and when I say 'knew' I don't mean they guessed. They *knew*. It worked like this. At one of his meetings of the committee the chairman would ask: 'How is old Jeff Black going to vote?' One of the committee would say, 'I tried feeling him out the other day and he wouldn't say.' 'Well, this won't do,' the chairman would say, 'we've got to know. Now, tomorrow I want at least four of you to go around to him and get him talking politics. Don't ask his opinions, just get him talking. And tomorrow night I want to know how Jeff Black is voting.'

"To give an example of how close the machines could estimate the votes, take Judge Timon's forecast of the H. G. Sherman and Roy Miller fight for mayor in 1912. Miller got three more votes than Timon said he would get, but even that didn't satisfy Timon. He scratched his head for days wondering where those extra three votes came from.

"On the night before an election, there was plenty of free liquor and Hispanic voters on the Hill got happy. The candidates would get them as drunk as possible and pen them up in houses and not let them out until it was time to vote the next day. Then they would hand them a marked ballot and lead them to the polling places, with stops on the way for free liquor. Every candidate would have a free whisky and cigars booth set up near each polling place. The candidates thought too much of their supporters to see one of them go around un-refreshed. The candidate or one of his helpers would be at every booth to hand out marked ballots.

"I will never forget the fix one candidate found himself in. He was at his booth with his pockets full of marked ballots. A pickpocket from the other side stole all the ballots out of his pockets and substituted opposition tickets. About five hours later the candidate discovered that he was handing out his opponent's tickets, and there wasn't any quieting him. He never was the same afterwards. People don't take voting seriously nowadays. In '95, every man had a vote, voted, and didn't let anything interfere with it. The words 'Don't die until after the election, grandpa,' would keep a man alive for an extra week. You don't find enthusiasm like that any more. Politics is not what it used to be."

As for the political machines, federal authorities did try to challenge the flagrant abuses of power. Those abuses stemmed, in large measure, from a combination of powerful political leaders, one-party dominance, and large numbers of illiterate voters.

In Corpus Christi, U. S. District Judge Walter Burns empanelled a federal grand jury to investigate alleged corruption in the general election of 1914 in Nueces County, probably the least corrupt of the political machines in South Texas. Summons were issued to more than 200 witnesses. A U.S. marshal took charge of ballot boxes. The grand jury indicted 42 for conspiracy, including County

James B. Wells of Brownsville was one of the most powerful politicians in South Texas, with Archer Parr in Duval County, Manuel Guerra in Starr County and Walter Timon in Nueces County.

Judge Walter Timon, District Judge W. B. Hopkins, Sheriff M. B. Wright, Tax Assessor Joe Bluntzer and others.

The case centered on a meeting in Timon's office where the question came up about how much it would cost to bribe voters on "The Hill." This was a euphemism for Hispanic voters concentrated on the bluff west of Upper Broadway. One man said it would cost $2,500 for the free whisky, cigars and cash handouts. Timon said $3,000. This was standard politics in Corpus Christi, spending money to buy votes on the Hill. The saying was, "As the money goes, so goes the Hill; as the Hill goes, so goes the election."

Charges against 18 people were dismissed. Sixteen were acquitted. Only five were convicted. The case against Timon was declared a mistrial. Federal prosecutors vowed to pursue political corruption in Nueces County, but the issue was quietly dropped as concerns about machine politics began to fade. That was old-fashioned democracy. Before our own enlightened age, politics was dirty, underhanded intrigue, not clean and honest like today.

UNION OCCUPATION

At the end of the Civil War, in April 1865, Corpus Christi was a desolate place. Many citizens moved away after Union warships bombarded the town in 1862. Those who stayed were nearly starving. County government was located at Santa Margarita. There was no city government. The town's newspaper, the *Ranchero*, relocated to Matamoros. Editor Henry Maltby wrote that Corpus Christi's population dropped to 400 people and that the town was under a veil of Egyptian darkness. "Corpus Christi that was, and Corpus Christi that is, are two very different places."

Corpus Christi was one of the few Texas cities subjected to prolonged occupation. When Gen. Phil Sheridan took possession of Texas for the Union, he ordered the 25th Army Corps to occupy Galveston, Indianola, Brownsville and Corpus Christi. Some 52,000 Union troops were stationed along the coast, out of 70,000 in the state. Small cavalry detachments were sent to San Antonio and Austin. Other units camped at Refugio and Goliad. Corpus Christi, with a mere 400 residents, was occupied by 3,000 Union troops. The sheer numbers were bound to cause trouble.

Texans wondered why such a large force was sent to occupy a defeated and demoralized state, which was as low, one said, as the tail of a whipped dog. But the Union forces were sent to Texas as a show of force, in response to French intervention in Mexico.

In June, Gen. Charles S. Russell was ordered to take a regiment to Corpus Christi. By late July, two regiments were in town. Russell occupied the home of Judge R. C. Russell (no kin) at Chaparral and Taylor. Because Confederates had to come to this house to take the "ironclad" oath to the Union, it was called the Ironclad House. In Matamoros, editor Maltby scoffed at all the oath-taking, writing that "the Yankees are the greatest people for oaths that we have ever seen."

Corpus Christi was occupied, off and on, by three Union regiments — the 10th, 28th and 36th — for more than a year. The 122nd may have been here for a short time. The regiments were designated as United States Colored Troops. They were under the command of white officers. This wasn't the first time area residents saw African-Americans in Yankee blue uniforms. When the barrier islands were captured by Union forces in 1863, two companies of black soldiers in the Corps d'Afrique were garrisoned on the island. They were auxiliary soldiers employed to dig fortifications. Corpus Christi was unfamiliar with the black soldiers that came in the occupation, who were combat veterans seasoned by the hazards of war. They had fought in battles in Virginia, around Petersburg and Richmond, in the last year of the war.

The Union soldiers erected tents on the beach and the bluff. Trouble quickly arose between residents and soldiers. The *Ranchero*, reporting from afar, wrote on July 28 that the troops plundered empty houses. "Among the houses sacked was that of Conrad Meuly (who died a few days since in Brownsville), a Union man . . . The furniture and all fixtures, including a rosewood piano, were carried off. The soldiers went into the backyard, broke open the family vault, and entered the coffin containing the remains of an infant and scattered the bones on the ground."

Margaret Meuly complained to the occupation commander about troops ripping up her house.

When Margaret Meuly, Conrad's widow, complained to Gen. Russell about the wrecking of her house, he said there was nothing he could do. The *Ranchero*, a diehard Confederate paper, reported that the white officers feared their own troops. "They are afraid to ascend the bluff (where many of the soldiers camped) in open daylight and after six o'clock in the evening they are afraid to walk the streets."

Soldiers were accused of drunkenness and vandalism. Helen Chapman, a Unionist, noted in her diary that there was "a good deal of bitter feeling about the colored troops." J. B. (Red) Dunn, in "Perilous Trails of Texas," said the Union soldiers subjected people to "all kinds of humiliation and insults." He wrote that two soldiers broke into his uncle's home and stole clothing and guns. When the Dunns returned home, they found the soldiers' uniforms left behind.

One of the boys, Matt Dunn, reported the theft to the officer in charge. "The officer denied that any of his men were involved. But next morning, Matt got there before roll call and saw that two names were not answered. He called the officer's attention to the matter, but the officer flew into a tantrum. He told Matt that if he was so sure about it, to go get the deserters and not come bothering him about it. Matt found them by Nueces Bay. When they saw him coming they pulled out their pistols and told him to stay back. Matt opened fire on them and when all his loads were gone but one, he charged and killed one of them. At that, the other one ran into the bay and got bogged in the mud. Matt roped him and dragged him to shore. He turned him over to the commanding officer."

Maria von Blucher wrote her parents that, "The federal troops have been ordered away; Corpus Christi will be rather lonely with 2,000 fewer men. We have gotten along very well with the officers, and upon closer acquaintance they have done all in their power to protect us from inconveniences and incessant thefts." In November, soldiers of the 28th Regiment, from Indiana, were shipped to Brazos Santiago, where they were mustered out. They were welcomed home in Indianapolis as returning heroes.

The departure of the 28th Regiment was not the end of the occupation of the city. Other units were shunted in from Brownsville and Indianola. The conjecture that Union regiments of black soldiers were removed because of friction with local citizens is dubious. It is doubtful that tough Union generals like Phil Sheridan cared much for the sensibilities of defeated Confederates. Sheridan didn't like Texas much anyway. It is more likely that the regiments were transferred because it was time for them to be mustered out as the vast Union army was being disbanded. It would be a long time before Corpus Christi recovered from the war, the occupation, and the coming Reconstruction. It would be a long time before that "veil of Egyptian darkness" was lifted.

MUSTANG GRAY

Mabry B. Gray lost his horse while hunting buffalo. Alone, on foot, he captured a mustang pony and from then on he was called Mustang Gray. He was said to be one of the finest riders in Texas and fearless in battle. But Gray's shadowy history reveals he was a killer without remorse.

When he was 19, Gray was with the Texas army at San Jacinto. As a veteran, he was granted a 640-acre land bounty by the Republic. This grant, called Gray's Ranch, was five miles north of Ingleside. (He may have owned another place called Grulla Motts on the Oso.)

After San Jacinto, Gray joined Texans raiding Mexican-owned ranches in South Texas. Some ranches had been abandoned. Stock left behind was driven east and sold. The raiders, called "cow-boys," expanded their activities to include robbery and killing. They operated out of Victoria and Corpus Christi.

In 1842, when the border region was in turmoil, seven Mexican traders from Camargo arrived at Victoria. They sold Mexican blankets and bought tobacco, bolts of calico, and other trade goods. On their way back, in camp near Goliad, they were sitting around a campfire cooking supper when Mustang Gray's party rode up. They were invited to share the meal. After eating, Gray's men pulled out their guns, tied the traders together, and told them they had a few minutes to pray.

The traders were shot by the light of the campfire. The raiders hid the trade goods and took the horses to sell. One of the traders was still alive. He had been shot, but he fell under the body of the man tied to him. When the killers left, the wounded survivor freed himself and walked to Refugio and was nursed back to health. He is variously identified as Manuel Escobedo or Manuel Escobar.

The survivor described the massacre to John J. Linn, who told the story in "Reminiscences of Fifty Years in Texas." Escobedo/Escobar went to Victoria and again told the story of the massacre. While the people of Victoria were shocked, nothing was done to charge Gray and his band of killers. But the massacre made it hot enough for them around Victoria that they moved on to Corpus Christi. They continued to prey on traders coming up from Mexico.

In another incident, Mexican traders on their way to Corpus Christi camped on Oso Creek. Mustang Gray, Andy Walker and others disguised as Comanches attacked the camp at night, whooping and shooting. Several traders escaped into the brush while others were killed.

Corpus Christi founder Henry Kinney urged President Lamar to crack down on the outlaw bands, which he called "robber Texians." These outlaw bands were semi-legitimate since they were authorized by the Republic as ranging companies or, as they were often called, as spy companies. They received no pay, which no doubt justified, in their own minds, taking plunder from "the enemy."

The attacks on Mexican traders invited reprisal raids from Mexico and threatened Corpus Christi's existence as a trading post. In 1844, Kinney was authorized to field a company of rangers for protection. He put some of the "robber Texians" at Corpus Christi on his payroll, including Mustang Gray.

When Zachary Taylor's army arrived in Corpus Christi in 1845, Gray and some of his men joined Samuel H. Walker's

First Texas Mounted Riflemen, the most famous unit of Texas volunteers in the war.

As Taylor's army pushed deep into Mexico, in the fall of 1846, there were reports (in error, it turned out) that Corpus Christi had been nearly wiped out by Comanche raiders. Mustang Gray and the men who volunteered with him formed a new company, with Gray as the captain, which was sent back to protect Corpus Christi. In early 1847, Gray's company was ordered back to Camargo.

Mustang Gray's rangers called themselves Mustangers after their commander. Among those in the company were Andy Walker, Reuben Holbein, David Hatch, Pat Quinn, William Clark. They were also known as the "Corpus Christi boys." Back with the army, they were assigned duty to protect army supply trains traveling to Monterrey.

On Feb. 22, 1847, a supply train was attacked by Mexican guerrillas. The teamsters were killed and their bodies horribly mutilated. It was believed the raid was launched from a village named China, a center of guerrilla resistance in northern Mexico. On March 28, 1847, Mustang Gray's company attacked Rancho Guadalupe near the village; 24 civilians were killed. S. Compton Smith, an army surgeon, wrote that Gray's company "in cold blood murdered almost the entire male population of the rancho of Guadalupe, where not a single weapon, offensive or defensive, could be found."

After the massacre, a proclamation urged Mexicans to kill any American they encountered, whether the American was civilian or military, armed or unarmed.

Gray's name was linked to other massacres, real or imagined. One supposedly occurred at a place called Rancho San Francisco, according to Samuel Chamberlain in "My Confession." Chamberlain, a Bostonian, loathed Texans so he may have exaggerated an incident or passed on a rumor. At Rancho San Francisco, he wrote, 36 men

Detail from Samuel Chamberlain's depiction of Mustang Gray riding into battle.

were tied to a post and shot by Mustang Gray's rangers. Most of them were killed, said Chamberlain, by a man called "Greasy Rube."

After the Rancho Guadalupe massacre, Gray's rangers were ordered back to Camargo, where they were mustered out of service on July 21, 1847. Gray stayed behind in Camargo. He died in February 1848, possibly of cholera, and was buried on the Texas side of the river in an unmarked grave.

After his death, a popular myth of Mustang Gray took its form in fiction written by Jeremiah Clemens from Alabama. Gray was also celebrated in a cowboy ballad that went: "There was a gallant Texan / They called him Mustang Gray / When quite a youth he left his home / And went ranging far away." The more accurate assessment was made by John J. Linn, who called him a cold-blooded killer and moral monstrosity.

LAND RUSH — 1

After the old cattle barons were gone, thousands of acres of their ranches were turned into plowed fields as farmers from the Midwest bought subdivided ranchland and moved to South Texas. This was the land rush and homeseeker era, which started with the railroads.

The Texas-Mexican Railroad was completed from Corpus Christi to Laredo in 1881. The San Antonio and Aransas Pass Railroad reached Corpus Christi in 1886. The St. Louis, Brownsville & Mexico Railroad (Brownie) made its first run in 1904. Ranchers could get their beef to market with this network of railroads, but railroads needed people and South Texas was covered by rangeland and cattle. In a sparsely settled land, no people meant no passengers and, except for cattle, no freight.

In the late 1880s, in a bad drought, ranchers began to sell some of their vast acreage. With fencing and stock breeding, they didn't need as much land. They could recover drought losses by selling excess acres, which brought more than they could make by grazing cattle. A Pearsall rancher was quoted in a San Antonio newspaper as saying, "All the vast tracts that have been used for ranches for so many years are being broken into small farms. Companies that own hundreds of thousands of acres are finding that to run cattle on land worth ten dollars an acre is unprofitable."

This undertaking had several dependent parts. Ranchers depended on the land promoters to promote and organize and sell their excess acreage. Railroads depended on the farmers (and more people) to make a profit on lines that were built on speculation. Farmers depended on the railroads to get their crops to market. Railroads helped the land promoters by offering low-cost passenger rates to homeseekers. Land promoters, buying the land outright or working on commission, subdivided large tracts of virgin ranchland into small farm-sized plots. Then they brought in hundreds of farmers and would-be farmers from the Midwest to make the sale.

The great land rush began with the Coleman-Fulton Pasture Company. The Texas Land and Cattle Company and King Ranch followed suit. The Benton pasture lands near Alice, part of the old Galveston Ranch near Falfurrias, the N. G. Collins properties around San Diego as well as chunks of the Welder Ranch were sold for farming.

In San Patricio County, the Coleman-Fulton Pasture Company (the Taft Ranch) was the first to turn to tenant farming, which began in 1886 and intensified in the 1890s. The ranch brought in Frank Ayers to supervise land sales. A house was built for Ayers at a railroad stop called Corpus Christi Junction. This was the first structure in the coming town of Gregory.

The 300,000 acre ranch sold 2,000 acres to Midwestern farmers from $10 an acre up to $25 an acre for smaller tracts. Prospective buyers were invited to come look at the soil. In "The Taft Ranch," A. Ray Stephens wrote that the selling job was made easy when a party of prospective homeseekers found a stray stalk of cotton that had grown accidentally from dropped seed. The stalk contained 80 cotton bolls. The excited buyers "started immediately for their families and farm implements."

Part of the sell-off resulted in founding Portland, the first of the land-rush towns. Two syndicates from Portland, Maine, bought land from the ranch and sold home sites across Nueces Bay from Corpus Christi. A Kansas firm, the Portland Harbor and Improvement Company, bought 640 acres next to property owned by the eastern syndicates. In 1890 and 1891, the Kansas firm developed a town site under the management of John G. Willacy, later a state senator.

The *Corpus Christi Caller* in July 1891 reported the sale of lots in Portland. "The steamer *Mascot* carried people over (from Corpus Christi) to Portland on Friday, making more than one trip . . . " In two days, $33,000 worth of town lots were sold. The area around Portland was one of the first to turn to truck farming. Grocery storeowner William Alexander McHarry built the first frame building "in a town of tents" in Portland.

A few years later, in 1895, the Texas Land & Cattle Company began selling acreage around Flour Bluff. This syndicate in Scotland had bought Mifflin Kenedy's Laureles Ranch. It sold land in the Encinal and Garden tracts outside Corpus Christi. Some Flour Bluff lands were sold in the early 1890s by E. B. Cole (for whom Cole Park was named). Cole would rent buggies with teams of horses, load up the buggies with ice, beer and picnic lunches, and pick up his prospects at the Steen Hotel. They would spend the day driving around Flour Bluff looking at land.

In 1904, 8,000 acres of the Grim Ranch, southwest of Corpus Christi, were sold to Stanley Kostoryz, a Czech newspaper publisher from Nebraska. He paid $52,000 for the tract, which he renamed the Bohemian Colony lands. He sold small plots to Czech farmers from around the country. In 1906, the first five Czech families arrived; the descendants of those Czech farmers, with names like Netek and Zdansky, are still with us.

Surprisingly, even King Ranch began to sell land. Ranch founder Richard King had always followed the advice of his friend Robert E. Lee, who told him, "Buy land, and never

About 1909 in Robstown, a new arrival of homeseekers from the Midwest gather for an excursion in buggies and wagons to look over tracts of land for sale.

sell." When King died in 1885, he owned more than 614,000 acres. In 1906, King's widow Henrietta sold more than 20,000 acres in the Rincon Bovedo tract to Theodore Koch, a banker from St. Paul, Minn. Koch began selling farm tracts and founded two towns, Riviera and Riviera Beach. At Riviera Beach, he built the Buena Vista Hotel, with a fine view of Baffin Bay, for prospective land-buyers.

T. R. Fehrenback wrote that, one way or another, all Texas is connected to a land rush. He was referring to pre-revolutionary Texas. Much of South Texas is connected to a second great land rush that began before the turn of the 20th Century and continued for the first decade afterwards. This land rush really took off with the arrival of young man from Iowa named George H. Paul.

LAND RUSH — 2

George H. Paul grew up near Washington, Iowa. He worked on a farm for $18 a month until he began selling land in Canada. He heard about ranchlands opening up in South Texas so he came down to see what was going on. He arrived in Corpus Christi on Jan. 3, 1907 and stayed at the Seaside Hotel.

The land that stirred his interest was part of the Driscoll Ranch north of the Tex-Mex Railroad, land once owned by Martha Rabb, but it was under contract to land agents from central Texas. Paul agreed to sell land around Hebbronville and soon had carloads of prospective buyers, called homeseekers, arriving. He was approached about the Driscoll land and he met Robert Driscoll in the law office of G. R. Scott in Corpus Christi. Paul agreed to sell the Driscoll lands north of what would become Robstown.

There were other land agents working the area, but the 30-year-old Paul was the standout. He quickly put together an organization and developed a strategy for selling the lands. He had two salaried employees at the start, but within a year he had 1,200 agents across the country. He was running a multi-million-dollar company that would have an immeasurable impact on the future of South Texas.

Paul bought four Pullman cars, one with kitchen facilities, to serve as the homeseekers' hotel for the 10-day trip from Kansas City until their return. With the Pullman cars, Paul was able to bring in 200 people and feed them. He would rent extra Pullman cars when he had more than 200 people. He charged $1.50 per day for bed and meals, well below his expenses.

Paul's homeseeker trains started at Kansas City. "If a state agent had enough people to have a car from his state, we would have a Pullman car located for him. This way we sometimes had several cars all converging on Kansas City to join our train," he wrote in an article in 1957. The railroads gave special Homeseeker Excursion Rates, $23 for a round trip from Kansas City or St. Louis.

In late 1907, Paul hired an Iowa contractor to build what became the State National Bank Building in Robstown. "People asked where we were going to get customers for the general store we established on the first floor of the building. We explained that we expected to bring them in and settle them on the lands in the vicinity of the town."

The sale of 12,000 acres of Driscoll lands north of the railroad began in 1907. Paul started on another 60,000 acres south of the railroad and was soon selling Taft Ranch lands in San Patricio County. For the Nueces County lands, the prospective buyers arrived in Corpus Christi every two weeks. The homeseeker train was switched to the Tex-Mex Railroad line for the short run to Robstown. They would reach Robstown on Friday morning and spend two days looking at land. Paul's Pullman cars were parked on a siding south of town.

All the carriages and buggies were assembled to take the homeseekers to see the land. Hiring enough vehicles was a great problem. Paul's agents would hire buggies and spring wagons from the three livery barns in Corpus Christi, one in Alice and one in San Diego. On the trips, the buggies would make a long caravan, sometimes 50 or more, traveling slowly and stopping often. Each agent carried a map showing lands for sale. Men on horseback would ride back and forth with questions for the agents. Paul's salesmen would show the land, answer questions, and let the customer decide whether to buy. They would say, "If you haven't been given the picture as it exists, Mr. Paul will refund the money for your trip."

On one trip, when the caravan reached a point south of Robstown, an Iowa woman signed a card to buy a 40-acre tract. Before her card was filled out, horsemen came back with orders for the next tract of 880 acres and another for 160 acres. "Before the teams moved again," wrote Paul, "we had signed cards covering 3,000 acres." On average, 85 percent of those who made the trip bought land. But not always. Mrs. O. E. Smith, whose husband sold land for Paul, recalled when 200 prospective buyers arrived just after a heavy rain. "The mosquitoes were so bad," she said, "we didn't sell an acre."

On a typical excursion, they would look at land on Friday and Saturday and return to Corpus Christi for church services or an excursion on the bay aboard the *Pilot Boy.*

Etta Doherty and husband Henry arrived in February 1909 to look over land near Sinton. She wrote a letter to her hometown paper in Fairmount, Ind. "We joined the George H. Paul Company's special car at Kansas City. From there on our trip was made without any change, as the engine, sleepers and diner are under control of the company. There were about 160 passengers. The evenings were spent in entertainment, consisting of music and speeches; the days in becoming better acquainted and seeing new countries. On reaching Sinton, we found Waldo Haisley and family well and enjoying their new home (they came the year before). We took a drive in the morning, passing a beautiful grove of live-oak. We came to a magnificent home owned by a wealthy rancher, which is certainly all that could be desired in the way of a country house . . . In the afternoon we went to Taft . . . Field after field of rich black soil plowed and harrowed, waiting for cotton seed so pleased Henry that I

George H. Paul, who grew up in Iowa, sold one-half million acres of South Texas ranchland for farms. He was known as the father of Robstown.

George H. Paul excursion train arrives at Sinton.

began to fear that I was going to have to call out some of the ranchers to lasso him to keep him from buying a team of mules, donning his blue overalls and going to work at once. It was a very interesting afternoon spent there. We met and talked with some of the farmers, who seemed very prosperous and contented."

LAND RUSH — 3

Flossie Harrop married Harvey Dunlap on July 1, 1908 in Lincoln, Neb. They arrived in Robstown 10 days later, a bright, sunny day. They came down on a George H. Paul homeseekers' train. Harvey Dunlap had bought a tract for a farm the year before.

On their first night in Robstown, the Dunlaps stayed in the Kuehm Hotel, a combination hotel, post office and saloon. About midnight, they heard an uproar and stuck their heads out to investigate. They were told it was only the Driscoll cowboys coming into town.

Next day, when they went to see their farm, three miles from town, the bride encountered a rude shock. "I was amazed at the chaparral and mesquite brush on the farm," Mrs. Dunlap said. "Mr. Dunlap assured me this brush was easily plowed out, that it just had surface roots, but the sequel to that was that it cost 30 dollars an acre for men to grub it out with grubbing axes; the roots were sometimes three feet deep."

The Dunlaps built a two-room house and spent $87 on furnishings. Their toughest task was to "grub out" the deeply rooted and thick growth of running mesquite. They hired Mexican-American workers to dig out the roots. They camped on the farm. The Dunlaps would take a horse and buggy the three miles to town almost every day to get the mail because they were homesick.

What brought people from Nebraska, Iowa, Kansas and Missouri to Texas was the deep longing for their own piece of land. In the Midwest, land prices were out of reach for many, but subdivided ranchland in Texas was cheap, on average $15 to $35 an acre, so homeseekers came here by the thousands.

After buying their plots, they went back to get families, farm equipment, and livestock. Railroads leased boxcars that were separated for household goods and livestock. Dr. Alfred T. Hightower, who bought a tract near Odem, put the family furniture, a wagon, horses, and his Reo automobile in an immigrant boxcar. The family camped under a mesquite tree while their house was being built.

Life was not easy as they struggled to adapt to a harsh land of brush, cactus and rattlesnakes. Some lived in barns or tents until a house could be built and a well dug. Pasture fences and two-story "Kansas barns" for livestock were usually the first priority.

Some homeseekers probably thought the land was ready to plow but, as the Dunlaps discovered, the land had to be cleared of brush and a tenacious underground growth of running mesquite. Underground mesquite was located by small switches showing aboveground. The mesquite roots spread far; people in South Texas, it was said, had to dig for their wood. The dense network of roots had to be dug out with grubbing hoes, mattocks and axes. Thousands of "grubbing crews" came up from Mexico to clear land. Some crews consisted of family units. They were paid by the acre; the rate was $12.50 an acre in 1910, which jumped to $25 an acre or more. S. J. Vickers, who bought a tract near Sodville, hired Mexican laborers to dig out the roots. They lived in tents on his land and worked to clear the running mesquite. The grubbed-out roots were burned in huge piles.

Root plowing was also done with huge steam tractors. It was said to be common to find chunks of coal that had been dropped while fueling the tractors. Some steam tractors burned the mesquite roots they dug up. Plowing out the roots was made easier when a root plow was invented by a Moravian blacksmith named Tom Mrazek, who came to Robstown in 1908. People wielding grubbing hoes and the powerful steam tractors moved across virgin pastureland until what had once been grazing range for cattle was converted into farmland. Cowboys called this turning the grass upside-down.

Some homeseekers met with difficulties and hardships and many went back north, especially in the drought years that began in 1914. Some hardy ones, determined to make good, survived and learned how to farm in South Texas. These hardy Midwestern farmers (many of them Republicans) were super-imposed (or grafted may be a better word) onto the culture of South Texas.

George H. Paul in 1957 said, "As we showed the lands we always stressed the need for more people and that with plenty of people this would become a very beautiful and prosperous section of the country. I remember talking to a young, single man from Nebraska. I think he was quite impressed by what I told him, for he bought a tract of land, then went back to Nebraska and got married and brought his new wife to Robstown. I believe they added eight children to the population, and now I am told that one of their sons has started off with twins, so the populating of Texas goes on. This young man from Nebraska was named Harvey Dunlap."

Paul had a powerful influence on the future of South Texas. Following the rapid expansion of grazing land into farmland, new towns were built, including Robstown, Bishop, Sinton, Taft, Gregory, Orange Grove, Premont, Falfurrias, Riviera, and others. In 1907, Paul sold 56,000 acres of Driscoll land. In 1908, he sold 56,000 acres of Coleman-Fulton Pasture Company land in San Patricio

At Banquete, a grubbing crew stands beside a mammoth kerosene-burning tractor that was used to plow up running mesquite roots to prepare land for farming.

County. In 1910, Paul sold 70,000 acres of John Welder's ranchland. In two years, he sold 200,000 acres in Nueces and San Patricio counties. Before the land rush was over, he sold half a million acres of Texas ranchland and, in doing so, made a fortune, but there is a sad sequel to his story.

Paul did not know about the deposits of oil under much of the half million acres of land that he had owned. If he had kept the mineral rights on that oil-rich land, it would have paid the rent. After business reverses in later years, Paul lived in extreme poverty in a basement apartment in Omaha, Neb. He died on August. 22, 1965. He was 88.

CHRISTMAS

The Republic of Texas celebrated its first Christmas in 1836 at Washington-on-the-Brazos. Sam Houston, hero of San Jacinto, made a speech in which he said a republic could only be founded by an industrious and sober people. This must have raised eyebrows, for Houston was a heavy drinker. His Cherokee friends called him Big Drunk. After the speech on sobriety, there was a Christmas party in which spiked eggnog flowed freely until the wee hours. The eggnog, I suppose, was spiked with a full measure of irony.

Of course that wasn't the first recorded Christmas celebrated in Texas. The first may have been in 1683 when a Spanish expedition to "Tejas" was led by Juan Dominguez de Mendoza. On Christmas Day 1683, near today's Presidio, Mendoza said that to celebrate the event, "On the top of a hill, I had a holy cross planted."

Perhaps the second observance of Christmas came three years later in 1686 on Garcitas Creek at Fort St. Louis (in today's Victoria County). La Salle's miserably doomed colonists celebrated Christmas with a midnight Mass, after which they cried, "The King drinks (after the custom of France), though we had only water. When that was over we began to think of setting out." After the colony was wiped out in a smallpox epidemic and Indian attack, after La Salle was killed by his own men, his loyal lieutenant, Henri Joutel, made his way back to France. That's how we know of the Christmas celebration on Garcitas Creek.

After Sam Houston's speech on sobriety, there was a Christmas party in which the spiked eggnog flowed freely.

Going forward to pre-Civil War times, there are interesting accounts of how Christmas was observed by plantation slaves in "The Slave Narratives of Texas," edited by Ron Tyler and Lawrence R. Murphy.

From that book, a slave named Edna Rains remembered that "Our biggest time was Christmas. Massa'd give us maybe four bits to spend as we wanted . . . On Christmas Eve we'd play games like 'Young Gal Loves Candy' or 'Hide and Whoop.' We didn't know anything about Santa Claus; never were we taught that. But we always knew what we'd get on Christmas morning. Old Massa always called us together and gave us new clothes and shoes. He always went to town on the eve and brought back our things in a cotton sack. That old sack would be crammed full of things, and we knew it was clothes and shoes because Massa didn't believe in foolishness. We got one pair of shoes a year, at Christmas. Most times they were red and I'd always paint mine black. I'd skim grease off dishwater, mix it with soot from the chimney, and paint my shoes. I was one [Negro] who didn't like red."

There are several accounts of Christmas celebrations on South Texas ranches. Mrs. S. G. Miller in "Sixty Years in the Nueces Valley" described one Christmas on the Miller Ranch (near today's Mathis) when they had unexpected visitors. "We set a fancy table for Santa Claus so that he could eat his supper on Christmas Eve night when he arrived with presents. All the goodies, including the roast turkey and a whole roast pig, were set on a big table in readiness for the great dinner on the morrow. In each of two corners was a barrel half full of apples. We had all gone into the living room to rest awhile. Suddenly, there was a tremendous crash in the dining room. We rushed in and were face to face with four of the biggest possums I ever saw." They ended up baked with sweet potatoes in the old-fashioned possum-and-taters dish.

Rachel Bluntzer Hebert grew up on a ranch near Banquete. In her book "Impressions," she wrote: "There was always Christmas to look forward to. When the time neared, Ramon Flores would go to the pasture to find a tree. It had to be large, even if of an unknown variety. He would set it up in the living room . . . Tomasa and I would make crepe paper chains and popcorn strings to drape around the tree. Mama would have one of the Mexican women make stockings of varied colors . . . After going to Robstown and buying crates of apples and oranges, bags of Christmas candy and nuts, we stuffed the stockings to capacity . . . Our family never made it a practice to exchange gifts, but Santa always came when we were young. When we reached 12 or 13, we ceased to get anything from Santa . . . It was the year of the drought. I was about 10. Santa no longer came (with gifts) for the older children. At the break of dawn, I was up when all were asleep. I crept down the stairs. I had left Santa some whisky and a piece of fruitcake. There on the hearth were some small things, a doll and some doll furniture and a tiny bathtub . . . The next Christmas, I went downstairs, hoping against hope, but there was nothing. The empty hearth left a gaping void that stayed with me all day."

Maude Gilliland in her book "Rincon" described Christmas on a South Texas ranch around the turn of the 20th Century. "At Christmas time, the boys went out in the pasture and cut down an ebony tree and put it in the upstairs room. On Christmas Eve the older boys and girls locked the door and we younger children had to wait until they finished decorating it before we could go in. The decorators first tied apples to the larger branches, then draped yards of popcorn strings around it. For other decorations they used colored paper chains and trinkets that might glitter, including rock candy which they tied to the branches with thread. After lighting the candles they opened the door. We stood there pop-eyed as we looked at the tree glistening in the flickering light of candles. I thought it was the most beautiful sight I had ever seen. This was Christmas Eve."

SALOONS

Corpus Christi in its early years, after its founding in 1839, had no churches but there was no shortage of saloons. That was especially true after Zachary Taylor's army set up camp in 1845.

Some 4,000 soldiers — half the U.S. Army — pitched their tents from North Beach to Artesian Park. Makeshift grog shops catering to the army were constructed of frame walls covered with cloth. When the army moved to the Rio Grande, grog-shop proprietors were told to stay behind, but they loaded wagons with barrels of Dicky Jones brandy and Monongahela whisky and followed the army. At Santa Gertrudis Creek (where Kingsville is today) some were sent back in irons and their liquor poured out.

Three years later, in the Gold Rush, Corpus Christi became a transit point on the way to California. The 49'ers could drink at the California House, a saloon and hotel on Chaparral. In the 1850s, Edward Harney opened the Ruby Saloon. After Dr. J. T. Yarrington shot and killed "Legs" Lewis, co-founder of King Ranch, men at the Ruby Saloon raised a toast to the doctor. Yarrington shot Lewis for carrying on with his wife. Lewis's reputation as a ladies' man had made him enemies among the patrons of the Ruby Saloon.

The La Retama Saloon opened across Chaparral from the Sierra Madre Hotel. On Aug. 4, 1860, John Warren, a butcher, got drunk and threatened to kill two men at the saloon. Sheriff Mat Nolan took Warren home and put him to bed (there was no jail). Warren later returned to the La Retama and stabbed the owner, leaving him near death. The sheriff and his brother Tom Nolan found Warren, who yelled, "Stand back or I'll shoot you!" When Tom tried to take his pistol, Warren shot him in the forehead. Mat and other men chased Warren into Zeigler's Hall and shot him to death. Tom Nolan died 11 days later.

In the 1870s, George Roberts' Favorite Saloon opened next to the Crescent Hotel on Chaparral. It was a large place with a billiard parlor and bowling alley. In 1883, Conrad Uehlinger opened a saloon across from Market Hall on Mesquite Street. Uehlinger's bar was in a small shellcrete building. After Uehlinger sold the place, it was renamed the Market Saloon. Uehlinger opened another saloon on Chaparral called the Wall Street Bar. Another Uehlinger, John, ran the Miramar Bar.

In this time of saloons, the city's greatest saloon was the Grande Saloon, later called the Ben Grande. Frank Grande Sr. built the Grande Saloon at Waco and Leopard. The family lived upstairs. In time, there was a whole Grande complex — the Grande Hotel, the Grande Restaurant, the Grande Pool Hall.

The Ben Grande Saloon had cockfights and, it was said, a man could ride up on his horse and a drink would be brought out to him. When he was a boy, William Fuller was wandering around while his father conducted business. He heard music coming from the door of a big two-story building. It was the Ben Grande. "Some men came out laughing and talking in a jovial mood. A female voice from the inside called goodbye a couple of times. I peeked in and saw the long shiny bar. The smell of whisky and beer was strong. A man at the bar turned, saw me, and yelled a good-natured hello. I scampered back toward Papa and his friends. It was my first sight of the famous, or infamous, Ben Grande."

A rancher shot and killed a man in the Ben Grande Saloon. The rancher, riding away, warned: "Tell Mike I'll kill anybody who comes after me." Sheriff Mike Wright rode out to the ranch. He was unarmed, as he usually was. The rancher met him with rifle. "I'll kill you before I let you take me in." Wright told him, "You see, I came, but I'm not wearing a gun." After a little talk, the rancher put down his rifle and rode back to town with the sheriff.

Most of the saloons were concentrated on Chaparral and Mesquite. At one time, eight saloons were clustered around Market Hall. On Mesquite were the Palace Bar, the Richelieu Bar, and, said to be toughest of all, the Buckhorn Saloon. On Chaparral were the Bluff City Saloon, The Club, the Stag Bar, the Tarpon Club Saloon, and the Dixie Bar. On Water Street were several beer joints. One was the Bay Saloon run by the Mircovich family of bay fishermen.

The town in 1916 had an astonishing 37 saloons (considering its size) with three others just outside city limits. Corpus Christi, said revivalist Mordecai F. Ham, was the rottenest town in Texas. Rev. Ham preached to packed revival meetings about the evils of Demon Rum. The revival dovetailed with an effort by the Nueces County Prohibition Club to force an election to determine whether the sale of intoxicating liquor should be banned in the county.

After a fierce campaign, Nueces County voted "dry" on March 10, 1916. It was closing time for the Ben Grande and the 36 other saloons. National Prohibition soon followed. Saloons were shut down and their proprietors found new lines of work. There must have been a bargain on bar furnishings. The Ben Grande became a grocery store. John Mircovich, who ran the Bay Saloon, opened the Bay Grocery.

Ben Grande behind the bar of his saloon.

A farm loan business moved into the Bluff City Saloon. The Buckhorn Saloon became a rooming house. The Market Saloon on Mesquite became the Alcove Chili Parlor, a favorite hangout of high school students.

For the patrons of the Ben Grande and the Buckhorn Saloon, it was a long time between drinks — 17 years. The bars would not reopen until the nation repealed Prohibition in 1933.

FREE MAIL DELIVERY

From 1846 through the 19th Century and in the first years of the 20th century, people in Corpus Christi got their mail by picking it up at the post office. That changed in June 1908 when free city delivery was inaugurated to homes and businesses.

In early 1908, a postal inspector recommended that carrier service be implemented in Corpus Christi. Postmaster T. D. Ward reported that home mail delivery would begin on Monday, June 8. I assume (and it may be a big assumption) that homes were already numbered. Old maps show that, early on, Corpus Christi adopted the Philadelphia system of having 100 numbers to the block, but I don't know if address numbers were displayed or whether this was done when free delivery was instituted.

There were four carriers in 1908: Hugh Long, Dudley Smith, Charles Rankin, and Berry Morris, and two substitutes: Harvey Ragsdale and Clyde Perras. Delivering the mail wasn't easy in those days. There were no sidewalks or paved streets and when it rained the carriers had to wade through deep mud. A year later, a rural route was added, which ran out along Dump Road (Staples) to the Sunshine community. D. E. Baland was the carrier for RFD 1.

Those first mail routes give us a good idea of the size of the city. The routes stretched from the north at Hall's Bayou, where the port entrance is today, to Buford Avenue in the south and from Water Street in the east to Last Street

Mail carriers and postal clerks stand outside the Federal Building on Starr Street in 1924.

on the bluff in the west. (Last Street is now Alameda.) That's it. There was not enough population density outside the downtown and uptown areas to justify door-to-door mail delivery. How much did it cost to mail a letter then? Two cents.

THE GREEN FLAG

I was reading about Southern Alkali and it led me to wonder what happened to the Green Flag. In 1934, the city gained its first big industry, Southern Alkali. A delegation led by Maston Nixon convinced the company to locate in Corpus Christi.

The city's advantages included the new port, cheap natural gas, a supply of alkali and brine, oyster shell lime, and an adequate water supply. The water supply presented a problem because of the collapse of the La Fruta Dam, which emptied the city's reservoir, Lake Lovenskiold. The city moved quickly to build a new dam, Mathis Dam, to impound a new city water supply at Lake Corpus Christi. Besides the water supply, another hurdle was the company's requirement of a 30-foot-deep inner-harbor channel to Avery Point. The port agreed that it would find the funds to dredge that channel.

When the deal was finalized, the Green Flag was flown over Leopard Street between the Nixon Building and the Plaza Hotel. The Green Flag was a symbol of the city achieving some great success. It was flown again when the Corpus Christi gained the Naval Air Station.

In 1934, when the Green Flag went up, the *Corpus Christi Times* reported that "business practically stopped everywhere except at the telephone switchboards while citizens congratulated each other." They knew that the Green Flag meant they had landed Southern Alkali. They also knew what that would mean for a job-hungry city in the middle of the Great Depression.

An office was opened on Leopard Street. Ben Garza, who helped found LULAC, sat at a card table and helped select workers to construct the plant. In the beginning Southern Alkali hired 250 workers in a city desperate for jobs. The plant opened on Sept. 1, 1934. It produced soda ash and caustic soda from oyster shell and brine. It was the first major industrial plant in Corpus Christi. It was also the first of many large chemical plants that would be built along the coast. But what happened to the Green Flag, symbol of civic success? It would be nice to have it, in case we ever get the chance to fly it again.

BOMBING THE ISLAND

A few weeks ago it was reported that the Army Corps of Engineers inspected an area near Padre Balli Park for leftover munitions or bomb remnants from World War II. That's when areas of Padre Island were used for target and gunnery practice. The Corps inspectors found no bombs or munitions.

After reading that story, I looked up an old map I have showing the restricted areas where aerial bombing and gunnery practice were conducted. There were three larger circular areas on the Gulf side, beginning near Packery Channel, and stretching south. A fourth area used for gunnery practice was on the Laguna Madre side.

Pat Dunn, the old Duke of Padre Island, was dead when this was going on. He sold the island in 1926 and moved into the Nueces Hotel. But he kept grazing rights on the island for his cattle. It was said that Dunn's cattle were so used to the Navy's aerial bombing sorties that they would run in the opposite direction when they heard the drone of planes overhead.

The island was off limits to visitors and fishermen during the war. It was patrolled by the Coast Guard, which maintained patrol and observation stations every six miles, all linked by phone. A few survivors from ships torpedoed by U-boats landed on the island and were rescued by the Coast Guard units.

After the war, the Navy still made use of the island for target practice, at least until 1946. When the JFK Causeway opened in 1950, any use of the island for target practice became impractical, unless the Navy wanted to use sunbathers stretched out on beach blankets as targets.

There's another little-known story about Padre Island in World War II. The first atomic bomb, in a test, was exploded near Los Alamos, New Mexico, on July 16, 1945. Only later it was revealed that one of the possible sites under consideration for that atomic blast was Padre Island. That really would have scared Pat Dunn's cattle.

KNIGHTS OF GOLDEN CIRCLE

Near the end of 1860, large groups of strangers began arriving in Corpus Christi by steamer from New Orleans. They left Corpus Christi on foot. Who were they? Where were they going? What was their purpose? No one knew. It was very mysterious.

Corpus Christi's newspaper, the *Ranchero*, edited by Henry Maltby, solved the mystery. The men belonged to a secret society called the Knights of the Golden Circle. The Knights had a plan to settle the problems Southern slave-holders had with their arch enemies, the so-called "bloody-fanged abolitionists" of the North. Their arrival in Corpus Christi was connected to that plan.

As an organization, the Knights of the Golden Circle was four years old, founded in Lexington, Ky., on July 4, 1856 by George Bickley. The secret society spread across the South. Local units were called "castles." Members were formed in three orders. Those with a military assignment (most of the members) were called Knights of the Iron Hand. Those with a financial calling were Knights of the True Faith and those with political skills (the leaders) were Knights of the Columbian Star.

The objective of the Knights of the Golden Circle was to "perfect" the institution of slavery in a new empire of slavery. This empire would be enclosed in a golden circle with Havana as the capital. It would extend to Central America and include much of Mexico and the West Indies.

In the United States, this empire would stretch from Kansas to Maryland and include Texas and all the states of the South. The empire, as they envisioned it, would hold a monopoly on tobacco, cotton, sugar, rice, and coffee. The South would control an empire that would become a world power, one to rival ancient Rome. Havana, in fact, would be called New Rome. With this wealth and power, the cities of the South would no longer be dependent on the abolitionist cities of the North.

That was the long-term goal. Short term, the Knights would assemble a force to conquer Mexico. If Mexico could be conquered, then carved into states and admitted to the Union, the added representation in Congress would make the South politically dominant.

It was a slave-owner's fairy tale, not to mention being morally repugnant, but the Knights had followers in Texas who were men of high rank. Ranger Capt. Rip Ford was almost surely a member. Alfred Marmaduke Hobby, later a Confederate leader, was a member. A large number of legislators were members. There were 30 "castles" in the state, with one in Corpus Christi. Reputed local members were hotelier Jacob Ziegler, George Pfeuffer, and Dr. Philip N. Luckett, an influential surgeon with the Texas Rangers.

In the fall of 1860, the Knights were on the march. The mysterious movement of men toward the border was part of the plan to conquer Mexico. The venture was badly organized. Several groups of men arrived in Corpus Christi and left on foot, walking toward the border. One rendezvous point was Brownsville and another was in Encinal County (this county was later added to Webb County, at Laredo). One group reached Banquete and settled down to wait for an army of thousands.

J. Williamson Moses, a former Ranger who was postmaster at Banquete, was disdainful of this wild scheme. "This magnificent order, at least in name," he wrote, "planned secretly to organize and when they had a sufficiently powerful host at their command, they were to swoop down on the land of Mexico, like Goths of ancient days. The leaders promised that the followers were to have a tract of 50 acres and five Mexican slaves, or peons, to till it for them. This was to be the allotment of privates. The officers, according to rank, were to get larger amounts of land and a greater number of slaves." Some of the more optimistic among them were learning Spanish.

The country above Brownsville was filled with Knights. "Their campfires are increased every night by new parties arriving during the day," a Galveston paper reported. So many arrived at Gonzales that Gov. Sam Houston ordered them to disband and return home.

Henry Maltby noted in the *Ranchero* on Sept. 15, 1860 that a detachment of Knights passed through Corpus Christi and, a week later, another detachment arrived. "Those who passed through last week are at Banquete," he wrote. "It appears they are bound to suffer disappointment, as they expected to meet a large force subsequent to a march on Matamoros." The paper said there were no large concentrations of Knights in Encinal County "or at any point in this section, hence the disappointment." The Knights who passed through were said to be "orderly and gentlemanly in their bearing, and one would suppose them not likely to be gulled by the prospect of a rancho in Mexico." But Maltby understood that they lacked the military force of arms to invade Mexico and he advised young men to stay home and forget the dreams of empire.

George Bickley, leader of the Knights, arrived in Texas and cited difficulties in raising money, buying weapons, and organizing such a large undertaking. He said he was postponing the Mexican invasion to await the outcome of the U. S. presidential election in November. The dispirited

J. Williamson Moses, postmaster at Banquete, said the Knights of the Golden Circle planned to "swoop down on the land of Mexico like Goths of ancient days."

phalanx of Knights who had come to South Texas to conquer Mexico headed home.

Corpus Christi's "castle" turned out on the fifth birthday of the K.G.C., July Fourth, 1861. The *Ranchero* reported that the local Knights "a numerous body, who have been regarded as a very mysterious order, marched through the streets, even as other members filed into Ziegler's Hall. George Pfeuffer made a telling speech and the Knights made a telling impression on the good things spread before them, and numerous pert toasts were made." That was their last hurrah before the "castle" disintegrated. Some of the first Confederate militia units were formed from the ranks of the Knights of the Golden Circle. Some secessionist leaders had been high in the order. But their dreams of preserving slavery in a new Empire of the Gulf was not to be, as the mysterious K.G.C. became one of the first victims of the Civil War.

TRAILING CATTLE EAST

Trailing cattle to Louisiana and Mississippi is much older than trailing cattle to Kansas. Thousands of Texas longhorns from herds belonging to Spanish missions in South Texas were driven to Louisiana to feed the Spanish army of Bernardo de Galvez.

Galvez, governor of Spanish Louisiana, was commissioned by Spain to mount a campaign against the British to assist the Americans in their fight for independence. From 1779 to 1881, during the American Revolution, 10,000 longhorns were trailed across bayous and through swamps to New Orleans. In 1779, a herd of 1,000 head, with 20 men from San Antonio hired to drive them, were attacked by Comanche warriors, who killed one drover, wounded two others, and slaughtered cattle.

Before the Texas Revolution, Victoria's Martin de Leon took a herd to New Orleans. They traveled over what became known as the Opelousas Route. From New Orleans, the cattle could be shipped to markets in the north. It was a lucrative business. In 1835, a steer that would sell for $5 in Texas would bring $35 in New Orleans. J. Frank Dobie ("The Longhorns") noted that when the battle of San Jacinto was fought, "a herd of Texas cattle was being trailed to New Orleans, which for decades continued as a market, cattle being shipped thence north by boat. Shreveport and Vidalia (opposite Natchez on the Mississippi) and New Iberia were other loading points."

After the Texas Revolution, with Texas under new ownership, the veterans of San Jacinto rounded up cattle abandoned by the retreating Spanish rancheros and drove them east for sale. They became known as "cow-boys."

James Taylor White, an early rancher (near the present town of Liberty), drove cattle to market in New Orleans during the late 1830s and early 1840s. Some ranchers would put their cattle together in a big herd and drive them to New Orleans. In their absence, women and children would "fort up" in one of the ranch homes, giving them the security of numbers, until the men returned from the drive, which would take several weeks.

For cattlemen along the coast, it was faster to ship by sea, but not cheaper. A man named James Foster of Indianola began buying and shipping cattle to New Orleans on Morgan Line ships. By 1851, he controlled the stock-carrying capacity of most steamboats sailing from Indianola to New Orleans. The longhorns made the journey in pens built between decks and on decks. Their horns, which could stretch five feet from tip to tip, were probably sawed off to make more room.

A cattleman named William B. Grimes, objecting to the high rates charged by the Morgan Line, decided in 1855 to send a herd over the Opelousas Route to New Orleans. One of his ranch hands, Abel Head "Shanghai" Pierce, was in charge of the herd. Pierce was 20 years old. He would go on to become one of Texas' greatest cattlemen, no doubt the most colorful of a colorful breed.

During the Civil War, Texas cattle were trailed east to feed Confederate armies. M. A. Withers, a trail hand, was 16 when he helped take a herd from Lockhart to Shreveport in 1862 ("Trail Drivers of Texas"). On another drive to Shreveport, the drovers found the buffalo flies so bad "the cattle would run off, crazed with misery, and it was hard to drive them back to the herd."

Cattleman Shanghai Pierce once drove a herd of cattle from Indianola to New Orleans.

W. D. H. Saunders was 17 when he was hired to drive a herd of 1,100 longhorns from Goliad to Mississippi in October 1862 ("Trail Drivers"). When they reached the Mississippi River, a thousand of the herd "took to the water and easily swam across." Some 100 cattle, quite sensibly, were unwilling to jump into the river. They were sold on the Louisiana side. The drovers and owners were arrested and detained on both sides of the river by Confederate authorities, who thought they were trying to take the herd to the Union Army besieging Vicksburg. Most of the cattle were sold below Natchez, while some were trailed on across Mississippi to Mobile, Ala., to be sold.

Trailing cattle across snake-infested swamps, bayous and marshy bogs of Louisiana had to be difficult, but details of these early cattle drives are scarce. The drive Shanghai Pierce made to New Orleans in 1855 for William B. Grimes became the basis for one of his famous campfire stories. His ability to elaborate on a story was legendary. His story of the Louisiana trip was told in the cowboy fashion of tall tales (taken from "Shanghai Pierce: A Fair Likeness," by Chris Emmett).

"The mud and water of the Louisiana swamps compelled us to pick every step," Shanghai said. "The public roads — where there were any — would bog a saddle blanket. My steers were nice, fat slick critters that knew how to swim, but they were used to a carpet of prairie grass. They were mighty choosey as to where they put their feet. They had a bushel of sense, and pretty soon over there in Louisiana they got to balancing themselves on logs in order to keep out of the slimy mud. They got so expert that one of them would walk a cypress knee to the stump, jump over it, land on a root, and walk it out for another jump. If there was a bad bog-hole between cypresses you would see a steer hang his horns into a mustang-grapevine and swing across like a monkey. The way they balanced and jumped and swung actually made my horse laugh."

BILLY'S MARK

At the start of the Mexican War, William Rogers survived a terrible ordeal near the Rio Grande. In later years, fantastic stuff was said about "Billy" Rogers and part of it may be true.

William Long "Billy" Rogers was born in Alabama in 1822, one of 10 children of Patterson and Elizabeth Rogers. Patterson fought in the Seminole Wars in Florida, where he was a friend of Zachary Taylor, then he ran a hotel at Fort Jesup, La. His son-in-law, Roswell Denton, was appointed sutler (a storekeeper who sold goods on a military post).

When Taylor brought half the U.S. Army to Corpus Christi in 1845, the Rogers family followed. When the army moved to the Rio Grande in March 1846, a supply depot was established at Point Isabel. Taylor authorized Roswell Denton to forward army supplies. Denton prepared a wagon train to carry supplies to Point Isabel, under the supervision of Patterson and two sons, Anderson and Billy. Once on the border, Patterson planned to open a hotel to cater to the army.

Denton, in New Orleans to buy goods, wrote to warn his father-in-law that it was too dangerous to move a wagon train to the border without an army escort. There were too many bandits and guerrillas operating on the Rio Grande. The warning came too late.

The supply train left Corpus Christi on April 25, 1846, two weeks before the first battles of the Mexican War were fought at Palo Alto and Resaca de la Palma. Besides Patterson Rogers and two sons, members of the supply train were teamsters, with three women and four children.

The wagon train followed the trail left by Taylor's army and arrived at the Paso Real on the Arroyo Colorado on May 1, 1846. Four miles south, they were surrounded by 50 or more guerrillas. Patterson Rogers and the teamsters, taken by surprise, surrendered and were forced to head back to the arroyo.

Two teamsters named Horton and Allenbrook were shot to death and a Mrs. Atwater was killed with a saber thrust. At the arroyo, 19 others were bound and stripped of their clothes; the bandits wanted the clothes without bloodstains. The women were raped. The throats of men, women and children were slashed and their bodies toppled into the river below. All were killed except one.

William Rogers missed death by an inch of a knife's blade. A deep gash severed his windpipe, but the blade missed his jugular. He was alive when pushed into the river. After the bandits left, he wandered, semi-conscious, naked, and sunburned. He staggered through dense brush and stayed alive by foraging for berries and drinking rainwater. He could manage this by lying on his back.

On the fourth day, more dead than alive, he came to the ranch of Juan Corona, 30 miles from the site of the massacre. He was taken in and nursed back from the brink of death. While recuperating, Rogers learned Spanish, which would prove useful when he began to search for the killers. The rancher Juan Corona was afraid that when word got around that someone had survived the massacre, attempts might be made on Rogers' life. Corona turned him over to the authorities in Matamoros.

War correspondent George Wilkins Kendall passed the site of the massacre. "We saw the remains of no less than seven of the unfortunate Rogers party, so cruelly murdered here a few weeks since," Kendall wrote. "Five skeletons, one of them apparently a female, were lying upon the banks, where they drifted after their throats had been cut; two others were discovered near the wagons. The wolves and buzzards had done their work."

In Matamoros, William Rogers was thrown into jail, his wound untreated. When he was not returned in a prisoner exchange, Gen. David Twiggs, a friend of Patterson Rogers, threatened to bombard Matamoros if Billy Rogers wasn't freed. He was released and his gaping wound treated by Army surgeon N. R. Jarvis. Gen. Zachary Taylor dispatched a ship to return Rogers to Corpus Christi, where he recuperated at the home of his mother.

Rogers traveled to the border to wed Julia Corona, the girl who cared for him after the massacre. It was the patient returning to marry the nurse. He became a prominent man in Corpus Christi. He bought a ranch, was elected sheriff of Nueces County, then county judge, and sent to the Legislature. Rogers bought the St. James Hotel and he was a co-owner of Market Hall. In 1871, after his home burned, he organized Corpus Christi's first volunteer fire department.

Rogers was a well-known citizen. What was not well-known, but whispered about, was that he once prowled the border searching for the bandits who killed his father and brother and left him for dead.

A few names of the bandits were known. The leader was one Juan Balli, also spelled as Juan Baillie. The plunder taken from the wagon train showed up in Reynosa. "Mustang" Gray's Rangers discovered that the Patterson Rogers killers were on a ranch near Matamoros. Gray's Rangers attacked the ranch and killed two dozen men, which accounted for half the killers.

A pattern of death was established for the others. One by one, it was said, bodies were found of men killed in a

William L. (Billy) Rogers survived a massacre on the Arroyo Colorado in 1846.

distinctive way. They were stabbed in the chest and their throats cut, almost symbolically. The story was that "Billy" Rogers and his brother Lieuen traveled up the Rio Grande on King and Kenedy riverboats. They would attend fandangos and when certain individuals were pointed out, they would be coaxed outside, into the shadows, stabbed in the heart and their throats cut. True? No one knows for sure.

But on the lower Rio Grande a slashed throat was called Billy's mark. The general belief was that Billy Rogers got his revenge, murder for murder. Simple, direct acts of retribution were understood, and appreciated, on both sides of the border. Years later, Rogers told a friend that he and Lieuen accounted for all the cutthroat killers except a man known as Capt. Santos who fled deep into the interior of Mexico. Billy Rogers died on Dec. 17, 1877. He was 56, still a young man, but his health had been poor, complicated by an old throat wound. He was buried in Old Bayview Cemetery.

MARKET HALL

Corpus Christi had been a settlement since 1839, a chartered town since 1852, and a growing municipality for three decades before the first city hall was built.

In the 1850s, the City Council (board of aldermen then) met in two shellcrete buildings on Chaparral: the Ohler building north of the Peoples Street intersection and the identical Hunsaker building south of the intersection. The council also met in Cornelius Cahill's two-story building across Water Street from Central Wharf. In the 1860s, the aldermen met in Charles Lovenskiold's academy.

In 1871, William Rogers and Richard Jordan offered to build a structure on Market Square that would provide space for city government, at no cost to the taxpayers. The builders would lease lower stalls to vendors and let the city utilize the upper floor. What was called Market Square — bordered by Schatzell, Broadway, Peoples, and Mesquite — was the site of sheds occupied by butchers and fruit and vegetable vendors. For years, people complained that butchers dumped rotting meat scraps around the square.

Unlike most towns in Texas, Corpus Christi didn't have a town square. There was uptown on the bluff, downtown on the beach below, and Artesian Square north of the main business district. If there was a focal point of the community, it was the area around Market Square.

In July 1871, the city agreed to the proposal. Jordan and Rogers hired E. D. Sidbury to construct a two-story building at a cost of $10,000. The building was to be 80 feet long, 32 feet wide, with a tin roof and brick floor. The lower floor would be divided into stalls for vendors and butchers. The agreement allowed the builders to charge rent for the stalls for 12 years, after which the building would become city property. To make sure the deal would be profitable, the city passed an ordinance making it illegal to sell meat or vegetables anywhere inside the city except at Market Hall.

When the building was finished, the city used the upper floor, where the mayor and aldermen met, and next to their offices was a large hall for dances and public events. One tenant was the recently formed Pioneer Fire Company No. 1, organized after fire destroyed the home of William Rogers. The Pioneer Fire Company and other volunteer companies — the Lone Star Hook & Ladder Company and the Shamrock Hose Company — fought fires in the city until a full-time paid department was established in 1914.

During Market Hall's existence, the big social event of the year was the firemen's parade and ball. The town's wards competed to have the most elaborately decorated hose cart for the parade. There was keen competition between firemen over who could move their wagon the fastest or pump the most water. The events were followed by an elegant supper and dance at Market Hall.

A bell tower on the top of Market Hall housed the fire bell, which sounded the alarm for fires (by ringing without stop). George Stevenson, the bell-ringer, would ring the bell to signal the start of the work day at 7 a.m. He would ring it at 8:45 on school days to alert the children that school would begin in 15 minutes. The council in 1874 stopped paying for a full-time ringer. After a hurricane wrecked the bell tower and sent the bell crashing to the ground, it was mounted on a concrete base and kept at ground level, at the back of Market Hall, next to the cistern, where men would gather to whittle and talk.

Photo of Market Hall, circa 1905, shows a ladder, used for training volunteer firemen, leaning against the building. The bell in the tower at right sounded the alarm for fires and signaled the start of the work day and school day.

When traveling shows came to town, they performed at Market Hall. In 1873, the Royal Japanese Troupe of acrobats played to a full house. The star of the show was a midget tumbler named "Little All Right." At a Christmas ball in 1876, the town was outraged when some culprit sprinkled cayenne pepper on the dance floor. The impersonator George Landrum appeared at Market Hall in a one-man play "A Pair of Spectacles" (reserved seats, 35 cents). The Spooner Dramatic Club, with Miss Allie Spooner, produced a play "The Pearl of Savoy." When photographer Louis de Planque moved to Corpus Christi, he put on an exhibition of photographs "in Polarscopic light" at Market Hall.

"Upstairs over Market House was a big hall, where the principal entertainments were held," Capt. Andrew Anderson once recalled. "Sometimes we had regular shows. Two of the popular shows then were 'Ten Nights in a Barroom,' and 'The Yankee in Texas.' Another play we liked was 'Rip Van Winkle.' The actors wore stovepipe hats, beaver hats. And we had medicine shows, too. I remember especially how they would sell Hamlin's Wizard Oil from a wagon. Four fellows would sing beautifully, and the whole street would be full of people listening to the singing. Finally, someone arranged for them to give an entertainment at Market Hall. You paid 25 cents to hear them sing, and they had a full house every night for a week. They sold a lot of Wizard Oil."

Market Hall was 40 years old when it was torn down in 1911 to make way for a new three-story brick City Hall on Market Square. What was once Market Square is now a small park below the towering buildings on the bluff. For a long time, the triangular area around Market Hall was the closest thing Corpus Christi had to a town square.

TALL BUILDINGS ON BLUFF

Corpus Christi was called the Bluff City. The bluff was where the town began, where Henry Kinney built a trading post, where Forbes Britton, Martha Rabb, Mifflin Kenedy and Henrietta King built baronial mansions on Broadway facing east on the edge of the bluff.

Kinney named Broadway at a time when Corpus Christi had only a few stores and a hundred citizens. Broadway opens a window into the city's history at a time of great change. People in mansions on Broadway had a wide-angle view of the terrible devastation of the 1919 storm. Corpus Christi languished in those years. A man could shoot a cannon down Chaparral, Eli Merriman said, and not hit anyone. That changed when the port opened in 1926. Suddenly, Corpus Christi was filled with cotton buyers, cotton brokers, cotton exporters and office space was at a high premium.

Maston Nixon planned to build a tall building to fill the need. Nixon grew up in Luling. His first job was to harness a mule that pulled the ice wagon. He saved his money and invested in an oil company that became Humble Oil. Nixon served as an artillery captain in World War I and after the war he moved to a cotton farm near Robstown. He organized the Blackland Special, a train filled with boosters that toured Texas promoting the farmland of the Coastal Bend.

Nixon and wife (Hallie Fincham) moved to Corpus Christi in 1925. Nixon had a curious way to start the day. He would get up each morning at 4:15, read the newspaper, drink a shot of Scotch, then go back to sleep for two hours.

In 1926, Nixon became interested in property at the corner of Broadway and Leopard. It was the site where Conrad Meuly's second home was ripped up for firewood when United States Colored Troops occupied Corpus Christi after the Civil War. When Nixon got options on the site, the Daimwood cottages were there, still in the Meuly family.

Nixon brought in H. L. Kokernut as a business partner with plans to construct the largest office building in the city. Newspaper ads said when the frame reached the 8th floor, if seven floors were leased, they would build to 10. When it reached the 10th floor, if nine were leased, they would build to 12. The 12-story Nixon building opened on April 2, 1927. It was soon filled with tenants, mostly cotton brokers.

Across the street was Dr. Henry Redmond's house, which had been Dr. Arthur Spohn's home after he married Sarah Josephine Kenedy. The house was known earlier as the old Pettigrew place, built in the 1860s. Kokernut looked across Leopard at the Redmond house and said, "Maston, we need a hotel on that corner." Nixon formed a Corpus Christi company to finance building the hotel and enlisted a San Antonio company to run it. The Spohn/Redmond house was moved to the Spohn Hospital. It was used as a dormitory for student nurses.

The Plaza Hotel opened in May 1929, giving Corpus Christi two "skyscrapers" on the bluff. The 14-story hotel, towering over Broadway, was known for its Pullman Coach lobby furniture and a roof garden resembling a ship's deck, called the Plaza Deck View.

Robert Driscoll, rancher and banker, was a major investor in the Plaza. He died soon after it opened. After his death, Jack White, who was operating the hotel, bought out the other investors. They were eager to sell during the lean times of the Great Depression. But Clara Driscoll, who inherited the family fortune, refused to sell. There was bad blood between her and Jack White. A court suit resulted, which White won, and he changed the hotel's name to the White Plaza.

Clara Driscoll's feud with Jack White led her to build a competing hotel next door. Before her brother died, he acquired property north of the Plaza. There was the First Presbyterian Church and the home of Mildred Seaton (formerly Rube Holbein's house). Miss Seaton taught Sunday School in the church next door and she had been Robert Driscoll's secretary.

The 20-story Robert Driscoll Hotel opened on May 25, 1942. The hotel catered to famous guests during the war. Tyrone Power kept a room there while he was stationed at the Naval Air Station. Mary Pickford stayed there while her husband trained to be a Navy pilot. A decade later, Elvis Presley had a room at the Driscoll when he performed at Memorial Coliseum. Clara Driscoll occupied a 20th floor penthouse (with 12 bathrooms) from where she could look down on the White Plaza below. She lived in the penthouse apartment until her death on July 17, 1945.

Maston Nixon worked to attract the city's first major industry, Southern Alkali. The firm's need for a dependable source of natural gas led Nixon to form the Southern Minerals Company — SOMICO. Nixon built a new headquarters for the firm at Broadway and Buffalo. The pink-and-green SOMICO building was later purchased by H-E-B.

In 1946, the Nixon building was for sale. Kokernut bought Nixon's share and intended to give the building to the Baptist Church, but the church objected to beer being served in the Nixon Café. Instead of giving the building to the church, Kokernut sold it to oilman Sam Wilson, husband

Three tall building on the bluff included the Nixon office building, the White Plaza Hotel and the Robert Driscoll Hotel.

of Ada Wilson. Nixon said it was a sad day when the name of the building was changed and the guardian gargoyles were removed. Another sad day came in 1962 when the White Plaza was razed to make way for the 600 Building. Nixon died four years later. He had been responsible for the commercial transformation of Upper Broadway. The bluff as we know it was largely his doing.

Not long after Maston Nixon died, the Driscoll Hotel closed. The building was stripped down to its frame and given a black granite facade. It is now the Wells Fargo building. Ada Wilson, whose husband was part of the transformation of the bluff, perhaps had the last word on the bluff development, which came at a time of tremendous growth for the city. "You know, honey," she told a reporter, "Corpus Christi is getting a lot bigger without getting a bit more interesting."

RECKLESS AUTO-ING

The first automobile arrived in Corpus Christi in 1901. It was an Oldsmobile shipped from Detroit to George Blucher. It was a chance encounter that brought the first auto to town. Blucher took his family to the Pan-American Exposition in Buffalo, N.Y. (where President McKinley was shot). At the fair, Blucher met Ransom Olds, who took him for ride and sold him one of his automobiles.

The automobile was shipped in a crate and arrived in Corpus Christi in October 1901. It had a tiller instead of a steering wheel and a curved dash like a carriage. The motor was under the back seat. It cost $650 and would get 40 miles on a gallon of gas, which cost 20 cents a gallon. It had two gears, forward and reverse, and would travel fast — up to 20 miles an hour.

Blucher drove his children to school the first morning after the car arrived. A son, Jasper Blucher, would always remember that the Oldsmobile was cranked up to take his sisters to school while he and his brother had to walk.

A few months after Blucher's automobile arrived, Dr. Alfred Heaney bought one just like it. He tried to take Father Claude Jaillet for a ride, but he refused to get in the devilish contraption. Dr. Heaney put the contraption to good use after Sam Anderson, ranch foreman of the Coleman-Fulton Pasture Co., was knocked unconscious when his horse fell on him. Dr. Heaney drove his new Oldsmobile to the reef road at North Beach, then rode a special bicycle across the SAAP railroad trestle, then a horse and buggy carried him on to the Anderson place. Anderson had suffered a concussion.

Dr. Heaney and Dr. Arthur Spohn were the leading physicians in Corpus Christi, and they were fierce competitors. After Heaney bought an automobile, Spohn ordered his own, a Cadillac, to keep up with Heaney. Then John G. Kenedy, son of Mifflin Kenedy, ordered his own. It was a rich man's indulgence. After a rain, the mud was so deep on roads outside town that horses and buggies had trouble getting through; never mind a car. In town, you could walk anywhere you wanted to go, at no expense but time. So there were some people who thought Dr. Spohn wasted his money.

Dairyman Peter McBride was on his way to town in a mule cart when he encountered the automobile driven by Dr. Spohn. "I kept trying to hold the mules back," McBride said, "but they were scared and there was no stopping them. Dr. Spohn stopped his automobile so we could get by."

By 1905, Corpus Christi, a town of 6,000, had six automobiles. One of the first auto ads in the *Caller* ran in 1906 for Noakes Brothers' machine shop. They were selling Cadillacs and Noakes offered to keep the machine in repair for six months, barring accidents or punctured tires.

In March 1908, the *Caller* reported that John D. Barnard and Dr. W. E. Carruth were traveling in a buggy on Broadway when an automobile ran into them. The collision threw both men out of the buggy and knocked down the horse. After the accident, the *Caller* started pushing for a vehicle ordinance to curb "reckless auto-ing." The rules of the road were rather vague; they could be reduced to the equivalent of might is right: Whoever was going fastest had the right of way.

The City Council passed an ordinance requiring motorists to sound a horn, bell, gong or trumpet as the driver

George Blucher takes one of his sons for a spin in his new Oldsmobile, which arrived in Corpus Christi from Detroit in 1901.

approached intersections. After it went into effect, the *Caller* editor complained that "auto-ists" were blowing their horns louder and longer than ever. "If they can't be a nuisance one way, they will another."

The auto-ists, feeling persecuted, were furious. They objected to the ordinance and many refused to comply. Wholesale arrests were made. One afternoon, five auto owners were fined in the city's Recorders Court. Some owners said they would sell their vehicles in protest. One man sold his car at a loss of $100. But the Police Department reaffirmed that arrests would continue when drivers failed to sound a horn, bell, or gong at intersections.

Roy Terrell, who grew up on a ranch on the Oso, recalled traveling by auto to Calallen. "There were no paved roads, not even the streets in town were paved. The only road that could be traveled in bad weather was a shell road from Corpus Christi to Calallen, following the old stagecoach road. I made this trip several times with my uncle Cal Allen who had one of the first automobiles. This road was made from oyster shells dredged from Corpus Christi Bay."

People in town knew everyone who had a car, Carlyle Leonard once noted. "If we saw a Hudson coming down Chaparral, we knew it was Mrs. Maude Miller. If we saw an open Benz with all the brass shining, we knew it was Mr. Driscoll. Mr. Grim could be heard before we saw him with his chain-driven car. If you were near Artesian Park and heard a four-cylinder Cadillac moving slowly, you would know it was Judge McDonald. If there were young fellows in a Hudson, you would know it was Mr. Morris Lichtenstein and his young friends."

In 1901, people probably couldn't imagine a world without horses, just as we can't imagine a world without cars. I was thinking of this the other day, locked in traffic at Everhart and South Padre Island Drive, surrounded by SUVs looking like heavy toads. Beyond the congestion and parking lots and angry drivers lurching from red light to red light, there was not much to look at, but in that kind of traffic, you don't look. But what an ugly landscape, this place made to accommodate the automobile.

PIERS AND WHARVES – 1

Piers and wharves on the waterfront once held a lot of the city's history. Hiram Riggs built Corpus Christi's first wharf for unloading ships in 1844, the year before Zachary Taylor's army landed. Riggs built a wharf out from where Lawrence Street is today. The base was green mesquite covered with shell and planked over. The wharf was washed away in the 1850s.

Hiram Riggs' wife, Mary Hefferman, was a member of a family massacred by Indians on Poesta Creek near today's Beeville in 1835. Riggs sold his eight-acre farm on the bluff to Felix Blucher and that area (behind where the Central Library is now) was known as Blucherville. Hiram died in 1855 and Mary, known as "Grandma" Riggs, died in 1903. Both were buried in Old Bayview.

When Taylor's army landed at Corpus Christi, beginning in August 1845, there were no wharves or piers. Ships would anchor off North Beach. Supplies were lightered to small boats. It was during one lightering process that U.S. Grant, a young lieutenant, fell into the bay. A bucket was lowered to haul him in, dripping wet. Every man aboard was laughing and Grant said he enjoyed the joke on himself.

Three years later, in 1848, William Mann built the town's second wharf, a 170-foot pier leading from a store and warehouse. Loaded flatcars were pushed by hand on a wooden track from ships to the warehouse. Mann's wharf stretched out from where Cooper's Alley is today. The building was used as a government storehouse, then a hotel — the Virginia House — and in later years as a packing house and an ice factory. The building was made of shellcrete bricks by Henry Berry, who dug the red clay out of the side of the bluff. Because of its reddish bricks, people called it Mann's red house. It was torn down in December 1901.

In the 1850s, when Corpus Christi was headquarters of the Eighth Military District, Government Wharf was built to unload army supplies, which were hauled by wagon trains to frontier forts. Because of mudflats blocking the bay, the Army moved back to San Antonio in 1857 and shipped supplies through the port of Indianola.

In 1853, John Willett built Central Wharf. It got its name because it was between Government Wharf and Ohler's Wharf. Cornelius Cahill built a two-story hotel — the City Hotel — across from Central Wharf. The ground floor was a store and living quarters with the hotel upstairs. It was built of crushed oyster shells, lime and clay — shellcrete.

Edward Ohler built a substantial wharf off Peoples Street. Near the foot of the wharf was his grocery store and warehouse with living quarters above, at the corner of Peoples and Water Street. Arriving immigrants got their first glimpse of Corpus Christi from Ohler's Wharf.

At the Lone Star Fair in 1852, Maltby's Circus Pavilion set up on the beach in front of Ohler's. Andrew Anderson as a young boy lived next door to the Ohlers. Each afternoon, he said, Edward and Mrs. Ohler would dress up and drive out to the Rincon (North Beach) in an elegant carriage pulled by four black horses handled by two slaves.

It was at Ohler's Wharf that Lt. John Kittredge, commander of the federal blockading fleet, stepped out under a flag of truce to demand Corpus Christi's surrender on Aug. 12, 1862. When his demands were rejected by Confederate authorities, Union ships bombarded the evacuated town. The following January, the steamer *Zion*, loaded with salt, a valuable commodity during the Civil War, sank at Ohler's Wharf.

After the war, W. N. Staples built a wharf where Riggs' wharf had been. Past the end of the Staples Wharf was the Lott, Kirsten and Ely warehouse. They had a heavy press used to compress 50 or 60 hides into a bale that weighed about 1,600 pounds. A lumber pier built by E. D. Sidbury was off Doddridge (a two-block street south of Cooper's Alley) where the old Government Wharf stood. Schooners unloading lumber from the pine forests of Louisiana and Mississippi were a common sight at Sidbury's. This wharf was sold to the Tex-Mex Railroad.

The Anderson pier was built near where Ohler's Wharf had been. It was where people gathered in a cold spell to get firewood. Capt. John Anderson's sloop *Flour Bluff* would sail up the Nueces River for wood, which was cut into firewood at Anderson's windmill. Anderson used four cannon balls from Kittredge's bombardment as ball bearings to turn the windmill into the wind.

A hurricane on Sept. 4, 1874 destroyed Anderson's wharf and the Staples wharf. Schooners docked at the T-Head of the Central Wharf were wrenched from moorings and driven inland. The schooner *St. Joseph* was lodged on the steps of Mann's red house. After the storm, the Central Wharf was repaired and expanded before an eight-foot channel, the Morris and Cummings Cut, was dredged across the bay.

One of the largest celebrations in the city's history was held at the Central Wharf on May 31, 1874. The ocean-going steamship *Gussie* docked at the T-Head of the wharf. About 3,000 people gathered to greet the ship. Ocean-going Morgan Line ships became a common sight at the Central Wharf. Shipping tycoon Charles Morgan had a ship built for the Corpus Christi trade named *Aransas*.

The Morgan Line steamship Aransas docked at the Central Wharf.

A shipping report indicates that cargo exported from Corpus Christi included "wool, dry hides, wet salted hides, skins, horned cattle, beef, horses, tallow, bones, lead." There was a cattle chute at the foot of Central Wharf where cattle were run out to be loaded on steamers for New Orleans. Once, the cattle bolted and in a panic jumped into the bay. Men went into the water on horseback to herd them to shore.

PIERS AND WHARVES – 2

From 1844 when Hiram Riggs built the first pier, the Corpus Christi bayfront was a working waterfront, based on shipping and trade. People went out to the piers to see ships coming in or to meet the mail boat from Indianola. By the 1880s, that began to change. People went to the bayfront for the fresh breeze off the water and a view of the bay. Entertainment began to replace commerce.

Corpus Christi's status as a seaport declined after the beef packing houses shut down, the wool market collapsed, and maintenance dredging on the Morris & Cummings Cut lagged. After railroads were built across South Texas, Corpus Christi was no longer an outlet for the Mexican trade and, in 1888, Morgan Line steamships were withdrawn. Not much commerce was moving in or out of the harbor.

The town turned to tourism. This was made possible after the San Antonio and Aransas Pass (SAAP) Railroad reached Corpus Christi in 1886. With the railroad, new waterfront structures were devoted to tourism and entertainment, changing the nature of what had been a working waterfront.

On March 28, 1891, the town was excited when a Mississippi River paddlewheel steamboat docked at Central Wharf. It was the *Alice Blair*. Capt. R. E. Blair brought the steamboat down the Mississippi and across the Gulf. When the *Alice Blair* lowered its gangplank, Central Wharf was packed with people. The *Corpus Christi Weekly Caller* reported that the boat "was boarded by many ladies and gentlemen; it was something new and they wanted to see it." On the following Wednesday, the ship left Central Wharf with 160 people for a trip across the bay. But the vessel ran aground in shallow water off today's Aransas Pass. Hot coffee was served all night and next morning sailboats rescued the stranded passengers. The *Alice Blair* made half-day trips to Ropes Pass, being dredged across Mustang Island, before the ship moved on to Galveston in June 1891.

About this time, Robert Ritter, who owned Ritter's Racket Store, built a hotel and opera house over the water off Belden Street. His hotel, with a ballroom and saloon, was a popular spot in the 1890s.

The Woman's Monday Club spearheaded an effort to build the Ladies Pavilion on the bay out from Peoples and Schatzell, where Ohler's Wharf once stood. The Ladies Pavilion opened on Aug. 7, 1903. After the Ladies Pavilion came the Natatorium, built off Twigg Street. "The Nat" featured bathing rooms where you could get a sulfur bath with water piped in from Artesian Park.

The Central Wharf, built in 1853, was sold in 1903 to Capt. J. B. Thompson and Gugenheim and Cohn, owners of a department store. A cotton gin was built at the foot of the wharf and an old bonded warehouse built by John Willett was used for a seed house. The wharf was remodeled with new creosote planks. The *Corpus Christi Crony* chided citizens for not using the bathing facilities: "The fine sea bathing to be found at Central Wharf continues to be ignored by many Corpus Christi people."

On Oct. 22, 1909, the revenue cutter *Windom* picked up President William Howard Taft for his visit to Corpus Christi. Taft was staying with his brother Charles at the Taft Ranch across the bay. Waiting at the Central Wharf was

Corpus Christi's "Welcoming Committee," all wearing top hats, Prince Albert coats, matching shoes and gloves. As the president made his way down the gangway, wearing an old coat and wrinkled gray trousers, it was said he was visibly amused by the overdressed Welcoming Committee.

That year, Jack Ennis built the Seaside Pavilion on a pier off Taylor Street. On the Pavilion's lower deck were booths with carnival concessions and on the second deck were hotel rooms with a view of the bay. J. E. Loyd opened Loyd's Pavilion and Pleasure Pier at the foot of Mann Street. Loyd's had bathing facilities, a room for motion picture shows, a restaurant, saloon, ballroom, ice cream and cold drink stands. Thousands attended the opening on June 6, 1914. The *Caller* said the new slogan in town was "Meet me at Loyd's."

The Natatorium and Ladies Pavilion were destroyed by the 1916 storm and Loyd's was badly damaged. The Seaside Pavilion was also damaged, but survived. What was left of the old Central Wharf was torn down. After the destruction, the City Council passed an ordinance prohibiting over-the-water structures on the bayfront. This pushed such development to North Beach, outside the city limits.

The Municipal Wharf was built in 1914 on a landfill off Cooper's Alley where the old Mann wharf once stood. It served as the town's primary shipping wharf. In January 1922, the City Council began discussing building a 1,000 foot Pleasure Pier off Peoples Street, with landing places for boats and a pavilion on the T-Head part of the pier. The pier, said to be the longest of its kind in the South, became a favorite place to stroll.

An old fisherman's shack at the foot of the Pleasure Pier, on the north side, was remodeled to become the Pier Café, operated by John Govatos. The restaurant extended over the bay. The Pier Café was moved into a new building on the south side of the pier in 1932. The café's furnishings were damaged in a hurricane in 1933.

In January 1939, the city warned tenants on the Municipal Wharf to move out. Standing in the way of progress were old fish houses and squatters living in shacks. When the seawall improvement project began, John Govatos moved up to the bluff to run the Nixon Café. His brother Jim took over the Pier Café. It was on Water Street, but the water was a block away. The once-popular café did not thrive next to an expanse of churned-up mud. "When they filled in the waterfront," John Govatos said, "it made a mess of the Pier Café. The water was gone and the glamour was gone."

Robert Ritter's Hotel and Opera House on a pier at the foot of Belden Street.

The Ladies Pavilion was built by the Woman's Monday Club in 1903 at the foot of Peoples and Schatzel Streets. Inside was a marvelous stage for perfomances and meetings.

The Natatorium at Twigg Street had 198 separate bathing rooms. Mineral water from Artesian Park was piped in for $1.00 sulphur baths.

Central Wharf was wide enough that wagons could pass each other on the wharf.

Cotton was stored on the edges of Central Wharf waiting for shipment. At the right the Pilot Boy coastal steamer is docked.

Seaside Pavilion Hotel at the foot of Taylor Street was part of Jack Ennis' Seaside Hotel complex. It had a saloon and dance hall as well as hotel rooms on the upper floors.

Loyd's Pavilion was heavily damaged in the 1916 hurricane. A portion of the pier was reopened, only to be destroyed in the 1919 storm.

Cotton Compress and Municipal Wharf, Corpus Christi, Texas.

The Municipal Wharf originally had a cotton compress. After the 1919 hurricane it continued to be used until the Port of Corpus Christi opened. Today the Corpus Christi Yacht Club is located on its former site.

The 1,200 foot Pleasure Pier was constructed after the 1919 hurricane. It survived the 1933 hurricane but was removed in 1939 when the seawall was under construction.

HENRY SCOTT, VIGILANTE

There were rough times in the 1870s. Citizens banded together to impose their own idea of law and order. Bodies were found hanging from mesquite limbs all over South Texas. Some were reported, as noted in Hobart Huson's "Refugio": "Archey Reeves at Ingleside found a Mexican hanging in the Nine-Mile Mott near Corpus Christi reef." . . . "James Hart was present at Corpus Christi when they took a Mexican boy and brought him to the mott (at Doyle's Water Hole) and five of Dan Doughty's company were seen to go into the mott with the Mexican who was found hanging. The Mexican boy formerly lived with Tom Welder."

Several vigilante outfits rode out of Refugio. One vigilante leader was Capt. Henry Scott, rancher and former Confederate officer. Scott's family came to Texas from New York when he was two; they joined the Power colony at Refugio. Scott was six when Texas prisoners were executed in front of the mission on March 16, 1836 by Gen. Jose Urrea's troops. The 20 or more executed men were members of Amon King's company. Scott watched as the Texans were marched in front of the mission, tied two by two, and shot. Amon King was the last man to die.

Four years later, 10-year-old Henry rode with his father, Capt. John Scott, on the trail of raiding Lipan Apaches. They caught the Indians near the border where Brownsville is today. In the fight, Capt. Scott was killed and Henry captured by Lipan raiders. The Indians took him deep into Mexico. One night, he slipped away and escaped on a pony. He rode through a rugged area, living on berries and roots, until he came to a rancho, and from there made his way to Texas.

In the Civil War, Scott was a Confederate captain. His company was stationed near the King Ranch to guard the Cotton Road. After the war, Scott enlarged his ranch from the original 4,000 acres (outside today's Woodsboro) to 35,000 acres between Medio Creek and Chocolate Bayou.

Scott's Minutemen were organized in Refugio in 1873 to protect against Mexican bandits. John Young ("A Vaquero of the Brush Country") said he joined Coon Dunman's regulators, a vigilante committee, which were absorbed into a larger company commanded by Capt. Scott. Young said members of Scott's company rode their own horses and paid their own expenses. "However, this expense did not amount to much as every home was open to us for anything we needed, without price. There was nothing for us to do except to put those criminals across the Rio Grande where they belonged, but too many of them would take their chances on being killed rather than return to Mexico where they would be lined up against a wall and shot. Where the evidence warranted, we gave them the choice to swim or fight."

Judge W. L. Rea said Scott's Minutemen restored order in Refugio County and they ranged into Goliad, Bee, San Patricio, and Nueces counties. "They tracked down and liquidated skinners, rustlers, bad men, desperadoes and common criminals."

A Minuteman related one encounter: "One night a band of Scott's men surrounded a gang of 15 Mexican horse thieves in a thicket . . . Captain Scott called the men about him and said, 'Boys, don't fire too quick. Get as close as you can and aim at the middle of their bodies. Just keep it in mind that Mexicans can't hit you.' Within an hour, Texas had a dozen fewer horse thieves within its borders."

Rough times. On May 9, 1874, four men were killed at Peñascal on Baffin Bay. A store owner, his brother and two customers were shot to death in a robbery. After the Peñascal slayings, a Committee of Public Safety was formed in Corpus Christi. An order required all adult males to register. Each man was given a certificate. Failure to produce the certificate was a serious matter.

One of Scott's friends was a deaf sheep rancher named Thad Swift. In June 1874, Swift took his wool clip to St. Mary's and sold it for $700, paid in silver dollars. On Saturday night, June 8, Swift was murdered in his bed, cut to pieces in horrible ways, apparently trying to make him reveal where he hid the silver dollars. His wife Irene was stabbed 25 times and her body left in the yard to be mangled by hogs. The couple's young daughters knew nothing of the slayings until they found the bodies on Sunday morning.

Minutemen were in the saddle after the alarm spread. Part of Scott's company went after a man named Marcelo Moya, who had been at the Swift home a few days before. Moya lived in Goliad County. After a shootout at the Moya ranch, three Moya men, the old man and his two sons, were brutally killed. Around Refugio, Mexican-Americans suspected of complicity in the Swift murders were chained in the courthouse. A lynch mob took three prisoners and hanged them from a tree in Thad Swift's yard.

Meanwhile, Scott and the rest of his Minutemen chased a man named Juan Flores, who had been with Swift to sell the wool and knew about the payment of silver dollars. At the border near Laredo, Scott paid $1,000 out of his own pocket to officials in Mexico for the return of Flores. Scott delivered him to Refugio County where he was tried, found guilty, and hanged.

Henry Scott, a rancher in Refugio County, led vigilante Minutemen during the lawless times of Reconstruction. He died in Corpus Christi in 1891.

Capt. Henry Scott, the grizzled vigilante, died at Corpus Christi on Feb. 27, 1891. He was 61. He had spent much of his life chasing border bandits during violent times when raiders struck across the border and Minutemen rode in deadly pursuit. They cut a furious swath across the land. T. R. Fehrenbach in "Lone Star" wrote that the bloody actions of the raiders and indiscriminate reprisals of the vigilantes kept blood feuds alive in South Texas for generations.

April 6, 2011

CECILIO BALERIO, UNION RAIDER

Cecilio Balerio, rancher and horse-trader, commanded 120 men in an irregular Union cavalry outfit that rustled cattle and attacked Confederate wagon trains carrying cotton down the Cotton Road. Balerio's raiders lived in the brush and prowled the remote Wild Horse Desert.

Before the war, Balerio traded horses and mules around Corpus Christi. Maria von Blucher in a letter to her parents in Germany wrote that the Blucher *remuda* of horses was stolen by Balerio, "a noted horse thief. Among them was my pretty chestnut mare; so probably she is gone, along with the rest."

When the Civil War broke out, E. J. Davis, former Corpus Christi judge who became a Union leader, enlisted Balerio to attack wagon trains carrying cotton down the Cotton Road between Corpus Christi and the Rio Grande. Balerio's outfit was, nominally, in the command structure of John Haynes' Second Regiment of Texas Cavalry. But Balerio operated on his own, committing what the Confederates considered opportunistic marauding.

Balerio was assisted by two sons: an older son named Juan and 19-year-old Jose Mario. Balerio was in contact with Union commanders in Matamoros and later in Brownsville. He supplied Union forces with beef cattle rounded up from South Texas ranches. He also was in contact with Union blockade ships standing off the Aransas Pass channel. The ships supplied Balerio with Burnside

Balerio's son Jose was captured in Corpus Christi, tried before a Confederate military court and sentenced to be shot.

carbines, Colt revolvers, blankets, and paid him in gold for his guerrilla raids against the Confederacy.

Balerio's cavalry was a thorn for the Confederates. His troops hid in the mesquite brush and launched surprise attacks against targets of opportunity, usually stray cotton wagons and unprotected ranches. Confederates searched for Balerio without success.

Early in March 1864, Balerio's cavalry raided King Ranch and drove off 100 horses. Soon afterwards, Balerio's son Jose Mario slipped into Corpus Christi to visit his girlfriend and gather intelligence about the movements of Confederate patrols. He was captured by Captain James Richardson, a Confederate officer, tried before a military court, convicted of spying and sentenced to be shot by firing squad.

Confederate Major Mat Nolan saw an opportunity. Nolan was in Col. John S. "Rip" Ford's command and he was also the sheriff of Nueces County. He told Jose his life would be spared if he would lead them to his father's hiding place in the brush. Balerio refused, but he broke down when he was taken before a firing squad. He told Nolan that his father's outfit was camped 50 miles below Banquete at a place called Los Patricios (near the present town of Falfurrias).

Nolan assembled a force consisting of some of his men and some from Richardson's company. Jose Balerio was placed on a horse, his feet tied to the stirrups and his hands tied to the pommel. Behind him rode one of Nolan's men with orders to shoot Balerio at any sign of treachery. They rode southwest and halted before dawn on Sunday morning, March 13, 1864. The Balerio camp was unguarded. At the last minute, Jose gave a warning shout — *"Cuidado!"* (Look out!)

Balerio had 80 men there and Nolan had 62. The fight in a dense mesquite thicket lasted 15 minutes. Balerio's guerrillas charged and, Nolan wrote in his report, fought gallantly. Two of Nolan's men were killed and two wounded. Five of Balerio's men were killed, their bodies found in the brush; blood trails indicated that others had been shot and dragged away. Wounded horses left behind had to be put down. The father and his two sons got away. Jose, who had been tied to his horse, apparently was allowed to escape as payment for leading the Confederates to his father's camp. Nolan's men captured 31 horses, 42 saddles, 25 sabers, 107 blankets, six Colt revolvers, five Burnside carbines, and papers indicating that Union Col. John L. Haynes was on his way to reinforce Balerio's band.

After this narrow escape, the Balerios crossed into the safety of Mexico and Cecilio went to see his nominal commander, Col. Haynes. For some reason, Haynes refused to see him. It was a deliberate snub, coming after such a hard-fought encounter. "Rip" Ford, Balerio's sworn enemy, in his memoirs made note of this slight. Ford described Balerio in admiring terms as a brave, crafty and resourceful officer, a tone suggesting he deserved better treatment from his Yankee overlords. "One thing is sure," Ford wrote, "after Captain Balerio's departure, no one came to take his place."

The war was over for the Balerio family after their defeat at Los Patricios and after Jose's near execution by firing squad at Corpus Christi. Balerio never attempted to reorganize his raiders. The Balerios returned to Mier,

Tamaulipas, where the elder Balerio was born. In 1868, Cecilio Balerio died, at age 72. Two years later, Reconstruction Gov. E. J. Davis awarded Balerio's heirs a quarter-section of land in South Texas for the services he rendered the Union during the Civil War.

INDIAN CAPTIVES

Settlers on the Texas frontier had many grievances against hostile Comanches, Kiowas and Lipan-Apaches, but nothing so inflamed them as capturing their children. What were the Indians' motives? To punish the whites? To increase the size of the tribes? To learn the customs of their enemies from the captives? Girls and young women were taken as sexual spoils of war. Boys were taken to perform menial tasks, such as herding horses, and they could become warriors in time. Because of the misguided practice of paying ransom — which could only encourage more hostage-taking — hostages could also be traded or sold.

The most famous captive story in Texas is that of Cynthia Ann Parker and her brother John, taken by Comanches in a raid on Parker's Fort, near Waco, in 1836. John Parker was six when stolen. He was ransomed in 1842, but he never could readjust. Cynthia Ann became the wife of a chief and her son Quanah Parker became a famous war chief. Cynthia Ann was retaken, against her wishes, and returned to "civilization." She languished, always trying to return to her Comanche husband, Peta Nocona, and her two children by him, before she died in East Texas. Of all the captive stories, her's is the saddest. She was captured by Comanches and recaptured by the whites 24 years later. Surely they had to know that taking her back, after such a long time, was a great cruelty.

Cynthia Ann Parker and her infant daughter, Topsannah (Prairie Flower), shortly after "rescue" by Texas Rangers.

Closer to our area is the story of Warren Lyons. In 1837, Warren and his father DeWitt were in a cow lot in Lavaca County (above Victoria). Comanche raiders killed the father and captured Warren, who was 11. In 1847, a surveyor visiting a Comanche camp saw a white man. He asked if his name was Lyons and Warren said yes. The visitor asked about a young Mexican boy, who seemed to be Warren's slave. "Yes," Warren said, "I caught him on the Rio Grande."

In his memoirs, J. Williamson Moses, one of the surveyors, said Lyons was very shy and when they tried to draw him into a conversation he answered only in monosyllables. He stuck close to one of the older Indians, whom he called his father, saying, in pidgin English, "Him killee my father; now him my father." Thus, wrote Moses, it seemed that the murderer of his father had adopted him. "The boys in the camp gave Lyons various articles of clothing, all of which he received very willingly, but he would not put on anything but a shirt and an old flannel blouse, the other garments he hung on his saddle horn."

Warren eventually returned home, married, and joined the Rangers, though he retained the mannerisms of a Comanche warrior.

After the Mexican War, John J. Thomas, a teamster, took his wife and five children to settle on the Lamar Peninsula. On Oct. 19, 1850, a Comanche war party raided his ranch and captured two daughters, Sarah and Eve, 10 and 11. The girls were taken in sight of their parents. That night, Eve tried to escape; the Indians stabbed her and left her for dead. They tied Sarah to a horse to keep her from escaping. Weeks later, an Indian agent swapped an Indian boy and some blankets for her. She returned home. Her sister Eve recovered from her wounds.

One of the strangest captive stories came out of South Texas, near Tilden. The story is told in the McMullen County History. In 1870, when raiding by hostile tribes had just about ceased, Thomas Stringfield and his wife Sarah, their 8-year-old girl and two boys, one six and the other four, were on a road in McMullen County when Indians attacked them.

The family ran to a mott of trees for cover and the father stood them off until he was shot. The girl, Ida, saw the Indians kill her father and stab her mother to death. When one picked up Ida, she bit his hand and he threw her off the horse. They lanced her seven times and carried off her younger brothers.

Ida never fully recovered from her wounds and she never ceased trying to find her missing brothers, Adolphus and Tommy. Years later, after she married, Ida learned that a man claimed to be Tommy Stringfield, the youngest brother who was captured the day her family was attacked. He called himself "Tommy Two Braids." She was thrilled when they met, then, over a period of months, she began to get suspicious. The man had brown eyes but her brother Tommy had blue eyes. The man could remember nothing of his life before he was captured. He was finally identified as an imposter, a man named Ora Woodman who was wanted for various crimes. He pulled the "Tommy Two Braids" hoax to promote a horse show he was staging. Ida Stringfield Hatfield never gave up searching for her long lost brothers. Not a sign of them was ever found, like so many captives who were carried off never to be seen again.

SECESSION AND WAR

One hundred and fifty years have passed since the start of the Civil War, that terrible conflict that would dwarf every aspect of people's lives. Corpus Christi's newspaper, *The Ranchero*, noted on Jan. 5, 1861: "Never before in the history of our country did a year commence which seemed to promise such a prolific harvest of startling events."

One of every four Texans wanted to stay in the Union. "I know neither North nor South," said Gov. Sam Houston. "I know only the Union." Houston, 70, struggled to keep Texas from seceding with other slave states. The hero of San Jacinto was called a traitor and heckled in Galveston when he warned, prophetically, "You may, after the sacrifice of countless millions of treasures and hundreds of thousands of precious lives, win Southern independence, if God be not against you, but I doubt it. The North is determined to preserve this Union."

Most Texans were ready, if not eager, to secede. The delegates at a state convention in Austin voted 152 to 6 in favor of secession. Henry Maltby, editor of the *Ranchero*, represented Nueces County at the convention. Maltby, though a native of Ohio, was an ardent secessionist. Delegates were sent home to urge the people to vote for secession.

Nueces County's Chief Justice H. A. Gilpin ordered a referendum held in Corpus Christi on Feb. 23. Only male property owners over 21 could vote. It was a soul-searching

273

time; some of the men voting for secession cried as they "bid farewell to the flag they were born under." Results showed 164 for secession, 42 against. Sen. Forbes Britton, who had died of pneumonia the week before, opposed secession, along with his son-in-law, Edmund J. Davis. Other Unionists in Corpus Christi included Swiss baker Conrad Meuly and Henry Berry, the county's first sheriff, but a majority cast their lot with the South and and the Confederacy.

On March 5, the secession convention approved joining the Confederate States. When Houston refused to take an oath to the Confederacy, he was deposed and the office of governor declared vacant. In the wake of this political earthquake, Lt. Gov. Edward Clark became Texas' first Confederate governor.

Mat Nolan, sheriff of Nueces County, was authorized to raise a company of cavalry. Nolan's Mounted Rangers, 98 strong, mustered at Banquete. They volunteered to serve six months, long enough, they thought, to win the war. Other companies mustered at Corpus Christi included W. S. Shaw's Light Infantry, James Morgan's Infantry Company, John Graham's Mounted Coast Guards, James A. Ware's Partisan Rangers, and the Corpus Christi Artillery Company. The artillery company soon adopted a flashy uniform with a red jacket with yellow piping and white pants with red stripes.

News of the April 12th bombardment and capture of Fort Sumter, S.C., reached Corpus Christi on April 18. They knew this meant war. With no inkling of the scale of misery and carnage this event would unleash, there was rejoicing in Corpus Christi. Ten guns were fired to celebrate, one for each Confederate state, one for Jefferson Davis, one for Gov. Clark.

As war began, U.S. military forts throughout Texas were seized by state militia or given up without a fight. On April

25, seven companies of U.S. forces at Saluria on Matagorda Island, near Indianola, surrendered to Confederate Col. Earl Van Dorn. The commander of the U.S. forces had planned to escape, but Van Dorn's men were able to board and capture their transport ship, *Star of the West*. This same ship had earlier tried to land supplies at besieged Fort Sumter and drew fire from Confederate batteries, the first shots fired in the Civil War.

As war fever gripped the town, county officials confiscated boats and tents that belonged to the U.S. Coast Survey. Grim times were ahead, as the *Ranchero* warned. "We are in danger and we should be prepared for any emergency. Corpus Christi lives at the mercy of any gunboat that chooses to steer over Aransas Bar up to our city . . . Let every able-bodied man in Corpus Christi come forward and equip himself with the best arms he can get."

Expecting a blockade to shut off supplies, merchants Norwick Gussett and John Woessner brought in a $25,000 shipment of groceries, including 700 barrels of flour, and other "antidotes to famine."

That summer, U.S. Navy ships arrived off the coast and Texas ports were declared in a state of blockade. When the blockade shut off the paper supply from New Orleans and the *Ranchero* ran out of newsprint, Henry Maltby wrote, "This is the first time we have missed an issue. We trust the devil will lay violent hands on Old Abe and anchor him in a lake of fire and brimstone."

The blockade cut off commerce and Corpus Christi came to a standstill. Stores closed; they had nothing to sell. The economy collapsed. The blockade tightened in the following year and blockading forces became active in the bays and around the islands. The war came home to Corpus Christi in the second year of the conflict when Union ships bombarded the city. The prolific harvest of startling events would continue until the war ended after four long hard years.

HENRIETTA KING — 1

Henrietta Maria Chamberlain moved to Brownsville in 1850. She was 18, a graduate of a finishing school in Mississippi where she learned needlepoint and flower arranging. Her father, the Rev. Hiram Chamberlain, came to Brownsville as a Presbyterian minister. He brought his third wife and four children. Henrietta was the oldest.

When Rev. Chamberlain could find no suitable house to rent, he installed his family on a surplus riverboat. The dark-eyed Henrietta first met Richard King at the dock. King usually docked his freight boat, *The Colonel Cross*, where Chamberlain tied up the houseboat. There was a sharp exchange between King and Henrietta.

King was smitten with the bright, intelligent, and pretty girl and got Mifflin Kenedy to introduce him. They were an unlikely match. The churchy Henrietta was very much the preacher's daughter who disliked parties and abhorred alcohol. She liked to sing hymns and read the Bible. By contrast, King was an orphan who grew up on riverboats in Alabama and Florida and was steeped in the rough ways of the waterfront. He came to Texas in 1847 to work on a boat captained by Kenedy. After the Mexican War, the two bought surplus Army boats to haul commerce on the Rio Grande. King spent his leisure time with hard-drinking friends at the Noah's Ark Saloon.

Though King became wealthy from the riverboat trade, he was far below Henrietta socially. But being in love with a preacher's daughter had some taming effects and King began to attend services to see Henrietta. She was engaged to a Sunday School teacher, a man of strict Christian decorum, but the engagement was broken off, clearing the way for King. Henrietta Chamberlain married Richard King on Sunday, Dec. 10, 1854. She wore a peach-colored dress and sang in the choir while King waited with Mifflin, his best man. After services, the marriage ceremony was conducted by Rev. Chamberlain. He gave his daughter an inscribed Bible as a wedding present.

Henrietta was 22 and King was 29. He called her Etta and she called him Captain. King bought a carriage for their trip to his ranch, purchased the year before, on Santa Gertrudis Creek. Henrietta later wrote of her honeymoon: "I doubt if it falls to many a bride to have had so happy a honeymoon. On horseback we roamed the broad prairies. When I grew tired my husband would spread a Mexican blanket for me and I would take my siesta under the shade of a mesquite tree."

The young couple stayed in a crude jacal at the cow camp. King was not acquainted with the country. He did not know how to manage a cattle ranch. He hired vaqueros (who brought their families with them) from a village in Tamaulipas. They knew the half-wild longhorns, they knew horses, they knew the land. They were called King's men, *Kineños*. Along with the land, they became the foundation of King's great wealth. For them, King was *El Patrón*; Henrietta was *La Madama*.

King and Henrietta made their first home in Brownsville in a cottage on Elizabeth Street. One early guest was Col. Robert E. Lee, a friend of King. At the ranch, King replaced the jacal with a low, rambling house on a hill between the Santa Gertrudis and San Fernando creeks. It was marooned in a lonely, dangerous country infested by bandits and hostile Indian raiding parties. Rip Ford said for King to carry

Riverboat captain Richard King first met Henrietta Chamberlain at a boat dock on the Rio Grande at Brownsville.

The Kings' first ranch house between the Santa Gertrudis and San Fernando creeks.

his wife to settle in the Wild Horse Desert, 50 miles from Corpus Christi and 110 miles from Brownsville, was an act of extreme audacity.

One day, Richard and Henrietta were camping on the ranch. A lone Mexican appeared and asked to join their campfire. As King tended the fire, Henrietta yelled, "Captain! Behind you." King, who learned to fight on riverboats, turned and grabbed the man by the arm, forcing him to drop his knife. He warned him to get off the ranch. In another incident in the early years, Henrietta was baking bread in the jacal with "Nettie" in a cradle. An Indian slipped into the jacal, brandished a club over the cradle, and pointed to the bread; he wanted it. A frightened Henrietta gave him all he could carry.

Their first child, Henrietta Marie (Nettie) was born in 1856. Ella Morse King was born in 1858, Richard King II in 1860, Alice Gertrudis King in 1862, and their fifth child, Robert E. Lee King, in 1864.

In late 1863, a Union cavalry detachment raided King Ranch. They shot and killed a ranch hand, plundered the house, and rounded up cattle. Henrietta decided to leave the ranch. On the way to San Antonio, at the home of friends in San Patricio, she gave birth to Robert E. Lee King.

HENRIETTA KING — 2

Henrietta Chamberlain, a Presbyterian preacher's daughter, married rancher Richard King in 1854. She bore him five children at two-year intervals in the late 1850s and early 1860s. The last child, Robert E. Lee King — known as "Lee" — was considered his parents' favorite. "Lee" died in St. Louis of pneumonia in 1883 when he was 19.

Richard King started drinking his favorite bourbon, "Old Rosebud," heavily after that and Henrietta stayed in St. Louis, perhaps to be away from King in his cups. Some years later she gave strict orders that no liquor could be sold on King Ranch or in the town of Kingsville.

During Richard King's Rosebud period, daughter Alice Gertrudis stayed at the ranch to look after her father. King was in bad health in 1885 and the whisky didn't help his growing stomach pains. Henrietta returned home to persuade him to go to San Antonio for treatment. Before he left the ranch, King's last instructions to his lawyer, James B. Wells, was to keep buying land and never sell a foot of "dear old Santa Gertrudis."

King died at the Menger Hotel in San Antonio on April 14, 1885. He was 61. Most of the family was by his bedside, along with Mifflin Kenedy, who had just buried his wife Petra. The eulogy of an old trail hand who worked for King summed up the cattleman: "He was a rough man, but he was a good man. I never knew a rougher man nor a better man."

King left the ranch to Henrietta. He started with 15,000 acres and kept buying land until he owned 614,000 acres. He also left a debt of $500,000. She took over management of the ranch, with the help of Robert J. Kleberg, who would marry Alice Gertrudis King the following year.

After King's death, Henrietta dressed in black. It was her uniform. Her bonnets, gowns and gloves were black. Her iron-gray hair was parted and plaited in a severe bun. It was said her eyes were open and friendly, but there was a glint hard as steel. At the ranch, she began the day by strolling through the vegetable garden, pointing out to a servant which vegetables to pick for dinner. She kept peppermints in a pocket for grandchildren and carried a stout cane if they misbehaved. She ruled from a rocking chair, accessible to all, but no one would forget she was *La Madama.*

One of the many accounts of King Ranch said dinner was announced by three bells: One to alert guests to get ready, which meant jackets and ties for men, corsets and gowns for women; the second to gather in the parlor; and the third started the progression to the dining hall with *La Madama* leading the way. After dinner, they would retire to the music room to sing hymns, such as "Rock of Ages." She was still the preacher's daughter.

In 1893, Henrietta built a mansion on the bluff in Corpus Christi so Alice's children could attend school. She allowed only one subscription to the *Caller*. She would get it first, read all the news, then sit on the paper in her rocking chair, and play a guessing game with members of the family about what was in the paper.

The original ranch house, built in 1856 and enlarged over the years, burned on Jan. 5, 1912. The fire was believed started by a disgruntled gardener. Family and guests escaped the flames, but the old house was destroyed along with family keepsakes. The *Corpus Christi Caller and Daily Herald* reported on Jan 5, 1912: "Santa Gertrudis, the

After Richard King's death in 1885, his widow Henrietta always wore black.

famous old ranch house, was totally destroyed by fire at an early hour this morning . . . In the middle of the night, while all the occupants were sleeping, flames enveloped the splendid old ranch house. So far had the flames progressed that it was with difficulty everyone was able to evade the fire . . . Within two hours of the discovery of the fire the building was in ruins . . . The loss has been estimated at $50,000, although in all probability it is much greater than this."

Mrs. King asked Kleberg to build a fireproof house that would be elegant, yet comfortable enough for a man in boots. The result was the 25-room "Big House" patterned after a Mexican hacienda.

Henrietta King, an invalid in her last years, died at age 92, on March 31, 1925. She died at the ranch where she had lived for seven decades. She lay in state in the front room of the great house as 5,000 friends filed by to pay respects. Some of the *Kineños* at the far end of the ranch rode two days to get there in time for the funeral. When her casket was lowered into the earth, horsemen waiting at the edge of the crowd rode forward, then galloped around her grave with hats held aloft in a final salute. Her accomplishments were many. She controlled the ranch King founded longer than he did. He ran it for 32 years; she controlled it for 40 years, with Kleberg's help, but with her making the decisions. She doubled the size of the ranch, from 612,000 acres to 1.2 million acres. She promoted the growth of Corpus Christi and Kingsville with generous gifts of land for schools, for Spohn Hospital, for the First Presbyterian Church. As it turned out, the skills she learned at a young ladies' finishing school in Mississippi stood the preacher's daughter in good stead as *La Madama*, matriarch of King Ranch.

FLOUR BLUFF — 1

The Sept. 8, 1838 *Telegraph and Texas Register* reported that Col. Edwin Morehouse was back from Corpus Christi Bay after his militiamen interrupted Mexican smugglers unloading cargo on the Encinal Peninsula, a wedge of land between the Cayo del Oso and Laguna Madre. The smugglers met a company of Mexicans on shore ready to load the goods on pack horses to carry into Mexico. When the Texas militia arrived, they dumped 100 barrels of flour and parts of a steam engine and escaped. That flour-dumping incident gave Flour Bluff its name.

Smuggling flourished around Corpus Christi Bay in 1838 when French warships blockaded Mexican ports. The French-Mexico conflict was over reparations that were owed to French merchants for damages caused by the looting of Mexican soldiers. Since one merchant was a French baker in Mexico City, the conflict was called the Pastry War.

With Mexico's ports blockaded by French warships, the value of imported goods, like flour, soared, making smuggling profitable. The new Republic of Texas wanted French recognition, so it tried to stop or discourage the smuggling. In late 1838, French forces fought a skirmish against Mexican militia at Veracruz. Gen. Antonio Lopez de Santa Anna was wounded (it cost him a leg) and nine of his men were killed. After that skirmish, the Pastry War came to a negotiated end.

A year later, Henry Kinney built his trading post at what would become Corpus Christi. He was engaged in the thriving Mexican trade, selling leaf tobacco and domestic calico to traders who came with pack-mule trains from Mexico. In May 1841, Philip Dimmitt built a competing trading post 12 miles away. Dimmitt was a hero of the Texas Revolution. His place, probably at Flour Bluff Point, could have marked Flour Bluff's beginning as a settlement if it had not been strangled at birth.

On July 4, 1841, Mexican cavalry under the command of Capt. Vicente Sanchez raided Dimmitt's store, plundered $6,000 in merchandise, seized Dimmitt and carried him to Mexico. Kinney's place, conspicuously, was not molested. In Mexico, Dimmitt took a fatal dose of morphine rather than face imprisonment in a Mexican dungeon.

The man who led the Dimmitt raid was an aide-de-camp to Gen. Mariano Arista, Kinney's friend. Dimmitt's friends suspected that Kinney used his influence with Arista to get rid of a competitor. Kinney and partner William Aubrey were charged with treason, but the case was dismissed for lack of evidence. Still, suspicion that they were behind Dimmitt's death never went away.

After the Dimmitt affair, Flour Bluff attracted little interest. When Zachary Taylor's army landed in 1845, Capt. W. S. Henry described Corpus Christi as a hamlet of 20 or 30 houses. He saw cattle grazing on a green slope and, to the south, he could see what he called "Flower Bluff."

In the Civil War, Flour Bluff became a sanctuary for Union sympathizers. Among the refugees on the peninsula were members of the Singer family from Padre Island and the Anderson family from Corpus Christi. After John Anderson was warned that Confederates planned to hang him, he took his family to Flour Bluff in an ox-drawn wagon. They moved into a salt storage house at the Point.

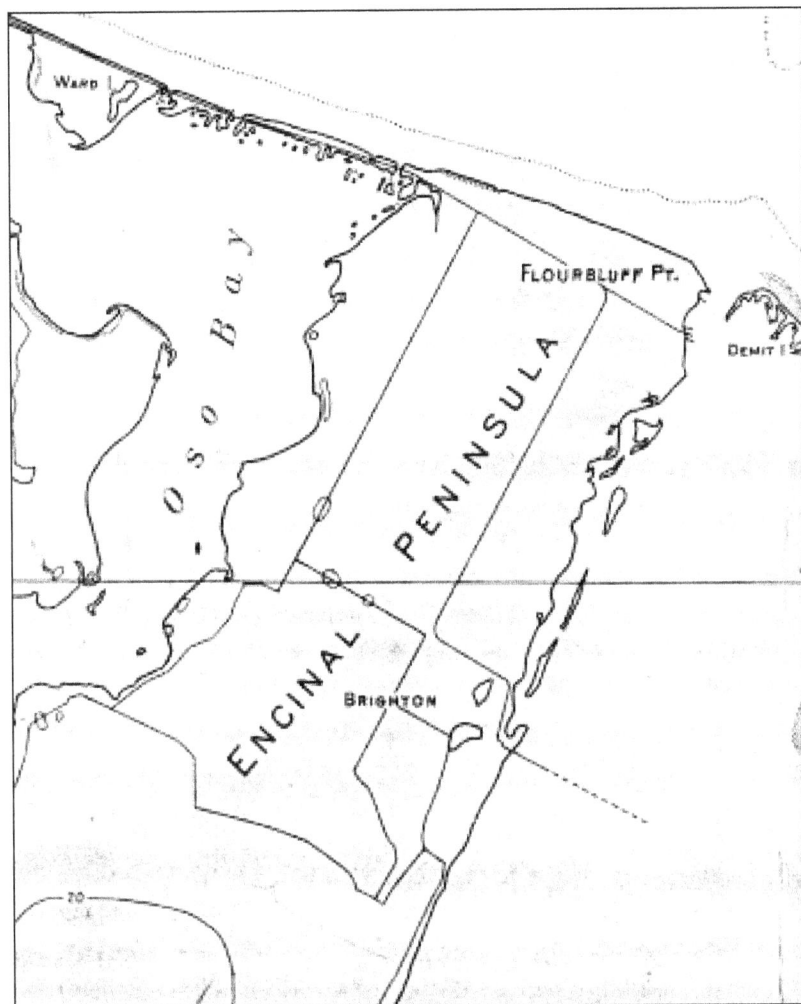

A 1909 map shows the Encinal peninsula between Cayo del Oso and Laguna Madre with Flour Bluff Point by the bay and the farming community of Brighton to the south.

In August 1862, Lt. John Kittredge, commander of the Union blockade, sailed his fleet into Corpus Christi Bay. He sent a shore party, with rat-tail files, to spike the guns of a Confederate battery. When they were beaten back, Kittredge's warships bombarded the town. Weeks later, he arrived at Flour Bluff to seek information from Union supporters or to get fresh eggs and buttermilk for the captain's mess.

When one of Kittredge's ships anchored off the Point, 50 Confederate soldiers were lying in wait. When Kittredge came ashore, he and his seven-man gig's crew were captured without a shot fired. At Corpus Christi, crowds came out to see "that pirate Kittredge," his bombardment still fresh on their minds. He was released on parole and sent north.

After the war, in 1867, James Doughty built a beef slaughter house, or packery, at Flour Bluff. He moved his operation to a rocky ledge at Aransas Bay, which became Rockport. That year, the Encinal Peninsula became part of Mifflin Kenedy's Laureles Ranch, which he bought from Charles and Cornelius Stillman. Kenedy also bought a beef packing house and moved it to the Point, across the way from Dimmitt Island (sometimes spelled Demit and Dimmit). After the packing house closed, the giant boiler was used "by old man Ritter" as a cistern.

FLOUR BLUFF — 2

Cabeza de Vaca was enslaved by Karankawas in 1528, perhaps on St. Joseph's Island. After he escaped, he described a white sand bank seen across a wide bay: "The side towards (the south) forms a point . . . having on it some large white sand stacks." Cabeza's sand stacks may have been the bank of white sand dunes at Flour Bluff Point.

Flour Bluff gained its name from an incident in 1838 when smugglers abandoned a cargo of flour at the Point. The place was a refuge for Union supporters during the Civil War and a center for gathering salt from the shores of the Laguna Madre. After the war, it was part of Mifflin Kenedy's Laureles Ranch. He sold the ranch to the Texas Land & Cattle Company. In 1891, the company sold part of the ranch — the San Jacinto Pasture that took in Flour Bluff — to Elihu H. Ropes.

Ropes tried to change the name Flour Bluff to Flower Bluff and filed a plat of Flower Bluff Farm and Garden Tracts. His promotional leaflets described the wonderful soil at "Flower Bluff" where farmers could grow pineapples, lemons, bananas and ventured that land values would reach $1,000 an acre. One of Ropes' salesmen, E. B. Cole (for whom Cole Park was named) would load up buggies with ice, beer and lunches and take prospects to spend the day looking at land at Flour Bluff.

When Ropes went bankrupt, the Texas Land & Cattle Company foreclosed and used Ropes' surveys to plat its own tracts. Ranchland was sold for farming. A man named Gurney bought land, planted salt cedars and started a nursery. He built a concrete reservoir for an irrigation system. Truck farmers planted cabbages, potatoes, squash and onions. South of Flour Bluff was a farming community called Brighton (after Brighton, Tenn.). The *Caller* noted on Feb. 28, 1896 that, "Postmaster C. C. Barnes of Brighton is a visitor to the city. He reports a big crop of onions has been planted in his section."

To get to Corpus Christi, Barnes could cross over the Oso by the Mud Bridge close to Brighton or cross the bridge at the mouth of the Oso and take a dirt road that would later become Ocean Drive. The latter route passed Aberdeen, the Chautauqua Grounds and the Alta Vista Hotel on the way to Corpus Christi.

As settlers moved in, a one-room school opened at Brighton and another opened at the Point. They would later be consolidated.

In 1907, King Ranch bought the Laureles from the Texas Land & Cattle Company. The King Ranch fence line ran across the Encinal Peninsula below Brighton. The rest of the peninsula was three miles wide from Cayo del Oso to the Laguna Madre, and six miles deep from the bay to the King Ranch fence line. The peninsula, surrounded by water on three sides and ranchland on the fourth, had an island character.

The late Bill Duncan, who was managing editor of the *Corpus Christi Times,* grew up on the peninsula. In 1962, Duncan described the Flour Bluff of his boyhood: "There were community fish fries, where people might gather and, with complete confidence, wait until grease in huge tubs began to heat before taking nets just off shore to catch fish." The families held communal cattle roundups. "Most of the boys first learned the strength of a Brahma calf on these roundups, and often came up short a front tooth at branding

The Don Patricio Causeway was built across the Laguna Madre in 1927.

Fishing from the Don Patricio was a popular pastime.

time." Shopping for food meant an all-day trek to Corpus Christi to buy staples only. Pork, fish, butter, eggs, and fresh vegetables were available at home, Duncan wrote. An occasional deer or wild hog, taken on a night foray on King Ranch, provided variety.

Flour Bluff experienced a spurt of growth in 1927 when the Don Patricio Causeway was built to Padre Island. The three-mile wooden causeway was built on pilings sunk into the Laguna Madre at a ford known as "the crossing." But

291

the boom was short-lived; the causeway was destroyed by a storm in 1933.

On the Laguna Madre side of Flour Bluff Point was Cline's Resort, which had been at Port Aransas before it was destroyed by a storm. Cline's was rebuilt at Flour Bluff in 1915, then washed away in 1916 and 1919, and rebuilt each time. Cline's had a pier, dining hall, cottages, and was famous for its food. Around Cline's pier were fishing shacks built on stilts that looked as if they were wading in shallow water.

It was a peaceful, leisurely life. When reporter Fred Gipson (later author of "Old Yeller") visited Cline's Point in 1935, he found a grocery store owner playing dominos with friends. Once in a while the game would be halted by a customer who wanted a gallon of gas or plug of tobacco. A leisurely passing of the time of day and the game continued. No hurry, no bother. There was plenty of time at Cline's Point, but dramatic change was coming.

FLOUR BLUFF – 3

Flour Bluff Point operated on a different pulse: No hurry, no bother. The Encinal Peninsula, almost an island, kept the world at bay, but that world intruded in 1935 when oil was discovered.

The late Bill Duncan grew up at Flour Bluff. He remembered when his mother came back from a visit to the discovery well, near their place, with oil spots on her dress. Fabulous riches were offered for mineral rights and oil-lease payments, said Duncan, were seen as "getaway money."

Five years later, the world really intruded. In 1940, Flour Bluff learned that a naval air station would be built at the Point. Flour Bluff was chosen for several reasons, including the possibility of a layout like that at the Pensacola naval air station.

Corpus Christi was thrilled over the economic prospects, estimating that the base payroll would exceed that of 25 chemical plants. But as Corpus Christi celebrated, Flour Bluff worried about the end of a way of life. Condemnation proceedings were filed in federal court in Houston on 128 tracts on 2,049 acres. An appraisal panel was appointed to establish values and hear complaints. "Vacate" notices were posted; families had to move. "I've lived here 33 years," one man said, "and it's hard to be told we have to get up and leave."

Powell's night club at Flour Bluff was located in almost the exact center of where the new Naval Air Station would be located. It was one of the first buildings razed to make way for construction of the base.

Up against the dunes at the Point, in the shade of ancient live oaks, were trailer homes of squatters. One story said they looked as if they had been blocked up on timbers for years. The squatters moved out on old trucks piled high with bedsprings and belongings; they were called naval base refugees. Three families of squatters slept on the beach until the Navy provided tents for temporary shelter.

Dispossessed landowners like the Cline, Curry, Powell and Timmins families, packed up to leave — amphibians moving inland from the water's edge. Mae Cline moved to Corpus Christi, didn't like it and moved back to the Bluff. "Monk" Simon closed his store and café and moved to North Beach. The J. W. Dorsey family moved to the Ozarks.

As the families moved out, Brown & Root moved in. Bulldozers at dawn. Sand dunes leveled. Fishing shacks and squatter trailers and Cline's demolished. Powell's Place, a large nightclub at the center of where the base was going up, was torn down. One problem was digging out voracious roots of the shin oak, sweet bay and ebony on the site. The terrain — from 40 feet to sea level — was leveled to a

The Naval Air Station under construction in 1940. It was dedicated on March 12, 1941.

uniform 12 feet. The railroad bridge across the Cayo del Oso was constructed in 35 days. The Naval Air Station was built in a frenzied nine months.

The base was dedicated on March 12, 1941. It represented an investment of $100 million, which paid off as Navy aviators trained at Flour Bluff played a major role in winning the war in the Pacific. At the time of the attack on

Pearl Harbor, young men who would avenge that attack were already being trained at the Naval Air Station.

On April 21, 1943, President Roosevelt and Mexico's President Avila Camacho came to inspect NAS and discuss the war. At the time of FDR's visit, 20,000 civilians worked at the base. At war's end, German POWs were housed in a barbed-wire compound at the Naval Air Station. The Naval Air Station was a big part of the nation's war effort, from beginning to end.

Five years later, in 1950, the Padre Island Causeway opened and Flour Bluff became a transit place again. Most of the time, day and night, traffic speeds across the Cayo del Oso and the Encinal Peninsula on the way to Padre Island.

The old contentious relationship between Corpus Christi and Flour Bluff returned in 1961. Corpus Christi wanted to annex the peninsula and whatever Corpus Christi wanted, it was assumed, was bad for Flour Bluff. On the same day Corpus Christi voted to annex the area, Flour Bluff voted to incorporate. Corpus Christi passed an annexation ordinance. Flour Bluff filed suit. The case went to the U. S. Supreme Court, but the high court declined to intervene.

Not exactly by choice, then, Flour Bluff became part of Corpus Christi, yet it has its own separate identity. Landmarks like the Buzzard's Roost and the rock house of Powell's Place have disappeared. The landscape was leveled and changed and the waterfront languor that governed life at the Point is long gone. The old Flour Bluff is no more, but there's a lot of history there.

A SOLDIER'S LIFE

A few years ago, I was asked to edit the memoirs of Daniel Powers Whiting, an officer in the 7th Infantry. He was with Zachary Taylor's forces at Corpus Christi. He was in the battles of Fort Brown, Monterrey, Veracruz and Cerro Gordo. This task renewed my interest in the Mexican War.

Whiting's sketch of the encampment at Corpus Christi, with rows of tents along the beach, and Monterrey scenes were published in his "Army Portfolio." His other war sketches were lost in a steamboat accident.

The Whiting project started in 2002. Herb Canales, director of Corpus Christi Public Libraries, attended a conference of Descendants of Mexican War Veterans. At the conference he met Roger Whiting, great-great grandson of Daniel P. Whiting, who sent Canales Whiting's original diaries with the hope of getting the work published. Canales asked me to edit the manuscript. The project languished, but recently I took it up again. Meantime, Roger Whiting donated a rare set of Whiting prints to the Corpus Christi Libraries. The set was appraised at $25,000. The five prints include the Corpus Christi and Monterrey sketches. A book based on Whiting's memoirs and lithographs is being readied for publication. ("A Soldier's Life" was published later that year.)

Whiting, the son of a judge in Troy, N.Y., entered West Point in 1828. Classmates called him "Dan Cupid" because of his good looks. He graduated in 1832 and, commissioned a second lieutenant, was ordered to Fort Gibson in Indian Territory (Oklahoma). Then he was assigned to Newport Barracks in Kentucky where he met Indiana Sanford, a Kentucky belle. He was such a frequent visitor to the Sanford farm that he beat a path the family called "Mr. Whiting's track." They were married in 1834. Their first daughter, Sue, was born in 1836. In 1838, a second daughter, Florida, "Florie," was born. In time, they had three daughters and two sons. Whiting called them the tribe of Dan.

When the Second Seminole War erupted, Whiting's regiment marched to Fort Smith, took keelboats to Little Rock then a riverboat to New Orleans. In March 1839, they landed at Tampa Bay. Whiting's men built a fort on the Suwannee River. They called it Fort Whiting, though officially it was Fort No. 4. In his free time, Whiting sat on a porch smoking a pipe and shooting at pine knots. After three years, he was detailed for recruiting duties and, "with great joy and satisfaction" left Florida. As a soldier, he expected to face danger, but in Florida danger lurked behind every tree and every swamp was a dark forbidden place. He found it hard to get out of the habit of looking for a hidden foe.

In August 1845, Whiting's regiment was ordered to Texas to prepare for a conflict with Mexico. Their landing on North Beach at Corpus Christi was contested by angry rattlesnakes. One day, Whiting saw the woman nicknamed the "Great Western" pick up a man who had offended her and set him down in a wash tub. The eight months spent at Corpus Christi, Whiting wrote, contributed to the esprit de corps that prevailed throughout the coming war.

At the Rio Grande, Whiting's regiment raised the flag on the river bank and occupied a makeshift fort called Fort Texas. Whiting was washing when he heard a round shot "with its peculiar rushing sound" that began the bombardment of the fort by Mexican batteries across the river. Maj. Jacob Brown was hit by a shell and died. The fort was renamed Fort Brown. They heard the sounds of battle of Resaca de la Palma and watched Mexican troops rushing toward the river chased by American dragoons.

Inside the fort, a chicken was killed by a shell fragment. Afterwards, when a shell hit, Whiting's sergeant would say, "There goes another chicken." In September 1846, they marched to Monterrey. Whiting's company was in the attack on the Bishop's Palace. His company was assigned to protect the artillery of Lt. James Duncan, known for his slovenly appearance but who kept his field guns like polished silver. American soldiers advanced from house to house, breaking through adjoining walls to avoid Mexican sharpshooters on the roofs. Whiting's men took shelter in a bakery and convinced the woman to bake some bread. Whiting ate three loaves, though, he noted, they were small loaves.

Whiting joined Gen. Winfield Scott's army at Veracruz. After the fall of Veracruz, the men captured mules loaded with casks of wine and sampled it "with a ready will." At the battle of Cerro Gordo, Gen. Santa Anna escaped, but left behind one of his wooden legs. Americans sang a song to the tune of "The Girl I left Behind" with the lyrics changed to "The Leg I Left Behind." Whiting was given leave and in May 1847 left Mexico.

Two years later, Whiting's wife "Indie" died in childbirth. He wrote that he faced "a lone and gloomy endurance to a shrouded future." He never remarried.

In 1858, Whiting's regiment was ordered to Utah to put down the "Mormon rebellion." After sending his children to boarding schools, Whiting left with "a heavy heart." The Utah Forces headed and marched 1,200 miles, averaging 20 miles a day. In September, when they neared Camp Floyd, their destination, the column crossed over the river Jordan

Daniel P. Whiting's memoirs relate his Army experiences from the 1830s to the 1860s, from the Seminole Wars, the Mexican War and the Mormon Rebellion in Utah.

and the regimental band broke into an old minstrel tune, "Jordan's A Hard Road to Trabble."

Whiting wanted nothing more than to get back to the States. He finally got leave and "shook the hated dust of Utah from my feet." He journeyed east, over the route they took, to be reunited with the tribe of Dan. In April 1861, with the outbreak of the Civil War, Whiting regretted that his poor health kept him from joining the fight. He hated secession and wanted to "punish this heresy." Whiting was placed on the retired list. He was only 55, but he was much older physically "because of the many years of exertion and exposure in my country's service."

Daniel Powers Whiting died on Aug. 2, 1892, at the home of his daughter in Washington. He was 85. The funeral cortege passed through Fort Meyer on its way to Arlington. Soldiers saluted the flag-draped casket as the sun went down and "Taps" sounded, the haunting notes hanging in the air, like a palpable presence, long after they sounded.

U. S. GRANT IN CORPUS CHRISTI

Ulysses S. Grant, a second lieutenant in the 4th Regiment of Infantry, thought he knew how the pulleys worked on the transport ship *Alabama*.

As soldiers were being transferred to smaller ships — lighters — to cross Corpus Christi Bay, Grant jumped up on the rail, grabbed a rope and fell head over heels in the bay. Soldiers were laughing as he was pulled back on deck like a wet parcel. Grant was laughing himself.

Grant, 23 years old, was among the soldiers who landed at Corpus Christi in the summer of 1845. Zachary Taylor's command, concentrated in Louisiana, had been ordered to move to the disputed territory of South Texas as Texas prepared to join the United States.

Taylor chose Corpus Christi as the staging ground for his army. It really wasn't a town. More like a trading post with a few hundred people. It would soon be an immense armed camp with half of the U.S. Army, 4,000 soldiers, in training for the coming conflict. Corpus Christi, Grant thought, was "a small Mexican hamlet."

Corpus Christi was also the cheap horse capital of the world, where mustangs could be had for a dollar or two. Grant, a fine rider who loved horses, bought four mustang ponies. The man Grant hired to cook his meals and clean his tent, a free black named Valere, was taking the horses to water and they got away.

"I heard that Grant lost five or six dollars worth of horses the other day," Taylor's adjutant joked. A slander, said Grant. They were worth $20.

Grant escorted a paymaster's wagon train to San Antonio. Wild game abounded along the way but they saw no people until they reached San Antonio. On the way back one night they heard wolves howling. Grant thought there were 20 or more in the pack. When they got close enough to see them, there were only two. Years later, when he was president, Grant remembered that when he heard the howling of members of Congress. "There are always more of them before they are counted."

That December, officers decided to stage "Othello." They looked for someone to play the beautiful Desdemona and Grant was urged to try out for the part. He had a trim figure and almost girlish good looks; his friends called him "Beauty." Though the costume fit perfectly, the officer playing the Moor couldn't look at Grant without laughing. They sent to New Orleans for a professional actress to play Desdemona. After that, Grant grew a beard to hide his girlish good looks. He was "Beauty" no more.

In March 1846, Washington ordered Taylor to move to the border and the army left Corpus Christi on March 6-8. The march south covered 174 miles over hogwallow prairies and sands glistening with salt. Grant rode out to see herds of mustangs that gave the region its name: the Wild Horse Desert. They covered the horizon. There were too many, Grant thought, to be corralled in the state of Rhode Island. It was rough traveling through the Big Sands, with ponds of potable water far apart. As soldiers struggled along with parched mouths and cracked lips under a tormenting sun, Grant admired the endurance of the enlisted men. After a three-week trip, the army reached the Rio Grande.

Grant was in the first battles of the Mexican War, at Palo Altoand Resaca de la Palma. Grant led one charge and

U. S. Grant, a second lieutenant in the Fourth Regiment, landed at Corpus Christi in 1845 with Zachary Taylor's forces.

captured a Mexican colonel who, it turned out, had already been captured. "My exploit was equal to that of the soldier who boasted that he had cut off the leg of one of the enemy," Grant explained. "When asked why he did not cut off his head, he replied, 'Someone had already done that.' "

The battles would have been won, Grant realized, if he had not been there. And he wished he had not been there, for he considered it an unjust war.

"I know the struggle I had with my conscience during the Mexican War," he wrote in his memoirs. "I have never forgiven myself for going into that. I had very strong opinions on the subject. I don't think there was ever a more wicked war than that waged by the United States on Mexico. I thought so at the time, when I was a youngster, only I had not the moral courage enough to resign."

Besides Grant, there were several future Civil War generals, Union and Confederate, with Zachary Taylor at Corpus Christi. The more famous were James Longstreet, George Meade, Braxton Bragg, John Magruder, E. Kirby Smith. (Robert E. Lee was not at Corpus Christi; he joined Taylor's army at Monterrey.) At the time, there was little to suggest that an obscure second lieutenant named Ulysses S. Grant would go on to become the most acclaimed general of his time, the Union commander in chief who would finally beat "Bobby" Lee to end the Civil War.

SALLY SKULL

One old mystery is what happened to the legendary Sally Skull. She disappeared in brush country never to be seen again. Her fifth husband, some thought, killed her for the gold she carried in a saddlebag.

Sally Skull may have killed two of five husbands, though she was never charged or convicted. They just disappeared. What is not in doubt is that she made her own way on the male-dominated frontier of Texas, at a time when gender roles were clearly defined and rigidly followed. She was self-invented, with no role models to follow. As J. Frank Dobie wrote, she was "notorious for her husbands, her horse trading, freighting and roughness."

She rode like a man, cursed like a man, and worked like a man as horse-wrangler and muleskinner. She demanded to be treated as an equal; men reluctant to concede that were advised to stay clear. She was a crack shot and carried a rifle, two pistols, and a blacksnake whip she could pick flowers with. Her name was used to frighten children: "You better behave or Sally Skull will get you."

Her real name was Sarah Jane Newman. In 1833, at age 16, she married Jesse Robinson. They lived above Gonzales. She bore him a daughter, Nancy, in 1834 and a son, Alfred, in 1837. When the couple divorced in 1843, Jesse accused her of adultery and gained custody of the kids. Eleven days after the divorce, she married gunsmith George Scull. Six years later, he disappeared. When asked where he was, Sally would say, "He's dead," with a look that ended questions. She kept the name, though she changed it from Scull to Skull.

She moved to Banquete, west of Corpus Christi, in 1852. When Eli Merriman was growing up at his father's place at Banquete, she paid them a social call. Merriman said she had the fierce stare of a hawk. "She came to our house bringing some of the finest butter ever made, large yellow balls of butter packed in a stone jar."

At the Lone Star Fair in Corpus Christi in May 1852, Rip Ford heard a shot and looked up to see a man falling and a woman lowering a smoking gun. "She was a noted character named Sally Skull," he wrote. "She was famed as a rough fighter and prudent men did not willingly provoke her in a row."

She bought horses in Mexico and sold them as far east as New Orleans. Some said she got the horses by other than legal means, but they didn't say it to her. One man learned the hard way. She heard he had made ugly remarks about her. When she ran into him, she whipped out a six-gun. "Been talking about me, huh? Well, dance, you son of a bitch!" He hopped around as she shot at his boots.

In October 1852, she married John Doyle, Husband No. 3. She dropped the name of Skull and paid taxes on her Banquete land as Sarah Doyle. Then John Doyle disappeared. Two versions have been told of his death. One said he drowned with a team of oxen crossing a river. Sally saw him drown and when a vaquero asked if he should retrieve the body, she said, "I don't give a damn about the body, but I sure would like the $40 in that money belt he had on him."

The second version said Doyle and Sally spent a night carousing at a Corpus Christi fandango. Next morning, he was anxious to gather their horses to leave and tried to wake her. He dumped a pitcher of water on her and she came up

Historical marker for Sally Skull is located north of Refugio on the Beeville-Goliad highway. The marker reads, in part: "Woman rancher, horse trader, champion 'cusser.' Ranched NW of here in Civil War Texas. Sally Scull (or Skull) freight wagons took cotton to Mexico . . . for the Confederacy."

shooting. She said she would not have shot him "had I knowed." Either version may be true.

She married Husband No. 4, Isaiah Wadkins, in 1855. She divorced him when he moved in with a woman named

Juanita in Rio Grande City. That might have been the safest way to leave Sally Skull.

During the Civil War, she hauled cotton down the Cotton Road. Fortunes could be made at the back door of the Confederacy. Cotton selling for a few cents a pound in east Texas sold for 50 cents or a dollar a pound at Matamoros, paid in gold. On her trips, she would visit her daughter Nancy Robinson at Blanconia in Bee County and her son Alfred Robinson at his ranch north of San Patricio.

On one trip, she ran into a freighter who owed her money. She raised an ax and said, "If you don't pay me, I'll chop the front wheels off every damned wagon you've got." He paid. John Warren Hunter saw her on the Cotton Road. He recounted the episode in "Heel-Fly Time in Texas." He said she was "superbly mounted, wearing a black dress and sunbonnet, sitting as erect as a cavalry officer, with a six-shooter hanging at her belt."

For Sally, husbands were easy to replace. She was 43 when she married No. 5, Christoph Horsdorff, called "Horse Trough," who was 20 years younger.

This time, she vanished, about 1866. The suspicion was that No. 5 blew the top of her head off with a shotgun to steal the gold she carried in a nosebag on her saddle horn. What happened to Sally Skull, and the circumstances of her death, can only be guessed at, but she was never seen again. Horsdorff left South Texas and remarried.

One story said her body was discovered by a man named McDowell who found one of her boots sticking out of a shallow grave. An unlikely story said she changed her name and started a new life on a ranch near El Paso. Whatever happened to Sally Skull, she was one of the most remarkable characters in the history of South Texas.

ON THE MILLER RANCH

S. G. (Sylvanus Gerard) Miller moved to the Nueces River Valley to start a horse ranch in 1859 and settled on land bordering both sides of the river. When the Civil War broke out, he joined Terry's Texas Rangers and saw a lot of action with Nathan Bedford Forrest's hard-riding cavalry.

After the war, his ranch was in ruins, the horses gone. He set about restocking the ranch and building a house with lumber hauled from Corpus Christi. To get ready cash, he cut down trees to make a ferryboat for Chihuahua wagons traveling to Mexico. Miller's Ferry became a major crossing place on the Nueces River.

In 1869, Miller took horses to sell in New Orleans and in Louisiana he met Susan Frances East, 19-year-old daughter of a plantation owner. They married on Jan. 31, 1870. They bought a buggy and a mare named "Lady Morgan," which cost $300. At Brashear (Morgan City), they took a steamboat to Galveston then a mail boat to Indianola. They left Indianola with the horse and buggy.

When they reached the ranch, the bride thought it beautiful. "It was vivid green in tall, waving mesquite grass. Added to this was a splash of wildflowers spread like colored lace over the green." Many Mexican families lived on the ranch. The women, dressed in black with shawl-like rebosos, were curious about the newcomer. They would pat her hair to see what she was made of and say, *"Muy bonito!"* and bring her pots of chili and prickly pear with eggs. She saw them often as they came to the ranch store to get supplies. Miller's store was about a mile from the ferry.

Their first child was born in 1871. A year later another son was born. It was a busy nursery; the sequence of births came regularly. In 19 years, from 1871 to 1890, Mrs. Miller gave birth to 13 children: Vivian Gerard, Ernest Elmer, Rollo Lee, Demrie Buford, Eilleen, Dean, Zenna Hortense, Adlia Lamar, Callie Lena and Susie Natalie. Three others died young or at birth. As the family expanded, the valley was being settled. Lagarto across the river was growing. Their ranch was located midway between Lagarto and the coming town of Mathis.

Miller put up a mesquite fence that angered some because it blocked the Corpus Christi-Gussettville road. Travelers would tear down sections of the fence rather than go through the gate. Miller, tired of repairing it, dug a ditch on the inside of the fence. One night, several wagons crashed into the ditch. "Such cursing and swearing you never heard," Mrs. Miller wrote, "but that was the end of the trouble."

In November 1876, Mrs. Miller returned from Louisiana on the sidewheeler *Mary*. The ship arrived as a norther hit. The *Mary* ran aground and pounded her bottom out as immense waves, black as pitch, lashed the sinking ship. With distress flags flying, bar pilots from the Mercer settlement tried to reach them in a pilot boat, but couldn't get close in the crashing seas. "Trial after trial was made to get to us, but each time the great waves carried our rescuers beyond our reach," Mrs. Miller wrote. After several hours, the pilot boat was lashed to the *Mary* by her gangplank. "To reach this gangplank, we waded through water waist-deep on deck. As I started across the gangplank, the *Mary* broke away and down I went into the sea. As I fell, the heel of my shoe caught on one of the slats. This broke my fall and enabled me to catch

Mr. & Mrs. S. G. (Sylvanus Gerard) Miller on their wedding day, Jan. 31, 1870.

hold of the plank. Scrambling to a sitting position on the gangplank, I bobbed up and down as each wave struck. It seemed an eternity before sailors caught hold of it and I was helped into the rescue boat."

The passengers, numb with the cold, went to the Mercer cabin to dry out before a roaring fire. When Mrs. Miller reached Rockport, she learned that her husband was in Corpus Christi "crazed with grief" after reports that all on the stricken ship were lost. "There are no words to describe our happy meeting, after he had mourned us as dead and we had given up hopes of seeing our loved ones again."

Back at the ranch, she was shown her husband's improvements. He put up an Eclipse windmill and built a gristmill to grind corn, living up to the family name of Miller. He drilled artesian wells, put in an irrigation system, planted fruit trees, imported rose bushes from Alabama, and planted crops of cabbages, onions and watermelons.

In 1907, Miller and his son Ernest bought a 110-000-acre ranch near Durango, Mexico. Ernest had married Gertrude Wade and after John Wade died, she inherited part of the Wade Ranch. Her inheritance helped finance the operation in Mexico. Ernest imported the first Herefords into Mexico and was supplying cavalry horses for the Mexican army when he was murdered by his American partner in 1908. That year, S. G. Miller died after a bout of typhus fever. He was 76. Another son, Adlia Lamar, called "Top," died in the Mexican Revolution of 1912.

This is told in the book by Susan Frances Miller, "Sixty Years in the Nueces Valley," published in 1930 and republished in 2001. She described the ranch's demise to make way for a reservoir and dam: "Eight thousand acres of the fertile land of the Nueces Valley is soon to be submerged in a great reservoir which the city of Corpus Christi is creating. A dam is being built below our ranch. The beautiful valley I have known for half a century will disappear beneath the water." The vivid green of mesquite grass, the splash of wildflowers, the roses brought from Alabama, what comprised the old Miller Ranch lies buried beneath the waters of Lake Corpus Christi.

U-BOATS IN THE GULF

In the quiet hours of the night, on June 16, 1942, the freighter *San Blas* of 3,600 tons was 97 miles from Port Isabel off the Texas coast. A crescent moon slipped behind a cloud and the *San Blas* was zig-zagging when a U-boat fired two torpedoes. One struck, one missed, but one was enough.

There was a roar when the torpedo struck the port side and ripped away the stern. Many crew members were killed by the explosion while others couldn't get on their lifejackets. As they lowered a boat, the ship rolled over and crushed it. The ship went down in three minutes. Heads bobbed in the water as 15 men swam to life rafts; 30 of their mates and the captain never made it. The rafts carried emergency rations of beef jerky, Graham crackers, malted milk tablets and 15 gallons of water. The survivors limited themselves to two cups of water a day.

As they rowed, with sharks alongside, they sang "By the Light of the Silvery Moon" to keep up their spirits. When one man died of injuries, the survivors recited the Lord's Prayer and slipped his body into the water. After 13 days, they were sighted by a PBY plane flying out of Corpus Christi. As the seaplane landed and began taking survivors aboard, those still on the rafts ate up the provisions and drank all the water they wanted. At the hospital, Milton Jacobson, 19, from New Orleans, looked at the water fountain and said, "I just let the water run through my mouth when I can't drink anymore."

German U-boats moved into the Gulf after the United States entered the war. A U-boat was sighted off Port Aransas on Jan. 28, 1942, leading to a blackout in Corpus Christi. For the next few months, the battle of the Atlantic shifted partly to the battle of the Gulf.

The *San Blas* was torpedoed during what U-boat captains called the "Happy Time" because it was so easy for them. They lurked off Gulf ports waiting for fat targets, especially tankers, and there were plenty, since Texas supplied half the nation's oil. No more dangerous job existed than being on an oil tanker in the Gulf in 1942. Men who sailed in tankers during the war, wrote Nicholas Monsarrat in "The Cruel Sea," were like sitting on a keg of gunpowder. The stuff they carried was the most treacherous cargo of all. A single torpedo could transform their ship into a flaming inferno.

The late Cecil Ferrell of Corpus Christi joined the Merchant Marine when he was 15, in January 1942. He was a mess boy on the tanker *Esso Dover* headed for Liverpool. When the ship left Corpus Christi, a PBY flew over and warned them to get back to port, a U-boat had sunk a ship ahead of them. They later saw an oil tanker on the bottom in shallow water. "We saw part of a man floating in a life preserver," Ferrell said. "Sharks had gotten to him."

Many seamen on oil tankers died in fiery explosions or were burned to death in a sea of flaming oil or died with their lungs and stomachs full of poisonous fuel oil. But it was dangerous for anyone, on a tanker or freighter, in 1942. In May and June, U-boat attacks in the Gulf claimed the highest total of ship losses for any other two-month period of the war.

Records released after the war showed that on May 6, the *Alcoa Puritan* was torpedoed and the *Ontario* was sunk 60 miles away, possibly by the same U-boat. Two days later, the *Torny* was torpedoed and sank in three minutes. The oil tanker *Aurora* was hit twice. Luckily for the crew, she was in ballast and managed to limp into Port Aransas.

On May 12, a U-boat torpedoed the tanker *Virginia* with 28 seamen killed. The tanker *Gulf Prince* dodged four torpedoes; a fifth struck a glancing blow, but failed to explode. The tanker *Gulf Penn* went down and 13 were killed. On the same day, the *David McKelvey* was sunk. On May 16, tanker *Sun* was hit by a torpedo but survived. Not so lucky was the *William C. McTarnahan*, attacked by torpedoes and gunfire; 21 men died in the action. Other ships sunk in May were the *Gulf Oil*, the *Halo*, the *Carrabelle*. The tanker *Hamlet* was hit by three torpedoes. The steamship *Ogontz*, the first cargo ship to enter the Port of Corpus Christi when it opened in 1926, was sent to the bottom.

In June, the oil-laden *Cities Service Toledo* was hit by four torpedoes; 14 of the crew were killed. Cargo ship *Moira* was torpedoed off Port Isabel. Tanker *Raleigh Warner* was torpedoed and blazed furiously for several hours; no survivors were found. The Mexican tanker *Tuxpan* was sunk and the British tanker *Empire Mica* became a roaring inferno after it was hit by two torpedoes; 33 crew members were killed. The list goes on. The last ship sunk by a U-boat in the Gulf was on Dec. 3, 1943 when the ironically named oil tanker *Touchet* went down with 120,000 barrels of oil. Ten men were killed.

U-boats cruising, off and on, in the Gulf in 1942 were identified later as U-67, U-106, U-128, U-166, U-504, U-564, U-157 and U-158 (which torpedoed the *San Blas* and *Moira*). Only one U-boat was dispatched by U.S. forces, at least officially. U-166 was sunk 200 miles east of Corpus Christi after it was hit by a depth charge from a Coast Guard plane. An oil slick, bits of wood, cork, fabric, soap and feathers, covered the surface. (After the war, German

THE EVENING SUN 5★★★★★STAR

Vol. ... No. ...   BALTIMORE, WEDNESDAY, JANUARY 28, 1942   30 Pages   3 Cents

SUBMARINE SIGHTED OFF TEXAS PORT
U. S. PLANES SINK ANOTHER JAP SHIP

Fight On $1-Men Hurts Defense, Nelson Says

THE HOME FRONT
Curbs Put On Use Of Metal In Lamp Bulbs

Rationing Of Gas 'Soon'

U. S. Says Nazis Dumped Loot In America

Bulletins

Churchill Critic Hits Pacific 'Insecurity'

Cruiser Also Hit In Macassar Battle

Sub Is Sighted Off Texas; 71 Saved In New Sinking

Still Holding Midway

Puerto Rico   Texas

The Baltimore Evening Sun reported a story about a German U-boat sighted near Port Aransas on Jan. 28, 1942.

records confirmed that *Unterseeboot* 166 was destroyed in the Gulf.)

U-67 was attacked and sunk in the Atlantic by planes from the *USS Cole*. The sub's survivors told Navy officials their boat had torpedoed and sank eight ships in the Gulf, their last cruise. One was the Mexican tanker *Oaxaca*, which went down 75 miles northeast of Corpus Christi.

The campaign against U-boats in the Gulf was conducted largely by the Eighth Military District, operating out of the federal building on Starr Street in Corpus Christi. Increased activity by anti-sub planes and ships made it too hot for U-boats, which returned to the Atlantic as the fortunes of war turned against them.

316

KING AND LEWIS

Richard King's Irish parents died when he was five. When he was eight, an aunt sent him to live with a jeweler in New York, who put him to work minding his kids. King ran away when he was 10 and stowed away on the *Desdemona*.

He was found and dragged before the ship's captain. He said he ran away because he didn't like minding the jeweler's kids. The captain put him to work as a cabin boy. At Mobile, King got a job on an Alabama steamboat. The captain sent King to school but he didn't like it and returned to the riverboat life in Florida.

King became friends with Mifflin Kenedy, captain of the *Champion*. When Kenedy was hired to operate steamboats for Zachary Taylor's campaign in Mexico, King joined his friend and became the pilot on the *Corvette*. King and Kenedy spent the war ferrying army supplies. After the war, they formed a partnership and bought surplus Army steamboats.

In late April or early May 1852, King and friends made up a party to visit the Lone Star Fair in Corpus Christi. One account says King visited the Bobedo Ranch near Baffin Bay, where he asked Manuel Ramirez about land for sale. Ramirez told him about the Santa Gertrudis grant to the north. The King party camped by a small stream called Santa Gertrudis.

King went on to the Lone Star Fair where he no doubt ran into Gideon K. "Legs" Lewis. Like King, Lewis may have

Legs Lewis, co-founder of the King Ranch, was accused of having an affair with the wife of Dr. Jacob Yarrington of Corpus Christi.

been an orphan; at least, he had no known family ties. He was born in Ohio in 1823, but worked as a printer's devil in New Orleans, then as a reporter in Galveston. In 1842, when he was 19, he joined the Mier Raid into Mexico. "Bigfoot" Wallace teased Lewis — "You better run or the Mexicans will get you sure."

Captured with other Mier raiders, Lewis was taken to Mexico. Santa Anna wanted to execute them all, but decided that one in 10 would be shot. The unlucky were chosen by lot. All were forced to take a bean from a clay pot filled with white and black beans. A white bean meant life, a black one meant death. Lewis drew a white bean.

After those who drew a black bean were executed, the captives were eventually freed. Legs Lewis returned to Galveston to work as a reporter. As war with Mexico threatened, he took off for the Rio Grande and, with Samuel Bangs, started a newspaper called *The Reveille*. Lewis left to join the Rangers and was cited for bravery in carrying dispatches.

In 1852, Legs Lewis was in Corpus Christi helping Henry Kinney put on the Lone Star Fair. He went to New Orleans to buy the engraved silver cups to be awarded as prizes. After the fair, he was named captain of a Ranger company at Corpus Christi.

Back in Brownsville, Richard King bought 15,500 acres of the Santa Gertrudis grant. He paid two cents an acre. The deed was filed on Nov. 14, 1853. This marked the beginning of the famous King Ranch. King took on Lewis as a partner. The Ranger captain could provide protection from bandits and hostile Indians. Lewis gave King $2,000 for a half interest in the ranch.

Lewis was tall and thin, with long legs, which gave him his nickname. He was described as good-looking, whose gifts with the ladies did not go unappreciated.

In 1855, Lewis was accused of having an affair with the wife of Dr. Jacob T. Yarrington of Corpus Christi. Yarrington found love letters between Lewis and his wife. Lewis was running for Congress and he wanted the letters back. He went to Yarrington's house and demanded the letters. Yarrington refused and warned Lewis not to come back. Lewis returned on April 14, 1855 and Yarrington shot him with a shotgun. Lewis fell against the house and died soon afterward.

The slaying of Legs, the boy captive of Mier, was big news in Texas. The San Antonio Herald wrote, "Few braver men could be found, where all were daring, than G. K. Lewis." Yarrington was taken to Galveston by the sheriff. Yarrington wrote a letter on the way, from Indianola, saying he "had the misfortune" of killing Capt. Lewis because "he seduced Mrs. Yarrington from me." He was never tried for the shooting.

Yarrington's wife, Anna Maria (Perlee) moved to Shubuta, Miss., where she taught school. She reportedly was an early teacher of Helen Keller, the exceptional deaf and blind woman from Alabama. Jacob Yarrington left Texas and established a business in Oakland, Calif., where he prospered as a merchant and lived until his death in 1894.

Lewis left no heirs, no family ties. His half-interest in the ranch was put up in auction. King asked Maj. W. W. Chapman to bid for the property by proxy. Chapman bought

Lewis's share of the ranch and left word for King that he had to bid more than expected because of the bidding by Capt. Fullerton. He signed a promissory note, which King paid.

Long after Chapman's death, his widow Helen sued King, claiming she owned half the ranch. King lost the case in 1883 and paid Chapman's heirs $5,000. A lawsuit in 2003 claimed Chapman's lawyer, Robert Kleberg, was already under retainer by King. The Texas Supreme Court ruled that the Chapman claim was based on a conspiracy theory that could not be proved and that there was no way of knowing, 150 years later, the true facts of the matter. Case closed.

Legs Lewis survived the Mier raid, the black-bean executions, the war in Mexico, only to be killed by a jealous husband in Corpus Christi.

D. C. RACHAL

When the White brothers, Frank and Edward, settled at what we know as White Point in 1856, they hired a young man from East Texas to help drive stock from their home at Liberty, Texas. His name was Darius Cyriaque Rachal. He was descended from the original Acadians who settled in Louisiana. He was 18.

He was known as Darius (usually pronounced "Di-reece") or D. C. He wanted to start his own ranch at White Point, but the Civil War broke out and he enlisted in the 5th Texas Infantry, part of Hood's Brigade. At Second Manassas, Hood's forces captured new ambulances and Cpl. Rachal was assigned to drive one of them. He was in major battles from the Wilderness to Gettysburg. After four years of hard living and hard fighting, he came home, married Julia Bryan in Liberty, and they had a daughter, Florence.

In 1867, Rachal bought land at White Point and began building a one-story house. A yellow fever epidemic at Corpus Christi hit White Point. Edward White and wife died, then Frank White died. Rachal tore off boards of his new house to make coffins to bury the Whites. The Rachals were lucky; their little daughter Florence came down with the fever but survived.

Rachal extended his pasturage and by the 1870s he was one of the largest ranchers around. D. C. and his brothers, Albert and E. R. "Nute," trailed huge herds to Kansas. "Nute" described one drive in 1871 in "Trail Drivers." It must have been a lively drive, with two stampedes and the herd mixed with another herd. "We drove 1,200 steers which we gathered and branded at the old Coleman Ranch, known as the Chiltipin Ranch. Bought them for $10 a head. My brother D. C. was in charge and I was second boss. We went from the mouth of the Nueces River to Ellsworth, Kansas without going through a gate."

The Rachals had their own technique for pushing cattle up the trail. Rather than let the cattle graze leisurely along, with trail hands dozing in the saddle, they would drive the cattle at a fast clip and then fatten them in Kansas. A trail boss trying to hurry his herd along would tell his hands, "Rachal 'em, boys, Rachal 'em."

The growth that began at White Point across Nueces Bay from Corpus Christi spread to Meansville (near today's Odem) and Sharpsburg. D. C. Rachal became a business partner of Sidney G. Borden and they built a cotton gin near Sharpsburg. They owned a store and ferry. (The ferry landing was above Nuecestown, one half-mile from Sharpsburg, built on a slight rise east of the river.) Sidney Borden (he was a cousin of Gail Borden, inventor of condensed milk) planted a grape vineyard and bottled wine for sale. The wines — "Sharpburg's Best" and "Rachal's Choice" — were sold in Corpus Christi, Victoria and San Antonio.

Rachal and Borden owned a schooner named the *Nueces Valley* that carried supplies up the Nueces River to and from Sharpsburg. The river was navigable then for shallow-draft boats. Residents would gather at the Sharpsburg landing when the boat came in because it brought the mail.

D. C. and Julia had a family of four boys and two girls and the one-story house Rachal built in 1867 became a little crowded. In 1883, the original ranch was enlarged and a second story, with a wide veranda, was added. The house faced east with a view of Nueces and Corpus Christi Bays.

D. C Rachal began ranching in the White Point area across Nueces Bay, in 1867. He drove herds of cattle to Kansas and became a successful rancher and farmer in South Texas.

The following year, Rachal and his brother Albert bought the old Rabb Ranch, 43,000 acres, for $4 an acre. Albert sold his share to Henry Scott, the vigilante leader and Refugio County rancher, for a quick profit of $40,000. But D. C. kept his share and sent his daughter Florence and her new husband P. A. Hunter to manage the his new ranch. But it was not the best time to buy a ranch: a drought in 1885-86 hit cattlemen hard and resulted in what they called a "die-up." When Rachal couldn't pay off the notes to the Rabbs, he sold the ranch to Jerry and Robert Driscoll. This land eventually became the property of Clara Driscoll and the foundation of the Driscoll fortune. It was rich in oil.

After the drought of the 1880s, Rachal, a cattleman at heart, turned to farming and produced large cotton crops on what had been grazing land. He remained a rancher, but he never gave up farming.

In January 1893, the Rachals held a dance to celebrate a good cotton crop. Furniture in the ranch house was moved to create a ballroom. Though D. C. and Julia didn't dance, they liked to watch. Falvella's band from Corpus Christi played until it played out, exhausted after two days, and another band was brought in. The party lasted three days. A story said, "It was the out-dancingest dance ever held."

Rachal was elected county commissioner in San Patricio County in 1880 and he held the position until 1896. In 1894, he became one of the stockholders in the Sinton Town Company. Rachal, true to the famous "Cajun" temperament, was known to have a short fuse. If Julia was nearby when he was about to blow up, she would step in with a warning cough and say, "Now, Darius, watch your temper," and he would calm down. After she died on April 7, 1911, D. C. would visit her grave first thing every morning.

Darius Cyriaque Rachal died on August 27, 1918. He was buried next to Julia in White Point Cemetery. The year after he died, the Rachal Ranch was a grisly scene where the dead and half-dead washed ashore in the 1919 storm.

MOSQUITO COAST

One pattern in the character of Henry Kinney, the founder of Corpus Christi, was revealed early. When he got into trouble, he took off for distant places.

The first time, he left home in Pennsylvania and went to Peru, Ill., after being attacked by a man who accused him of having an affair with his wife. A few years later, when he got into financial difficulties in Illinois, in a canal-building venture, he left for Texas. He opened a store at Live Oak Point then in 1839 moved to the bluff overlooking Corpus Christi Bay. It was originally called Kinney's Rancho.

More than a decade later, Kinney lost $50,000 on the Lone Star Fair in 1852 and was in deep financial difficulty. He had borrowed money to put on the fair and the creditors closed in. While Kinney had a vast amount of land, there were no buyers. He had cattle on his ranches, but there was no market. Kinney's solution once again was to leave for distant places. He made his friend M. P. Norton his business agent and left Corpus Christi on Sept. 4, 1854, headed for the Mosquito Coast of Nicaragua.

Kinney planned to establish a colony in the Mosquito Indian region. Some said that his ultimate goal was to establish a slave state that would eventually be annexed by the United States. Kinney's venture was one of two filibustering expeditions against Nicaragua in 1855. The other was mounted by William Walker of Tennessee. Sam Houston wrote that Kinney's scheme was financed by New

York speculators. "He contracted for 30 million acres of land in the Mosquito territory . . . He planned to set up a new empire." In the language of the time, Kinney was a filibuster or freebooter.

In New York, Kinney wrote his friend M. P. Norton on Nov. 8, 1854: "The Central American Company met at my rooms last evening. Several of the great men of the nation attended and made speeches. All agree that I shall go down at the head of the New Government of Central America."

When rumors of Kinney's scheme reached Washington, Secretary of State William Marcy asked Kinney to put in writing the purpose of his venture. Kinney wrote that his aim was to occupy and improve the lands within the Central American Company's grant. Marcy replied that the government would not object if it were a peaceful enterprise, but that "it is assumed your colony proposes to take possession of a part of the Mosquito country for which Nicaragua claims jurisdiction." Marcy said that would represent an invasion of Nicaragua and thus violate U.S. neutrality laws.

After this, Kinney parted ways with the Central American Company and concocted his own plans for Nicaragua. He borrowed money and formed a partnership with Joseph Fabens, the U.S. consul at San Juan del Norte; Fabens claimed ownership of a large tract of land at Lake Nicaragua. Kinney and Fabens called their company the Nicaraguan Land and Mining Company and they proposed to work the mines in the region, cultivate the lands and cut mahogany trees for export. They also planned to set up their own government with Kinney at its head.

Kinney chartered the steamship *United States*. As the ship was made ready to sail, Kinney and Fabens were indicted by a federal grand jury and charged with violating the neutrality laws. They were arrested and released on bond; the case against them was postponed several times.

President Franklin Pierce ordered the commander of the Brooklyn Navy Yard to prevent the Kinney expedition from leaving port. Kinney's chartered steamship, docked in the East River, was blocked by four Navy destroyers.

On June 6, 1855, Kinney wrote Norton that he was sailing that afternoon. He had secretly chartered another ship, the schooner *Emma*, and organized a demonstration to protest the blockade of the ship *United States*. While the attention of authorities was focused on the protest, Kinney sailed away on the *Emma*, free on the high seas. In letters to Norton, he wrote that he expected to make a million dollars.

The schooner *Emma* wrecked on a reef off the Turks and Caicos Islands. The ship was a total loss. When the ship struck, passengers said Kinney took charge and helped save lives and part of the supplies. After the disaster, Kinney sailed on the *Huntress* for Greytown (also known as San Juan del Norte). On Aug. 17, Kinney wrote Norton: "I am at last on Central American soil with 100 men and more. This is a beautiful place and is to be the principal of the world. My force will be augmented in three weeks to 2,000 men, when I shall move up country. I have a larger space to act in than I had at Corpus Christi and the result of my undertakings in Central America can hardly be imagined."

Kinney's followers elected him governor. By his own authority, he could raise armies and establish martial law. He appointed a Cabinet, flew his own Mosquito flag, and established a newspaper called *The Central American*. Kinney's government lasted 16 days before he resigned. He still struggled to establish control over the territory he claimed, but he was fiercely opposed by William Walker, who had become a power in Nicaragua.

When Kinney went to meet Walker, he was perhaps lucky that Walker didn't have him hanged, as he had threatened to do. Kinney ran out of options and hauled down his Mosquito flag and with it his dreams of empire. He was

Henry L. Kinney planned to establish his own empire in the Mosquito region of Nicaragua.

broke, drinking hard, and had lost any influence he had in Nicaragua. He gave up his residence in San Juan del Norte and in 1858 returned to Corpus Christi.

In his own town, he was hailed as a hero despite the bad debts he left behind and the muddled failure of his Mosquito Coast filibuster. Those who knew him thought he was a shell of the man who had left four years before.

THE FEDERAL BUILDING

The Commercial Club, which existed before the Chamber of Commerce, asked Congressman John Nance Garner to push through a bill in Congress to construct a new federal building in Corpus Christi. Garner was successful and on May 30, 1908 Congress authorized the building.

The problem was that only $70,000 was appropriated to buy a site and construct the building. It was not enough. A site was chosen in 1908 at the upper end of Starr Street, next to the bluff, but the project was delayed until 1913 when Garner was able to get Congress to double the amount to $140,000.

Construction began in 1915. When work was finished in December 1916, the Post Office, Customs office, and federal court offices were moved into the new building. This was part of a growth surge in Corpus Christi in the second decade of the 20th Century. The federal courthouse — a three-story structure of tan brick and white stucco with a red tile roof — was finished about the time the bluff balustrade was built and downtown streets were paved.

In past years, federal offices were leased. This was the first building constructed to house local federal departments. In the 1919 storm, the U.S. Weather Bureau office at Corpus Christi was located in the City National Bank Building at Peoples and Chaparral. The following year, it moved to the third floor of the new federal building.

In 1929, the Post Office occupied the first floor of the building. On the second floor were the offices of the postal inspector, U.S. attorney, U.S. marshal, law library, federal judge and courtroom. Besides the weather bureau, offices on the third floor included witness rooms, Navy and Army recruiting offices, an IRS office, a customs office, and an immigration office. Because Customs offices were in the building, confiscated liquor was destroyed (poured down municipal drains) at the federal building.

On May 19, 1939, Postmaster Gilbert McGloin and Assistant Postmaster Albert Dittmer were found shot to death in McGloin's office on the second floor. Both men were shot in the head. A .45 caliber handgun was found near Dittmer's body. Two bullets had been fired. Investigators believed McGloin was sitting at his desk when he was shot. Dittmer was shot behind the ear. No official explanation was given, but it was considered a murder-suicide. Dittmer apparently shot McGloin then himself but no motive was ever provided. Mrs. Ameta McGloin was appointed to succeed her husband as postmaster.

After Corpus Christi gained an appropriation to build a new post office on Upper North Broadway, which opened in 1939, the federal building was remodeled to provide more space for federal court and other federal offices.

Soon after the Japanese attacked Pearl Harbor on Dec. 7, 1941, recruiting offices were flooded with volunteers. One group of 135 Corpus Christi men, calling themselves the Pearl Harbor Avengers, was sworn in in front of the federal building. When German U-boats were taking a deadly toll on shipping in the Gulf, the federal building was a beehive of activity. Countermeasures against U-boats were coordinated from Eighth Naval District offices on the second floor.

After Hurricane Celia hit Corpus Christi on Aug. 3, 1970, virtually the entire building was commandeered by the

The Federal Courthouse on Starr Street was built in 1915 and occupied in 1916.

Office of Emergency Preparedness. A dozen federal agencies set up shop. A radio station was installed on the first floor and law offices were converted into a communication center.

That year, President Nixon appointed Owen Cox to a new federal judgeship in Corpus Christi. Judge Cox became the focus of attention when he signed school integration orders that led to protests and demonstrations.

Judge Cox's courtroom also became the focus of national attention when George B. Parr, the "Duke of Duval," was arraigned on charges of income tax evasion. A jury found him guilty on all counts. A year later, on March 31, 1975, Parr failed to appear before Cox for a hearing and the judge ordered the U.S. marshal to find him and bring him to the courtroom. Next day, April 1, 1976, in an early morning fog, they found Parr slumped over in his car, the engine still running, on his Los Horcones Ranch south of Benavides. Earlier that morning he put a .45-caliber pistol to his head and pulled the trigger.

After a new, larger federal courthouse opened on Shoreline Boulevard on Feb. 12, 2001, the 83-year-old federal building on Starr Street was purchased by Thomas J. Henry to house his law firm.

A lot of history was recorded at the old federal building — from the 1919 storm to the campaign against German U-boats, to the relief efforts after Hurricane Celia, to school integration and the trial of George B. Parr. Not long after it was built, Corpus Christi gave John Nance Garner a gold watch in recognition for his work in gaining the port and getting the appropriation passed for the federal building. Garner carried the watch for the rest of his life. The building itself should have carried his name. It should have been called the John Nance Garner Federal Building.

RAIN BATTLES

This year's drought has been called the worst in Texas history, worse than the terrible drought of the 1950s which San Angelo's Elmer Kelton wrote about in "The Time It Never Rained." The title came from a joke. A West Texas rancher bet three friends it would never rain again. After six years of drought, he collected from two of them.

It never rained in South Texas, either. In the long dry summers of the 1950s, grain and cotton stalks withered and died. Grazing land was stripped of grass and hope. Blowing sand drifted against fence lines and drought cracks opened across the land. That drought lasted from three to six years, depending on the region of Texas.

Droughts are no strangers to this land. The earliest in recorded history was mentioned by Cabeza de Vaca in 1534. During his sojourn in Texas, Indians begged him, as a powerful medicine man, to make it rain so they could plant their corn. They told Cabeza de Vaca there had been no rain for two years.

Closer to our time, droughts afflicted South Texas in almost every decade of the last half of the 19th century. The droughts were often followed by frigid winters which claimed the lives of thousands of cattle weakened by a lack of grass and water. Cowboys called those times die-ups.

There was a terrible drought in 1856 and 1857 and during the Civil War, a drought compounded the war's miseries. Thomas Noakes, at Nuecestown, wrote in his diary on Jan.

A book titled "War and the Weather" by Edward Powers noted that artillery fire in the Civil War often brought rainstorms.

24, 1864: "No rain worth mentioning since the 10th of last July. Dead animals meet your gaze in every direction, look where you will; the atmosphere is quite oppressive on account of decomposition."

Ten years later, in 1872, a drought was followed by a die-up winter. Cattle drifted away from the howling norther and bogged down along the creeks. That's where they died — bogged down in mud where the river receded, too weak to pull themselves out. Ranchers put their hands to skinning carcasses for the hides. Rustlers and thieves also worked the ranges, taking hides from dead cattle and often killing live cattle. The fight between ranchers and hide rustlers was called the Skinning War.

A bad drought hit Texas again in 1886. J. Frank Dobie in "I'll Tell You A Tale" wrote that it was a year without a spring, a year of August-like weather. "The only winds were whirlwinds — the sign of more dry weather. The grass roots had died; the bull nettles in the fields were runty and withered. Drought cracks seamed the black land everywhere . . . Dry, dry, dry, and not a cloud to try."

Dobie wrote about another drought in 1888 in "Tales of Old-Time Texas." Several ranchers thought it would be a good idea to consult an old preacher and get him to pray for rain, to intercede with the Almighty in their behalf. "He listened to them sympathetically, then said, 'As long as this wind keeps steady out of the west, it won't do any good to pray.' "

A bad drought in the 1890s led to an unusual experiment. A book titled "War and the Weather" by Edward Powers noted that artillery fire in the Civil War often brought rainstorms. Powers' theory was that clouds could be bombarded into dropping moisture.

It sounded plausible enough that the U.S. Department of Agriculture decided to conduct a cloud-bombarding experiment in Corpus Christi. On Sept. 26, 1891, experimenters took two howitzers outside town and fired the shells timed to explode at 500 feet. After the shells exploded, a few raindrops fell. By the time the last shot was fired, people at the experiment were soaking wet.

Scoffers pointed out that the howitzer shots had nothing to do with the rain because on the day of the exercise, thunderclouds were over the city and it had rained the day before. But there had to be clouds to bombard for the experiment to work.

The experimenters went on to San Diego, where there had been no rain for a long time. This time, they used 10-foot balloons filled with gas and carrying explosive charges. The balloon explosions were synchronized with artillery fire on the ground. Judge James O. Luby, a spectator, carried an umbrella just in case. The mortars thundered and balloons exploded from 9 p.m. until midnight. The spectators gave up and went home, thoroughly dry. But about 4 a.m. after the last balloon was exploded, a heavy rain fell.

This was followed by another experiment conducted in the Alamo Heights area of San Antonio. The first shot took off the top of a mesquite tree and concussions from the cannon shots shattered the windows of the nearby Argyle Hotel. But there was no rain in San Antonio. However, there was a violent downpour in Laredo. A telegram sent from Laredo, perhaps only half in jest, thanked the man in charge, John T. Ellis, for the rain.

That ended the experiment of bombarding clouds until 20 years later. C. W. "Charlie" Post, who invented Grape Nuts and founded the West Texas town of Post near Lubbock, set up his own dynamite blasting stations to make it rain. He called his bombardments "rain battles." After one exercise in 1911, it rained for 10 days and a man actually sued Post for damages caused by the deluge.

A deluge is what we need, or what the old *Nueces Valley* newspaper called a cistern-filler. In a drought in 1871, the Mercer log — a diary of events kept by the Mercer family of bar pilots at Port Aransas — noted: "The wind shifted and it commenced to rain, an article very much needed in this section of the country, for everybody and everything was in want of it. Did not milk the cow this morning. It rained so hard a fellow would've got wet, so the calves had it all to themselves. It quit raining about noon. So ends this day. Wind N. E. First rain of the year."

DUKE OF DUVAL – 1

Archer (Archie) Parr of Matagorda Island was 11 years old in 1871 when he went to work as a cowhand for the Coleman Fulton Pasture Company, one of the great cattle ranches of South Texas.

Archie was an experienced hand by 1883 when he was hired, at the age of 23, as foreman of the Sweden Land and Cattle Company near Benavides in Duval County. Parr was carrying a battered suitcase when he got off the Tex-Mex train at Benavides, 15 miles southwest of San Diego, and asked a boy at the station if anyone from the Sweden Ranch was there to meet him. The day Archie Parr stepped off the train in Benavides marked the beginning of a long and fateful relationship between Parr and the people of Duval County.

As the foreman of the Sweden Ranch, Archie Parr hired mostly Mexican-American vaqueros. He learned Spanish and was trusted by the vaqueros who worked for him. One San Diego resident said, "When Archie told you something, you knew it was so. He stood hitched."

Archie Parr married Elizabeth Allen, a student at Sam Houston State Teachers College, in 1891. They had six children, including George B. Parr. Archie was elected to the Duval County Commissioners Court in 1898. His political power was based on his long association with Mexican-Americans in Duval County.

A special election was being held on May 18, 1912 on a proposal to incorporate San Diego as a city. Hispanic voters, led by Parr and the Democrats, supported incorporation, while Republicans and cattle barons opposed it. On election day, at the only polling place in San Diego, C. M. Robinson, his brother and two friends ran into three county officials, all Hispanic. Angry words were exchanged and gunfire erupted. All three Hispanics were shot to death. One of the gunmen went in search of Parr, but Parr had been warned that violence was possible and he had taken his family to Corpus Christi.

The following day, Parr returned to San Diego to find Mexican-Americans arming themselves to retaliate. Parr urged them to put away their guns and let the law take its course. Three suspects were taken to Corpus Christi and put in jail. They were tried in Fort Bend County, on a change of venue, but not convicted. Key witnesses disappeared or had memory lapses.

From the time of the shootout, Parr's influence with the Mexican-American voters became stronger than ever. In 1914, he was elected to the state Senate. His election was virtually assured because he controlled the Hispanic vote in Duval County and was allied with James B. Wells of Brownsville, the boss of political bosses in South Texas.

Parr took his 13-year-old son George Berham Parr with him to the Senate to act as his page, to learn the art of politics. "You'd better try to make some new friends every day," Archie told George, "just to take the place of the ones you're bound to lose when you're in politics."

Archie consolidated his hold on power. He became the dean of the Senate and fellow senators began calling him "the Duke of Duval." Back home, he was called *jefe* or *padron grande*. He controlled the Hispanic vote through paternalism, by giving handouts to supporters, and through fraud and coercion. Marked ballots were used, armed guards (special deputies appointed by Parr) patrolled the polling places and election returns were changed and inflated, to suit the need. Parr's minions knew how to stuff a ballot box.

Criminal prosecutions of Parr and allies were blocked by control of the prosecutorial and grand jury process. Patronage was the reward for those who could help keep him in power. So long as he controlled the system, Parr was safe.

Archie Parr was investigated by the state in 1914 over allegations of misuse of county funds, but at a critical stage in the investigation, the Duval County Courthouse burned and with it all the key records were destroyed. Missing and lost records became a trademark of the Parr regime.

It was a lesson young George B. Parr, the heir apparent, learned well. George grew up on his father's ranch near Benavides, the Rancho los Horcones (ranch of the forked poles). He was known to be in training to take over his father's political dynasty. George spoke Spanish before he learned English. He graduated in 1921 from Corpus Christi High School. He played end on the football team that won the South Texas title that year. He went on to college and the University of Texas Law School. He dropped out before getting a degree, but he passed the state bar exam in 1926. That was the same year he was elected county judge of Duval County. To insure George's election, Archie made sure there were no other opponents on the ballot.

It wasn't long before George was in trouble. He was indicted in 1932 by a federal grand jury in San Antonio for income tax evasion, for not reporting a $25,000 kickback from a road-building contractor.

Vice President John Nance Garner, a Parr ally, tried to have the indictment quashed, but George was convicted and given a probated sentence. One probation requirement was that he stay away from politics. When that was violated, he

Archer (Archie) Parr, a former cowhand, became the first Duke of Duval County.

was sent to the El Reno Reformatory in Oklahoma. During his nine months there, he worked in the prison library

Meantime, Archie Parr was defeated in 1934 in his state Senate re-election campaign. He had lost power outside of Duval County after it was reported that he received a $100,000 kickback. He retired from politics and turned over his "dukedom" to George.

Archie moved to Corpus Christi, where he lived on Saxet Drive. He died in 1942 at the home of his daughter, Mrs. B. G. Moffett, at the age of 82. Among the honorary pallbearers at his funeral was Gov. Coke Stevenson. The new Duke of Duval, George Parr, would help defeat Stevenson in the 1948 Senate race against Lyndon Johnson with a stuffed ballot box, the infamous Box 13.

DUKE OF DUVAL — 2

George B. Parr dominated Duval County politics after his father Archie died. He married, divorced, and remarried a high-school sweetheart, Thelma Duckworth of Corpus Christi. As a convicted felon, George couldn't hold office, but he could call the shots in Parr territory.

In 1945, Duval County commissioners loaned Parr $662,000 to buy the 55,000-acre Dobie ranch. In 1946, through the influence of powerful Texas politicians, President Truman granted George a pardon, which restored his civil rights and allowed him to return to politics.

A Senate runoff election between Lyndon Johnson and Coke Stevenson in 1948 was a fierce contest. For five days after the election, Stevenson believed he had won the closest senatorial election in American history. Out of nearly a million votes cast, he had a 112-vote lead.

On the sixth day, Precinct 13 in Jim Wells County reported an amended return, with 202 additional votes, 200 of them for Johnson. On election day, Box 13 reported 765 votes for Johnson and 60 for Stevenson. Six days later, the total was Johnson 965 votes and 62 for Stevenson.

Stevenson showed up at a bank in Alice which had the precinct boxes. This was a Parr bank. George's brother Givens Parr was the bank's executive vice president. Stevenson looked at the tally sheet and found that the last 202 names on the list for Box 13 were in alphabetical order and written in the same color ink. Stevenson challenged the results, arguing that all the votes in Jim Wells' Precinct 13 should be discarded.

Stevenson also challenged the results in Duval County, where the vote totals also changed dramatically after the election. On election night in Duval County, the county chairman reported Johnson with 4,187 votes, Stevenson with 38. Six days later, the official canvass increased that to 4,622 votes for Johnson, 40 for Stevenson. Johnson gained 425 votes and Stevenson 2.

When Box 13 was opened in court in Alice, the tally sheet Stevenson had seen was missing. The State Democratic Executive Committee certified Johnson as the nominee and a bitter Stevenson said, "I was beaten by a stuffed ballot box." Those who understood South Texas politics had no doubt it was Parr's doing.

Parr never admitted to the Box 13 fraud, but he explained why he backed Johnson over Stevenson. "We went to ask him (when Stevenson was governor) to appoint Jim Kazen district attorney (in Webb County) when a vacancy came up," Parr said. "He refused. This election is the first time we've had an opportunity to vote against him. We befriended the Mexicans and they cast their vote for the man (Johnson) whom we believe to be our friend."

On July 29, 1949, crusading radio commentator in Alice, Bill Mason, a critic of Parr, was shot to death by a deputy sheriff, a friend of Parr's. The deputy was convicted and later hanged himself in prison. The violence was a sign of things to come.

Jake Floyd, an Alice attorney, was a leader of anti-Parr forces in Jim Wells County. Parr called him *"la vibora seca,"* the dry snake. On the night of Sept. 8, 1952, Floyd got a call from Nago Alaniz, a lawyer connected to Parr. Alaniz asked Floyd to meet him at Jewel's Drive-In. At the drive-in, Alaniz warned Floyd that two hit men had been paid to kill him. "One of them," Alaniz said, "is standing in your garage right now." "Has George Parr got anything to do with this?" Floyd asked. "I don't know," Alaniz said, "but somebody is putting up the money."

Floyd rushed home. He found his son shot in the driveway. He died soon afterwards. Parr denied any connection to the shooting but Floyd said, "I know in my heart who tried to have me killed and killed my boy instead."

Two men were convicted of the murder, Mario "El Turko" Sapet, a Parr "special deputy" and a Mexican national, Alfredo Cervantes, who said it was a contract killing but he was not paid because he shot the wrong man.

The Box 13 episode and the murder of Jake Floyd Jr. shed a bright light on the Parr machine, which operated best in the dark. Investigators were all over San Diego and Alice and, at one point, some 400 indictments were returned against Parr and his associates.

Investigators followed a trail of corruption. County monies, school district monies, water district monies, were spent with abandon. Authorization for huge expenditures of public funds was often missing. Generous payments were made out of public funds on the basis of scribbled notes by Parr, even when he was out of office. Not only did Duval County loan Parr the money to buy the Dobie Ranch, it paid for expensive irrigation equipment for Parr's Los Horcones Ranch. Parr family members were paid by county government for uncertain purposes. Hundreds of people in Duval County were put on the county payroll just before an election and taken off after the election.

In 1958, Parr was found guilty of mail fraud by a federal jury and assessed a 10-year sentence. Seven of his cronies received prison terms. The convictions were thrown out by the Supreme Court. Parr filed bankruptcy and was forced to sell his Dobie Ranch.

George B. Parr, the son of Archer Parr, became the political boss of Duval County after his father's death.

The downfall of George B. Parr began in 1972 with an IRS investigation for tax evasion. He went on trial in federal court in Corpus Christi before Judge Owen Cox on March 4, 1974. A jury returned a guilty verdict on all eight counts. The following year, on March 31, Parr failed to appear before Judge Cox. Next day, on April 1, in an early morning fog, federal investigators began searching for Parr and they found his car, with the engine running, on the Los Horcones Ranch. A few hours earlier he had put a .45-caliber pistol to his head and pulled the trigger.

Archie Parr and son George and their political cronies were able to corrupt everything within their reach and that reach extended a long way. How much of the Parr legacy of corruption still survives in the dark shadows of South Texas politics?

E. BARNES COLE

E. Barnes Cole was in Kansas on his way to Colorado when he read about a land boom at a place called Corpus Christi. He decided to take a look. A fight between two bulls on the track held up the train and Cole talked with a man who had lived in Corpus Christi. Cole asked if the land was worth anything. The man said, "Most of it is not worth a damn."

Cole was born on April 23, 1856 on a farm outside Chicago. He grew up in Elkhart, Ind., went to school until he was 14, and worked as a hotel clerk. He bought a small hotel in Elk Falls, Kan., then sold out to raise sheep. He married Anna Haynes, daughter of a Union colonel in the Civil War. Cole lost his shirt when the wool tariff was lifted, allowing in cheap Australian wool. He was on his way to Colorado when he changed his travel plans and came to Corpus Christi, which was booming.

This was during the Ropes era. With access to capital backing, E. H. Ropes began dredging a channel across Mustang Island and bought land along the shore for a development called "The Aransas Cliffs." Land values soared. Ropes bought land for $8 an acre that later sold for $1,000 an acre. Land was selling like hot cakes and the town was full of prospectors.

Cole went to work for Ropes, selling land at Flour Bluff. He would load up buggies with ice, beer and packed lunches and pick up prospects at the Steen Hotel. They would drive around Flour Bluff looking at land. When they were late getting back, Cole would send a boy ahead on horseback to hold up a lantern to cross theCayo del Oso. Cole would spend half the night drawing up contracts.

The bottom fell out in 1893, Ropes went broke and people who bought land during the boom lost fortunes. Corpus Christi underwent a flood of bankruptcies and property values plunged until, as the man on the train said, they weren't worth a damn.

Land speculators left town, but Cole decided to "wait for the good times that were coming." Land was dirt cheap and Cole started to buy, as he could afford it, bit by bit. People thought him mad. The only thing he was sure of, Cole said, was that Corpus Christi would grow. He predicted it would become the second largest city in Texas. "We can't beat Houston," he said, "but we can beat everybody else."

Cole knew the black land was fertile, but the only crops were grown out toward Calallen. Then the Poenisch family settled south of town and showed what good land it was with fine crops of cabbages. A man offered 7,000 acres of the old Grim Ranch for sale through Cole. "The old settlers wanted to know what I was going to do with it. I told them I would settle it with farmers. They laughed and said the farmers would starve. I sold all of it and never had to take a single bit back." Cole sold the land to Stanley Kostoryz, who resold it to Czech farmers.

A Wisconsin woman wanted to invest in Corpus Christi property. Cole sold her 13 acres in 1900 at $75 an acre, near today's intersection of Agnes and Port. The land she bought for $975 later sold for $40,000.

In 1902, Cole began buying land near the bayfront and by 1917 he had a block of 200 acres. A man wanted to buy it. "I won't sell," Cole said, "unless the party who buys it promises to subdivide it, restrict it, and put in all the conveniences." The man was shocked. "You mean if I buy

E. B. Cole was on his way to Colorado when he changed plans and came to Corpus Christi.

the land I can't do what I want to with it?" Cole said, "That's right."

Wallace L. Dinn convinced investors in San Antonio to develop Cole's 200 acres. They paid Cole $150,000 for the tract and Dinn and two partners were hired to develop and sell the property. The result became the Del Mar addition. The opening sale was on Dec. 5, 1925. In four months, $1 million worth of residential lots were sold. Suburbia, in Corpus Christi, started at Del Mar.

Cole bought a 56-acre tract on the city's outskirts for $11 an acre. That was Six Points. He put together 300 acres in the Cole tract and refused to sell, even after the area was built up. As with Del Mar, he wanted a first-class subdivision. He finally sold in 1944. That area today is Lindale.

Cole tried to convince the city to turn North Beach into a park. When he was pushing the idea, Zachary Taylor's old rifle pits were still there. The city showed no enthusiasm for the idea. Cole had bayfront land in front of Del Mar that he had refused to sell. He gave it to the city for use as a public park if certain conditions were met. He wanted improvements made to protect against erosion and a large sign designating it the E. B. Cole Park. The improvements were completed in 1933 and Cole and his wife were honored at the park in 1939. It was his 83rd birthday. His wife died July 3, 1946 and E. B. Cole followed on June 18, 1951 when he was 96. He was a real estate pioneer who was not afraid to invest in the city's future.

JACK HAYS — 1

Texas found an unusually effective Ranger captain in the last years of the Republic with John Coffee "Jack" Hays, a boyish-looking man who came from the same area of Tennessee as Sam Houston. Jack Hays' time as a Ranger lasted from 1836 until 1848, but he seemed to be in every fight in the three-sided conflict between Texans, Indians and Mexicans. He was the model of leadership all Ranger captains came to be measured against, though no other Ranger ever reached the measure of Jack Hays.

Hays was small, five feet eight inches tall, and weighed 150 pounds. There was no hint of self-importance about him. He was almost shy, always courteous, and didn't speak often, but when he did, things happened. He was uncommonly brave. He never ran from Indians and was never defeated by them. He knew how to improvise on a battlefield, which was borne out in his battles at Bandera Pass, Uvalde Canyon, Enchanted Rock, Salado Creek, and the Pinta Trail Crossing. How did Jack Hays come to be the most deadly Ranger of them all?

He was born at Little Cedar Lick, Tenn., near Nashville, on Jan. 28, 1817. He was 15 when his father and mother died. He went to live with an uncle in Yazoo, Miss. The uncle wanted Jack to work in a store, but Hays wanted a military career. He left for Texas, arriving soon after the battle of San Jacinto, and joined the Texas Army.

In June 1836, Hays was in a detail of soldiers sent to bury the remains of some 400 of James Fannin's men killed by Mexican forces at Goliad after they surrendered. Hays then joined a company of Rangers commanded by "Deaf" Smith. He was with Smith's company when they were sent in March 1837 to assert Texas' claim to Laredo, considered by its inhabitants as a Mexican town. Smith and 20 Rangers were attacked by soldiers from Laredo. Hays said the gunfire of the Rangers "threw them into confusion." Ten men from Laredo were killed.

After the Laredo expedition, Hays was promoted to sergeant and led patrols in search of bandits, horse thieves and hostile Indians. In one encounter, Hays shot a bandit from his horse and chased down three outlaws, who were hanged. Hays was with Capt. Henry Karnes on a foray in 1839 on the Pedernales River. Hays and two scouts found the Comanche camp and the Rangers attacked. Twelve Indians were killed.

Hays in 1840 was given command of a Ranger company headquartered in San Antonio. In choosing recruits, Hays wanted men of courage, of good character, who owned a horse worth at least $100. Their lives depended on their horses.

In 1841, Hays with 40 Rangers rode up the Medina River toward Bandera Pass, separating the Medina and Guadalupe valleys. The Comanches saw the Rangers first and prepared an ambush, with warriors hiding among the rocks. When Hays' men were halfway through the pass, the Indians opened fire, taking the Rangers by surprise. There was much confusion as the Rangers tried to regain control of their frightened mounts; they couldn't aim their guns and control their horses at the same time. Hays shouted, "Steady, boys. Get down and tie those horses."

In hand-to-hand fighting, one Ranger charged an Indian with his five-shot Colt pistol. As he was about to fire, the

Jack Hays and his company of Rangers in camp near San Antonio in 1844.

barrel fell off and he was left holding the handle. The Ranger and Comanche each had half a weapon. The Indian was too close to string his bow, so he stabbed the Ranger with an arrow. The Comanche chief attacked Kit Ackland and Ackland killed him with a Bowie knife. After the fight, the Indians moved toward the north end of the pass, where they buried their chief. The Rangers went to the south end where graves were dug and wounds bandaged. Five Rangers were killed and six badly wounded. The battle at Bandera Pass was one of Hays' toughest fights.

That June, Hays took 30 Rangers up the Sabinal River toward Uvalde Canyon. Near the canyon, circling buzzards denoted the presence of an Indian camp. The Indians were roasting venison. When Hays led an attack on the camp, the Comanches ran into a thicket. Hays had his men surround the thicket and Hays took a Ranger with him to drive out the Indians. The men heard shots; Hays came out carrying the wounded Ranger. Hays went back in the thicket and after several shots, Hays' men went in search of their captain. They found him with eight dead Comanches.

Between fights and scouting expeditions, the Rangers enjoyed their time off around San Antonio. That month, a ball was held to honor President Mirabeau Lamar. Hays and Rangers Mike Chevalier and John Howard attended, but they had only one dress coat. Mary Maverick wrote that the

351

Rangers took turns wearing that coat on the dance floor. "The two not dancing would stand at the hall door watching the happy one who was enjoying his turn and they reminded him when it was time for him to step out of that coat."

In August, Hays and 50 men, with Lipan-Apache Chief Flacco scouting, went after Comanches on the Llano and attacked a camp with 200 warriors. In the battle, Hays' horse ran away with him, toward the Indian lines. Flacco, thinking that Hays was making a charge, rode after him. Both men were able to ride straight through the Comanche lines and come out on the other side. Flacco would later say, "Me and Red Wing (his horse) not afraid to go to hell together. Captain Jack not afraid to go by himself."

JACK HAYS — 2

Jack Hays' first law of fighting was never back down. He knew that sheer determination of a few could whip larger forces. He seemed to possess a certainty of how things would come out in battle and that certainty inspired his men.

What may be true or may be legend was a fight in the fall of 1841 at the Enchanted Rock. Based on Hays' character, the story is believable. Hays was scouting alone, away from where the Rangers were camped, on Crabapple Creek near the Enchanted Rock that dominates the Llano Valley (near today's Fredericksburg). When Hays discovered Comanches behind him, he raced to the Enchanted Rock, slapped his horse on the rump, and scrambled to the top.

As Comanches ran up after the man they called Devil Yack, he picked them off from the summit. Hays saw a cloud of dust as the Rangers, alerted by his rider-less horse, raced to his rescue. The Indians took off, leaving 15 warriors dead on the Enchanted Rock, all killed by Hays.

The following year, Hays was instrumental in defeating and turning back Mexican Gen. Adrian Woll after he captured San Antonio in September 1842, known as the Woll Raid. Hays was not in charge of the Texans; Gen. Matthew "Old Paint" Caldwell was in command. But Hays with a few chosen Rangers drew Woll's forces out of San Antonio to a place picked by Hays for the battle, at Salado Creek.

In January 1844, Sam Houston told Hays the Texas Navy, being dismantled, had a supply of Colt revolvers. After Hays got them for his Rangers they came in handy in a fight on the Pinta Trail crossing on June 8, 1844. This battle has also been called the battle of Walker's Creek and the battle on the Pedernales, but Rangers called it the fight on the Pinta Trail. It was one of the hardest fights Hays had since he was ambushed at Bandera Pass.

Hays and 14 Rangers were scouting on the Pedernales, 80 miles from San Antonio. They camped near the Pinta Trail, an old Indian route, when they discovered Indians following them. When the Rangers advanced, the Indians feigned alarm, making for the cover of a wood. Hays had been in too many fights to be taken in. He made no move to chase them. Fifteen warriors came out of the sheltering wood and Hays recognized Chief Yellow Wolf. The Indians yelled insults in Spanish, calling the Rangers cowards. Hays yelled back his own insult: "Yellow Dog, son of a dog-mother, the Comanche liver is white!" The chief was so incensed he nearly fell off his horse.

Hays saw a larger force waiting on the ridge. The Indians made for the top of the hill and waited for the Rangers to attack. Hays noticed a ravine that could not be seen from the hilltop. He led the Rangers into the ravine, rode around the base of the hill and up behind the Indians. The Indians, watching for Hays to come up the front of the hill, were taken by surprise when they were attacked from behind.

The Indians, yelling and whooping, came to lance-throwing distance and the Rangers fired their newly acquired Colts. Two dozen warriors dropped from their ponies. As Yellow Wolf harangued his warriors to make another charge, Hays asked Richard "Ad" Gillespie to "make sure work of that chief." Gillespie's rifle made a dull crack and Yellow Wolf fell dead. The Comanches rode off a short way, then fled.

Jack Hays, the famous Ranger captain and Indian fighter, died in California in 1883.

Thirty Indians were killed. Of the Rangers, two were killed and five wounded. In his report, Hays said: "Whenever pressed severely, the Indians were making the most desperate charges and efforts to defeat me. Had it not been for the five-shooting pistols, I doubt what the consequences would have been."

There has been much dispute about which battle Hays and his men first used Colt firearms. Some accounts place it in a fight near Corpus Christi two years earlier and others at a battle in the Nueces Canyon. Several Rangers, and Hays himself, obtained Colt firearms as early as 1839. One man used a Colt rifle at the battle of Plum Creek in 1840 and

Ranger Andrew Erskine was firing a Colt pistol at Bandera Pass in 1841 when the barrel fell off. But the Pinta Trail battle in 1844 was the first time an entire Ranger company was armed with Colt revolvers.

Before the emergence of Colt revolvers, Comanches could let fly half a dozen arrows and ride 300 yards in the time it took a Ranger to reload a .48 caliber flintlock rifle, which couldn't be done on a horse. With Colts, Rangers could fight like Indians from horseback.

When war loomed with Mexico, Hays raised a regiment of Rangers, which trained at Corpus Christi with U.S. troops in 1845 and early 1846. Many of Hays' Rangers enlisted. During the war, an officer in the Army pointed to a "little fellow" at the head of the First Regiment, Texas Volunteers, and asked who he might be. He was surprised when someone said it was Jack Hays, the world-famous Ranger and Indian fighter. If the war had lasted longer, Rip Ford wrote, Hays would have been in line to be promoted from colonel to brigadier general in the Army for his actions at Monterrey and Mexico City. The boy who ran away from his uncle's home because he didn't want to be a clerk, but wanted a military career, achieved his goal, though it was a roundabout way.

Hays married Susan Calvert of Seguin in 1847. They went to California in the gold rush of 1849. He speculated in gold mining, became the first elected sheriff of San Francisco, and helped found the city of Oakland. But he was always best-known for his exploits on the Texas frontier when Comanches knew him as Devil Yack. He died in 1883 at age 66. It did not escape notice that he died on San Jacinto Day.

NUECES COUNTY SHERIFFS — 1

Going back to 1846, Nueces County elected some colorful and unusual, famous and infamous, sheriffs. The county's first sheriff was a hired gunslinger. After him came ranchers, range bosses, stockmen, sheepmen and former Texas Rangers. Two sheriffs were killed in office and two others were tried for murder.

The first sheriff, Henry W. Berry, may have been a wanted man somewhere else, like so many others who came to Texas, a place of second chances. His background was a closely held secret and he used two different first names, Henry and Harrison. He arrived in Corpus Christi in 1843, coming from Ohio or Tennessee. He was one of Henry Kinney's hired gun hands paid to protect the trading post.

Berry earned his pay in May 1844 when a Comanche raiding party struck Kinney's Rancho. Kinney, Berry and 10 other men chased the Indians and in a fierce fight Berry was shot in the groin with an arrow. He pulled it out and kept it as a souvenir. Berry was elected sheriff when Nueces County held its first election in July 1846. He served until Aug. 7, 1848, then became a building contractor. He and John A. F. Gravis built Mann's "red house" and Cornelius Cahill's shellcrete building on Water Street. One of their buildings still stands on the bluff; we call it Centennial House today. After Gravis died in 1854, Berry married his widow Irenah and became the stepfather of four Gravis children, including two boys, Charles and Frank.

During the Civil War, Berry was identified by Mat Nolan as one of several renegades helping Union soldiers load confiscated cotton. Berry was accused of treason, but he never stood trial as the war came to an end. With Union men in power, Berry was again appointed sheriff, holding office for a second time for two years. He died on May 15, 1888.

Nueces County's second sheriff, William Long "Billy" Rogers, was elected on Aug. 7, 1848. He followed Berry's first term. Two years before Rogers was elected, he was the survivor of a bloody massacre. In 1846, at the start of the Mexican War, Billy Rogers left Corpus Christi with his father, Patterson Rogers, in an army supply train headed for the border. There were two dozen people, including wagon-drivers, women, and children in the train. They were captured by Mexican guerrillas and killed, most of them with their throats cut. Billy Rogers' throat was cut and he was thrown in the Arroyo Colorado. He wandered the brush for days before he was taken in by a family and nursed back to health. The story was told that Rogers in time tracked down the killers one by one and slit their throats. A cut throat on the Rio Grande was called "Billy's mark."

Billy Rogers served as sheriff until Aug. 5, 1850. He bought a ranch, owned the St. James Hotel, and built Market Hall. He organized Corpus Christi's first volunteer fire department and was elected to the Legislature. He died on Dec. 17, 1877.

After Billy Rogers, between 1850 and 1858, came a succession of sheriffs — Thomas Parker, John Vernon and John Graham. Matthew Nolan, better known as Mat Nolan, was elected sheriff on Aug. 5, 1858, defeating Samuel Miller, who operated the first Miller's Ferry on the Nueces River.

Mat Nolan, his younger brother Thomas and sister Mary were young Irish immigrants whose parents died after they

reached New York. The boys enlisted in the 2nd Dragoons as bugle boys and Mary became an Army nurse. They landed in Corpus Christi with Zachary Taylor's army in 1845. Mat and Tom served in the Mexican War and after the war joined the Texas Rangers. When the Rangers were disbanded, they returned to Corpus Christi.

When Mat Nolan was elected sheriff, he appointed Tom as a deputy. One of Nolan's problems was that he had no place to put prisoners. With no jail to hold prisoners, the sheriff put them up in a boarding house, at his own expense, or let them go. The lack of a jail led to a tragedy.

On Aug. 4, 1860, a drunken butcher named John Warren threatened to kill James Barnard, the owner and bartender at the La Retama Saloon on Chaparral. Sheriff Nolan arrested Warren but, with no jail, he had to take him home and put him to bed. Warren went back to the La Retama and stabbed Barnard several times with a Bowie knife, leaving him near death.

When Sheriff Nolan and his brother Tom went in search of Warren, they found him at Richardson's store, next door to Ziegler's Hall. Warren pointed a gun at the Nolan brothers and warned, "Stand back or I'll shoot!" When Tom reached for the gun, Warren shot him in the forehead at close range. The sheriff and bystanders chased Warren into Ziegler's Hall, where they shot him to death.

Tom Nolan died 11 days later. The obituary in the Ranchero said, "Reared in arms, educated on battlefields, the thunder of cannon and the whizzing of shells, shot or bullets was familiar music to Thomas Nolan." After Tom's death, Mat hired former sheriff Henry Berry, the former sheriff, to fill the deputy sheriff's vacancy.

Mat Nolan served as a Confederate officer during the Civil War, fighting several engagements in Texas and Louisiana. While he was away, John R. Peterson was elected sheriff, serving from 1862 to 1864. Nolan, back in the area and recently promoted to lieutenant colonel, was re-elected sheriff of Nueces County on Aug. 1, 1864.

A few months later, three days before Christmas, Nolan was shot to death on Mesquite Street. Before he died, he said Berry's two stepsons, Charles and Frank Gravis, shot him. They were indicted for murder, but the war ended and the indictments were quashed. Nolan was the first of two Nueces County sheriffs killed in the line of duty. He was buried in Old Bayview next to his brother, also slain in the line of duty. Mat Nolan's headstone says nothing about his high Confederate rank or holding the office of sheriff, but tells of his earlier days as a bugle boy in the Mexican War. It reads: "Matthew Nolan, Co. G, 2nd U.S. Dragoons."

NUECES COUNTY SHERIFFS — 2

In 1867, two years after the Civil War ended, John McClane was appointed sheriff by the military authorities governing Texas. McClane replaced Henry Berry, who was appointed in 1865. McClane came to Corpus Christi in 1856 when he brought a shipment of merino bucks for Richard King from his father's sheep farm in Pennsylvania. McClane stayed in Texas and soon had his own flocks of sheep.

During the war, McClane was a blockade runner, carrying cotton to Matamoros in an old sloop and bringing back military supplies. His blockade-running ended when he had to abandon his ship and wade ashore to escape capture. When the war ended, he switched sides, joined the Grant Club and became friendly with Republicans who were gaining power. McClane was a friend of E. J. Davis, soon to become the Reconstruction governor of Texas.

During the war, McClane stockpiled his wool clips. As a blockade-runner, he could have sold his wool in Matamoros, but he held it for better times. After the war, he made a deal with Union Army quartermaster Daniel Haverty to sell 52,000 pounds of wool in New Orleans. Haverty sold the wool and pocketed McClane's $21,000.

Sheriff McClane followed Haverty to Chicago, where he arrested him and brought him back to Corpus Christi. He locked him up in what was called a jail but was really an iron lockup, a cage, that was added to the upper floor of the

1854 courthouse. Haverty had influence with ruling military authorities and in June 1868 a military board ordered Haverty's release. To show its displeasure, the board declared the office of sheriff of Nueces County vacant.

McClane was removed as sheriff and Haverty was freed to return to Chicago. McClane followed him and filed civil suit to reclaim his $21,000. There was no love for ex-Confederates in Chicago; Haverty had McClane arrested for kidnapping and McClane was held in the Cook County Jail for eight months until he dropped the suit against Haverty. The wool money was gone.

The military authorities appointed Peter Benson, who served a year, then Dennis Kelly was elected in 1869, the first election held since the end of the war. Kelly served until June 13, 1870 when he was stabbed to death by a man who thought the sheriff was going to arrest him. After Mat Nolan, Kelly was the second sheriff killed in the line of duty.

With E. J. Davis in the governor's mansion, McClane was appointed sheriff again. Two years later, he was elected and served until 1876. No other sheriff of Nueces County faced as troubled times, outside of the Civil War, as McClane did during Reconstruction.

The year he was appointed, in 1870, the Corpus Christi newspaper reported that there was no security for person or property between the Nueces and Rio Grande. Stolen cattle were driven to the border for sale. Hide-peelers skinned thousands of cattle on the ranges. Vigilantes were in the saddle and bodies were found hanging all over the country. Such were the times during McClane's tenure as sheriff.

On May 9, 1874, bandits killed four men at Morton's store at Peñascal on Baffin Bay. Seven of the alleged killers were brought to Corpus Christi. A mob of posse members, most of them from San Patricio County, gathered at the jail with a rope ready at hand. McClane prevented a lynching.

Sheriff John McClane, a sheepman from Pennsylvania, was a blockade-runner during the Civil War.

Two suspects were found guilty and sentenced to hang. On Aug. 7, 1874, McClane gave the men a drink of whisky and escorted them to a scaffold on the second floor of the 1854 Courthouse, where they were hanged.

The following year, bandits raided and terrorized Nuecestown, 12 miles up the river. When the alarm spread to Corpus Christi, McClane rode up and down the streets, shouting, "Close your windows! Bar your doors! Arm yourselves! Protect the town!" A wounded bandit, left behind, was brought to Corpus Christi, trussed-up in a two-wheeled cart. People in town, having heard that he was on the way, started to erect a scaffold on Mesquite Street from which to hang him. McClane put a stop to it. When the cart came in on Leopard Street, members of the posse, joined by people in town, looked for a place to hang the wounded bandit. They went to a field where a new gate had been put up. A cross pole between the gate posts was high enough to give clearance. William Ball put the noose around the bandit's neck, the rope was thrown over the pole, and the cart driven on, leaving the man hanging from the crossbar.

When McClane's tenure ended in 1876, the books were audited and McClane was short $13,000. He sent word by Pat Whelan to his friend Richard King about the problem. King told Whelan, "Well, tell him I'll fix it." King hired an accountant who found that McClane's books balanced to the penny. John McClane died at his home on April 1, 1911.

After McClane came Thomas Beynon, a former Confederate cavalry officer and a trail boss for King Ranch. Beynon was elected on Feb. 14, 1876, and re-elected on Nov. 5, 1878 and Nov. 2, 1880. He served three terms. Afterwards, he operated a livery stable on Tancahua and ran a stage line to Brownsville. He died on March 16, 1913.

Beynon was followed by Pat Whelan, a close friend of John McClane. Whelan had been a bricklayer and a city marshal in the 1870s. He served as sheriff from 1882 through 1896. He died on May 29, 1921. After Whelan came John McTiernan, a bookkeeper at Sidbury's lumber yard before he was elected sheriff in 1896. McTiernan served until he died, at age 42, on July 21, 1901. John Bluntzer was appointed to complete his term.

NUECES COUNTY SHERIFFS — 3

Michael Bennett Wright, a cousin of Texas Ranger Will Wright, raised livestock at Banquete before he was elected sheriff of Nueces County in 1901. One of his first cases was the murder of Eunice Hatch, who lived on a farm west of Corpus Christi.

She was found in her home on April 21, 1902, her head split open with an axe, her baby crying in a crib nearby. Suspicion focused on Andres Olivares, a hired hand on the nearby McCampbell place. He had been a guest in the house, but Eunice told her husband Jim Hatch not to bring him back because she didn't like the way he looked at her.

Wright found splatters of blood on Olivares' clothes and his shoes matched prints at the murder scene. The trial lasted one morning. The jury deliberated that afternoon, finding him guilty and assessing the death penalty. The judge ordered Olivares to be hanged on June 3, 1902.

The day of the hanging, Olivares spent the morning with Father Claude Jaillet. And then was taken to a scaffold platform. He yelled *"Adios amigos!"* seconds before Sheriff Wright sprang the trap. The newspaper commended the sheriff, writing, "Everything was in perfect readiness and the program was carried out to perfection, like clockwork."

Two years later, the sheriff was the hangman again when Apolinario Hernandez, who killed his wife, was hanged two days before Christmas 1904. When the black cap was placed on Hernandez and the noose adjusted around his neck, the doomed man confessed to killing his wife and said to pardon him if he had offended anyone. Mike Wright was the last sheriff of Nueces County to serve as executioner.

As sheriff, Mike Wright arrested a murder suspect 27 years after the crime was committed. The case involved a fatal shootout at a Ranger camp at Banquete. Josh Peters, son of a nearby rancher, rode up to the camp and asked the Rangers who tied a tin can to his horse's tail. It was a prank. Peters' gelding was grazing peacefully when a Ranger, George Talley, took a tomato can with gravel in it and tied it to the colt's tail. It spooked the horse and he nearly ran himself to death.

Peters said, "Who tied that can to my colt's tail? I'll whip the sorry bastard who did it." Talley said, "I done it." Both men pulled guns. Talley shot Peters in the temple; he was dead before he hit the ground. Talley was indicted for murder and put in jail by Sheriff Beynon. After he was released on bond, Talley left Texas and worked on ranches in New Mexico and Arizona.

In 1905, Talley returned to the area. After he had been tipped off, Sheriff Wright approached Talley in the street. Talley said his name was Smith. Wright had him lift his pants leg, which showed an identifiable scar. A trial in Corpus Christi ended with a mistrial. In the second trial, a jury found Talley not guilty.

Mike Wright was a curious sheriff, almost a pacifist. He rarely carried a gun. A rancher shot and killed a man in the Ben Grande Saloon. Riding away, he yelled: "Tell Mike I'll kill anybody who comes after me." Sheriff Wright rode out to the ranch. The rancher met him with a rifle and said, "I'll kill you before I let you take me in." Wright told him, "You see, I came, but I'm not wearing a gun." After a little talk, the rancher put down his rifle and rode back with the sheriff.

Klan supporters attend the funeral service of W. F. "Wildfire" Johnston.

Wright served as sheriff until 1916. On June 6, 1917, he was riding his prized horse "Garza" when he slumped over, dead in the saddle. The obituary noted that Wright pulled a gun only twice in his 15-year career as sheriff. "In all truth," said the obituary, "he was a man unafraid yet withal considerate of the rights of others."

Frank Gravis Robinson was a foreman on the Driscoll Ranch before he was elected sheriff in 1916. Thomas Beynon, elected in 1874, also had been a foreman and trail boss for King Ranch. Robinson's tenure as sheriff ended with his shooting to death of reputed Ku Klux Klan leader Fred Roberts. On Oct. 14, 1922, Roberts was shot to death by Sheriff Robinson and a deputy.

On Oct. 14, 1922, Sheriff Robinson and Deputy Joe Acebo entered a grocery store in Corpus Christi, on Railroad Avenue, owned by G. E. Warren. The sheriff hassled Warren, accusing him of being in the Klan. "You are a Ku Kluxer, aren't you, Warren? By God, you know you are." The sheriff slapped Warren, then the sheriff and deputy left and crossed the street.

Warren called Fred Roberts, who came to the store, talked to the Warrens, then went to his car. Sheriff Robinson walked over and fired three shots at Roberts, killing him. Acebo fired one. Robinson and Acebo and two others were indicted for murder. The sheriff resigned. In the trial, which was moved to Laredo, the former sheriff said he shot Roberts because he thought he was going for a gun. The jury found all four not guilty. After the trial, Robinson, said to be afraid of Klan retaliation, moved to Mexico where he lived for a decade. His daughter was the longtime county clerk, Marion Uehlinger. Robinson died in Laredo, at age 67, on Jan. 22, 1941.

After Robinson resigned, W. G. Cody was appointed and served about a month, then George Peters was elected sheriff of Nueces County, the first Republican elected to the office since John McClane. Peters' opponent, W. F. "Wildfire" Johnston, was considered the Ku Klux Klan candidate. The election was close, with Peters winning by 60 votes. Johnston challenged the vote count; a recount showed Peters winning by only 40 votes. When Johnston died three years later, a contingent of white-robed Klansmen attended his funeral at Rose Hill Cemetery.

NUECES COUNTY SHERIFFS — 4

Ben Lee was elected sheriff of Nueces County in 1924, after the Fred Roberts shooting episode, and re-elected every two years through 1932.

In September 1931, a body was found on the Oso with a hole in the skull. Sheriff Lee's deputies identified the dead man as Alfred Steinbach, who shared a room with V. Don Carlis, a mechanic. The evidence pointed to Carlis. Bloodstains were found on one of his tools, a hammer, which fit the hole in Steinbach's skull.

During the trial, the skeleton was brought into the courtroom and the district attorney told the jury the dead man was there to tell of his fate: "Here, see this hole in my skull, that's where the murderer hit me with a ball-peen hammer," said the district attorney. The jury found Carlis guilty; he was sentenced to 99 years. But the macabre skeleton stunt got the case overturned and Carlis was brought back to the county jail for a new trial.

Carlis convinced Sheriff Lee he could prove he was innocent if the sheriff would take him to see certain people. The sheriff took him out of jail and drove him to San Antonio. As Sheriff Lee later explained, "I took him out to make further investigation. We went to San Antonio and he prevailed upon me to take him to a certain address. He went in the front door and out the back door." Lee said he guessed he should not have trusted him.

369

Carlis was captured in Missouri and returned to Nueces County. In a second trial, he was found guilty, but sentenced to only eight years in prison.

In his time in office, Sheriff Lee was known to obtain confessions by making a suspect stand on bare feet on a block of ice until he talked. When a reporter asked about this practice, Lee bristled. "I didn't spend one penny of county money for that ice. I paid for it out of my own pocket." Lee died at age 80 on March 28, 1963.

After Lee, James Galbreath was elected and served a few months before he died in office. Paul Cox, appointed to fill the vacancy, served out the end of the term.

William Y. Shely was elected sheriff in 1934. He served through the end of 1938. Before he was elected sheriff, he was in the Texas Rangers and before that he was a deputy sheriff of Nueces County. Six members of Shely's family served as Rangers.

When Shely was a deputy, a foreman at the Laureles Ranch reported that a vaquero stole two horses. Shely started after him. The horse thief had 12 hours head start. He was riding one horse and leading the other, leaving a clear trail. At night, Shely would strike matches to find the tracks. He came upon a jacal, with two horses grazing nearby. He slipped up to the house on foot and, looking in, saw his man asleep on the floor, his rifle beside him. Shely eased inside, picked up the rifle, woke the horse thief, and put on the handcuffs.

Shely had been without sleep for 30 hours. He was tired. Shely, his prisoner, and the stolen horses started for Alice. Shely got sleepy and decided to camp. He placed the guns at a distance and handcuffed the prisoner to him. With his saddle for a pillow, he went to sleep. Shely woke with a start. The prisoner, using corn shucks he carried to roll cigarettes, had almost worked free of his handcuffs. Shely finally put the horse thief in jail. He later said he and the

Nueces County Sheriff John B. Harney, elected in 1938, always wore a Stetson and sported a badge decorated with diamonds.

horse thief became friends, as if they had accomplished a difficult task together.

Shely solved the Flat Iron Murder case in 1935. A young prostitute named Annabelle Evans had her skull crushed by a flat iron for the money she carried in a Bull Durham sack. Shely was able to identify the body and arrest a suspect, who was convicted of the murder. Shely, after he left office, was on his oil lease near Shreveport in 1939 when he died of heart attack. He was 71.

After Shely came John B. Harney, who was elected sheriff in 1938. Some thought him the image of a Texas sheriff, at 6-3 and 280 pounds, wearing a Stetson, with a badge decorated with diamonds.

In 1942, a suit was filed by the Texas Attorney General seeking Harney's removal from office for official misconduct. The case centered on the arrest and death of William King, from West Virginia. He was arrested on Feb. 1, 1941 without a warrant, held for seven days in the jail, then taken out and shot by Harney, the state contended. Harney claimed he was taking him to look for stolen property when he shot the prisoner in a scuffle over a gun. The jury exonerated Harney. He kept his badge and was re-elected to another term.

In 1952 Harney was defeated for re-election. He died of a heart attack on Sept. 23, 1959. He was 59.

After Harney came Odem Dolan, then Johnnie Mitchell, who served 20 years, the longest tenure of any sheriff, then Solomon Ortiz, James Hickey, J. P. Luby, Larry Olivarez, Rebecca Stutts, the only woman to hold the office, and Jim Kaelin, the 31st sheriff of Nueces County. The long line of high sheriffs goes back to the county's first sheriff, Henry W. Berry, bricklayer, builder, and hired gunslinger.

RISE AND FALL OF INDIANOLA

In the summer of 1840, a Comanche war party of 500 braves passed around San Antonio and struck south. They burned houses, stole horses and captured hostages at Victoria and headed for Linnville on Lavaca Bay, where they plundered stores and burned the town. They took away captives and plunder as a large force of Texans chased them. The Texans caught them at Plum Creek, where the Comanches suffered a crushing defeat.

After Linnville was sacked and burned, its commerce moved south to Lavaca; residents rebuilt their homes on a bluff overlooking the bay. Lavaca ("the cow") got its name when it became a shipping point for cattle and grew when Charles Morgan made it a port of call for Morgan Line ships. The name was changed to Port Lavaca to reflect its status as a seaport.

Twelve miles down the beach from Port Lavaca, Prince Karl of Solms-Braunfels, head of the German Immigration Society, picked a spot to land 200 German families. The immigrants landed at Indian Point, which Prince Karl named after himself, calling it Karlshafen (Karl's Harbor). The strip of beach along Lavaca and Matagorda bays was surrounded by lakes, bayous and marshes.

A tent city grew up on the sandy shore as thousands of German settlers arrived at Karlshafen, then moved on to New Braunfels and Fredericksburg.

Up the coast, Port Lavaca made a fateful decision to raise its wharf fees and Charles Morgan was quick to react. He built a wharf 12 miles below Port Lavaca, on Powderhorn Lake, down the beach from Karlshafen, and established regular steamer service between his docks and New York. This became a center of commercial activity; the community sprouting up around it was known as Powderhorn, then Indianola.

Wharves stretching into the bay were piled high with hides, pecans, oats, corn, cotton, gold bullion destined for the U.S. Mint at New Orleans. Longhorns were driven to the docks for shipment east. John D. Young helped drive longhorns, which the cowboys on the coast called "sea lions." "Our route to Indianola was across bayous and along lakes and the 'sea lions' gave us as much trouble in the water as wild cattle ever gave anybody in the brush."

Secretary of War Jefferson Davis launched an experiment to study using Arabian camels to carry Army supplies from Texas. The first contingent of camels arrived at Indianola on May 14, 1856.

D. A. Saltmarsh ran a stagecoach line from Indianola to San Antonio. One passenger found that the roads were so bad he had to walk most of the way and help pull the coach out of mud holes, "the hardest and dirtiest work I have ever done." Capt. Peter Johnson ran schooners from Indianola to Saluria on Matagorda Island and from there he ran a stagecoach line down Matagorda, across Cedar Bayou, to the town of Aransas on St. Joseph's. His line carried the mail from Indianola to Corpus Christi.

The Old Cart Road from Indianola to San Antonio was said to be the busiest freight route in Texas. In 1857, what came to be called the Cart War broke out on the Old Cart Road. When Hispanic freighters charged lower rates than their Anglo competitors, Anglo freighters began destroying carts and some cartmen were killed. When the stream of

374

goods to San Antonio slowed, merchants complained to Gov. E. M. Pease, who called out the Rangers to put an end to violence on the Cart Road.

In the Civil War, Indianola was occupied when Union forces captured Galveston in 1862 and again in 1863 after Gen. Nathaniel P. Banks' army captured Brownsville, Fort Semmes on Mustang Island, and Fort Esperanza on Matagorda Island. Indianola was held briefly by Union forces before they were withdrawn, ending Banks' campaign in Texas.

After the war, Indianola, the Queen City of the West, passed Galveston and became one of Texas' greatest cities. Then it was nearly destroyed when a storm struck on Sept. 16, 1875. The Signal Service, forerunner of the U.S. Weather Bureau, called it one of the most perfect types of tropical storm since the tracking of hurricanes began.

Indianola, low and exposed, at near sea level, surrounded by water, was terribly vulnerable. When the storm surge hit, the streets turned into rivers. Trains couldn't run with the tracks underwater. People were trapped in wooden buildings that collapsed in the storm surge. People clung to lumber and cotton bales. A four-year-old girl, her hand caught in a rooftop, was found 15 hours later, alive, but half-crazed from the ordeal. Huck's Lumber Yard, the Casimir House hotel, the *Indianola Bulletin* newspaper, Louis de Planque's photo studio, and three of every four buildings were destroyed. Some 200 lives were lost. Twelve new bayous cut through the devastated town. But people, used to living in the place, began to rebuild. They were not beaten.

History repeated itself. On Aug. 20, 1886, Indianola was hit by another powerful hurricane. Some who experienced both storms said the sequel in '86 was even worse. It was followed by a fire that consumed what the storm left standing. The last disaster sealed the fate of Indianola. This

Main Street (above) in 1873, two years before a hurricane destroyed much of Indianola. One home stands islanded (below) amid destruction after Indianola was hit by a second destructive storm in 1886.

time, they were beaten. People didn't have the heart to rebuild the ruined city. Buildings were salvaged and erected in Port Lavaca, Victoria, Beeville and other towns. Commerce moved to Rockport, then Corpus Christi. Two catastrophic storms a decade apart spelled the end of Indianola. Today, it is a small fishing village, with a store or two and more history than houses.

DEATH OF AN INDIAN CHIEF

Near San Antonio, on the way from Laredo, the party camped for the night. The leader was a Lipan-Apache chief named Flacco. With him were an elderly Lipan-Apache who was a deaf-mute and two Texans. They were driving a *caballada* of 40 horses belonging to Flacco. In the late hours of the night, Flacco and the deaf-mute were murdered in their sleep and the two Texans left with the horses.

That was in December 1842. Flacco was the youngest of two chiefs, father and son, both named Flacco. Flacco the Elder, a friend of Sam Houston, was made a colonel in the Texas Army for services to the Republic of Texas. He could write his name and signed his signature as "Flacco Colonel." His son, Flacco the Younger, led Lipan scouts for Jack Hays' company of Rangers and taught Hays how to trail. He also taught him Comanche battle tactics. He and Hays were close. Flacco, it was said, constantly watched Hays and nothing the Ranger captain did escaped his notice.

In many of Hays' fights with Comanches from 1840 through 1842, Flacco was there, with his Lipans as scouts and warriors. Several times Flacco saved Hays' life or Hays saved Flacco's. On one foray in search of hostile Comanches, Rangers invited Flacco to share a meal. "No," he said, "warriors never eat much on warpath. Captain Hays is great chief, but Rangers eat much too much on warpath. Too much eat, too much eat."

Flacco the Lipan chief said of Jack Hays: "Me and Red Wing not afraid to go to hell together. Captain Jack not afraid to go by himself."

In 1841 in a battle on the Llano, Hays' Rangers attacked 200 Comanches and during the fight, Hays' horse ran straight at the Indian lines. Thinking that Hays was charging, Flacco rode after him. Both men rode through the Comanche lines and came out the other side untouched. Flacco said Captain Jack was "bravo too much." The Lipan chief added, "Me and Red Wing not afraid to go to hell together. Captain Jack not afraid to go to hell by himself."

In 1842, at some soiree at LaGrange, Flacco was one of the invited guests. He dressed for the occasion, wearing his breechclout and leggings of white buckskin and a string of beads, amulets and silver wrist bands. He was in the company of Capt. Mark Lewis. A young lady played the piano for the chief's amusement and afterwards, someone remarked that the young lady was a particular favorite of Capt. Lewis. "Oh, no," she said, "I am not tall enough for the captain."

Looking over and sizing up the young lady, who was somewhat short and overweight, Flacco said, "You tall too, but the Great Spirit, him put hand on head and mash you down."

In 1842, Flacco joined Jack Hays as part of the punitive Somervell expedition into Mexico that led to the disastrous Mier raid. When Somervell was forced to turn back, he gave permission for those of his men who needed fresh mounts to confiscate horses from an old ranch near Laredo, since the herds were a source of supply for bandits. Flacco rounded up a *caballada* of 40 horses, a valuable herd. On the way to San Antonio, Flacco and his deaf-mute companion were murdered and the horses were stolen.

There was no real mystery about who killed Flacco, but Sam Houston, in his second term as president of the Republic, was anxious to prevent hostilities with Lipan-Apaches, should they learn that their young chief had been killed by two white horse thieves. Houston spread the word that Flacco was killed by a Mexican bandit named Agaton. Houston asked Noah Smithwick, who lived near Flacco the Elder, to tell him that Mexican bandits killed his son. Smithwick said it was simply a ruse to prevent the Lipans from going on the warpath. A Houston newspaper added to the misinformation, reporting that the bandit Agaton had been sighted on the Nueces River and some traders said he was responsible for murdering Flacco. Hays' Rangers were sent to capture or kill Agaton.

The real killers were James Ravis and Tom Thernon, the two men helping drive Flacco's horses. They were seen in Seguin with the horses shortly after Flacco's murder. They were not pursued or arrested or charged because their arrest and trial would not fit the concocted story that the Mexican bandit Agaton was the killer.

Sam Houston sent the Lipan Apaches a poem about the death of their young chief. It was headed, "To the Lipans in memory of their chief, Flacco, from the Executive Department, Washington, Texas, March 28, 1843.

Perhaps no single piece of Houston's writings have been reprinted as often as the words he wrote in condolence to Flacco the Elder on the death of his son, part of which follows:

> *My heart is sad!*
> *A cloud rests upon your nation.*

Grief has sounded in your camp;
The voice of Flacco is silent.

His words are not heard in council;
The chief is no more.
His life has fled to the Great Spirit,
His eyes are closed;
His heart no longer leaps
At the sight of the buffalo.

The voices of your camp
Are no longer heard to cry
"Flacco has returned from the chase."

Grass will not grow
On the path between us.
Let your wise men give counsel of peace,
Let your young men walk in the white path.
The gray headed men of your nation
Will teach wisdom.

—Thy brother, Sam Houston.

After the death of their son, Flacco and his wife began to fast, a Lipan custom. When they visited Noah Smithwick, they had starved themselves until, said Smithwick, they looked like mummies. Smithwick convinced them to end their fast and share a meal cooked by his wife. The name of Flacco the Younger is remembered due to his connection with Jack Hays and Sam Houston. He is remembered because of his devoted friendship with Hays and because of Houston's elegy on his death, who wrote of Flacco that — "His heart no longer leaps at the sight of the buffalo."

Nov. 23, 2011

CATCHING MUSTANGS

The land between the Nueces and Rio Grande was called the Wild Horse Desert because of herds of wild horses — mustangs, or *mesteños* — of vast number and great beauty. How long had they been there? Many accounts say they were the offspring of horses lost during Spanish expeditions to Texas in the 17th Century. They were left behind because they were lame or too weak to travel, but they recovered and adapted to the open grasslands of South Texas and spread across the coastal plains after generations of breeding.

While that may be right to some extent, there were wild herds in northern Mexico that no doubt drifted across the Rio Grande, extending their range north and east and giving an identity to what the maps would show as the Wild Horse Desert.

Blas de la Garza Falcón, governor of Coahuila, in 1735 saw huge herds of mustangs on his way to the Rio Grande. He believed they were descended from horses that escaped during stampedes and turned wild. When José de Escandón began establishing settlements in South Texas and along the Rio Grande in 1747, he found wild horses. On an inspection tour of missions in Texas in 1768, Fray Gaspar José de Solís saw wild horses around Laredo. Father Juan Agustín Morfi in 1777 saw mustang herds north of the Rio Grande "so abundant that their trails make the country, utterly uninhabited by people, look as if it were the most populated in the world."

Manuel de Mier y Terán, who toured Texas in 1828, ran across great concentrations of wild horses below the Nueces where, he wrote, "it is necessary to post sentries to watch packhorses and mules to keep them from running off with the wild horses."

Herds of wild horses were prevalent in the region in 1845 when Zachary Taylor's army was concentrated at Corpus Christi. Ulysses S. Grant, a young second lieutenant, found that mustangs could be bought for a few dollars a head, so Grant bought four mustang ponies. When the army marched south in March 1846, Grant rode out to see the huge herds of mustangs, too many, he thought, to be contained in the whole state of Rhode Island.

Capturing, breaking and selling wild horses was a major occupation in South Texas. Thomas Dwyer, a lawyer from London, arrived in Corpus Christi in 1848. He went to work as a mustanger. Dwyer wrote that, "Many Mexicans, whose families resided at Corpus Christi, Goliad, and San Antonio, supported themselves by running, that is, catching wild cattle and by mustanging, that is hunting wild horses." The mustangs were caught, tamed, and killed. The best of the breed were broken to the saddle and sold, but many were killed for their hides. Henry Kinney, founder of Corpus Christi, had a pen and slaughter-house on North Beach where mustangs were killed and stripped of their hides, which were salted down and sold in New Orleans.

To catch one prized mustang, rather than a herd, mustangers would sometimes resort to what was called "creasing," which required an expertly fired rifle shot in the neck, close enough to the spinal column to temporarily paralyze the animal. If the shot missed a little low or a bit wide, it was bad news for the horse.

An 1835 sketch titled "Catching Wild Horses."

J. Williamson Moses became captain of a mustang crew in the early 1850s. He described the mustangers' methods of catching herds. A crude pen called a *"corral de aventura"* was built with an opening that could be quickly closed. Wings built of brush shaped like a "V" stretched about some 700 yards. Mustangs were chased into the open end of the "V" and run toward the corral. Men chasing them were *"aventurers."* When the horses were in the wings, *"recibidors"* moved in behind them. When the herd was in the small corral, the closer, called *"enserado,"* stepped into the gap waving a white blanket to keep the horses from running out again. Then the cutter or *"cortador"* cut off their escape by sliding mesquite poles across the opening. When the gate was closed, the horses were trapped. They would run, wheeling round and round the corral, looking for a way out, until they could run no more. Then the hard work of breaking them began.

Once a herd was funneled toward the corral, there was no way to tell how big the catch might be. What happened if the herd was too large for the pen to contain it was described by Moses. It happened at a place near Amargosa Creek, in today's Jim Wells County. "We made such a large drove that when we got them going for the pen, the rush they made was uncontrollable. The *cortador*, whose job was to cut off the herd when the pen was full, was unable to do so. They went with such a rush he could do nothing. The animals in a wild stampede ran over one another. The bottom of the corral was covered with crippled and dying animals. Others rushed, crushing and bruising themselves against the pickets until the pen gave way. The furious, thundering horses, clambering over their dead and dying companions, vanished in a cloud of dust."

During Moses' time, mustangs were so numerous that no one would have believed they were vanishing, but the immense herds that made the horizon seem alive with movement were mostly gone by the end of the 1850s. They were hunted like the buffalo to near extinction. They were not natural to the land but they were wild and beautiful and lent much to the character and spirit of early Texas.

BOMBARDMENT OF FORT BROWN

On Sunday morning, March 8, 1846, the first units of Zachary Taylor's army marched out of Corpus Christi for the Rio Grande. Drummers beat out the traditional marching-away tune, "The Girl I Left Behind Me." Capt. Daniel P. Whiting left at the head of his company in the 7th Regiment. By the time they reached Twelve Mile Motts, Whiting regretted he was a captain of foot. They marched 16 miles the second day, camped at Agua Dulce, and reached Santa Gertrudis Creek on the third day.

Whiting's company, with the rest of Taylor's army, camped on the Rio Grande on March 25 and raised the American flag next to the river. The soldiers went to work building a fort, opposite Matamoros. They called it Fort Texas. While they were building the fort, Capt. Seth Thornton led a squadron of dragoons into a trap, where they were attacked by Mexican troops. Sixteen dragoons were killed, 47 were captured. Taylor notified Washington — "Hostilities may now be considered as commenced."

Taylor worried about his supply base at Point Isabel, near the mouth of the Rio Grande, 26 miles away. He took 2,000 men to Point Isabel to get supplies and left behind 500 men of the 7th Infantry to garrison the new Fort Texas. Whiting wrote in his memoirs that when the fort was finished the 7th camped in the interior. When the rest of the army left for Point Isabel, they left their baggage at the fort.

On May 3, 1846, Whiting was washing his face when a round shot passed over from the Mexican side. Whiting rushed out to find men running to get ready for an attack. Twenty-six miles away, Taylor's soldiers heard the beginning of the bombardment of Fort Texas by Mexican batteries across the river.

As Whiting's company was forming, a bomb hit the ground nearby, the fuse burning, and Whiting and his men threw themselves on the ground. "No sooner had we done so than the shell exploded, tearing up the ground for several yards, but all the fragments flying upward cleared the fort without further injury. The next minute grapeshot struck a sergeant near me on the head; he was never aware of the fatal cause. Except this instance and that of Maj. Brown, our commander, who was afterwards killed, no deaths occurred, though many were wounded by fragments."

During the night, soldiers erected bomb-proofs — covered ways for protection — with whatever they could find, including the baggage and bedrolls and belongings of the absent troops. Some chicken coops were knocked open and a chicken was killed by a shell. Whiting's personal valet, an Irish enlisted man named Mac, cooked it for Whiting's dinner. "Frequently after, without waiting for an 'accident,' Mac served a fowl for our repast, remarking, whenever a shell burst in the fort, 'There goes another chicken.' "

Whiting wore a slouched black hat that looked like the chapeau of a field officer. He was standing near a bastion when shots struck nearby and someone cried, "Why, captain, they are shooting at you! It must be your hat." The Mexican forces had several sharp-shooting guns of small caliber. "I squatted on the ground and, putting the hat on a stick, I raised it above the line and as often as I did so, whiz!, came one of the balls. This convinced me that I should be cautious how I showed my hat, especially when my head was in it."

Gen. Mariano Arista's forces crossed the river and took a position to block Taylor's return from Point Isabel. Their pickets were seen from Fort Texas. On May 6, Major Jacob Brown, commander of the fort, was struck on the leg by a shell. He was carried into one of the bomb-proof shelters, where he died. He was buried near the flagstaff.

On May 7, with supplies loaded, Taylor started to return to the besieged Fort Texas, traveling over a prairie until they reached a stand of timber called Palo Alto. On May 8, as they approached Palo Alto, they faced a Mexican army of 6,000 men, three times their strength, drawn up in line of battle in front of the timber, their bayonets glinting in the sun.

At Fort Texas, they heard cannon fire and saw columns of smoke, which told them Taylor's forces were engaged with the Mexican army.

At Palo Alto, Taylor formed a line of battle and orders were given for a platoon from each company to stack arms and fill canteens for the rest of the companies. When they were back, the order to advance was given. Gen. Mariano Arista opened fire with artillery and the American guns replied. During the artillery exchange, the tall grass caught fire and smoke obscured the battlefield.

Under this smoke screen, Arista attacked the left of Taylor's line and was driven back by Taylor's artillery. Near sunset, the Mexicans fell back as Taylor's troops advanced. The first battle of the Mexican War ended as darkness fell. American casualties were nine killed and 47 wounded. Arista lost some 200 men killed and wounded.

Next day, May 9, Arista retreated and Taylor followed. In the afternoon, they reached some ponds, an old channel of the Rio Grande, called Resaca de la Palma. Arista's forces formed on the opposite bank. Taylor's troops advanced. At Resaca de la Palma, the second major battle of the Mexican

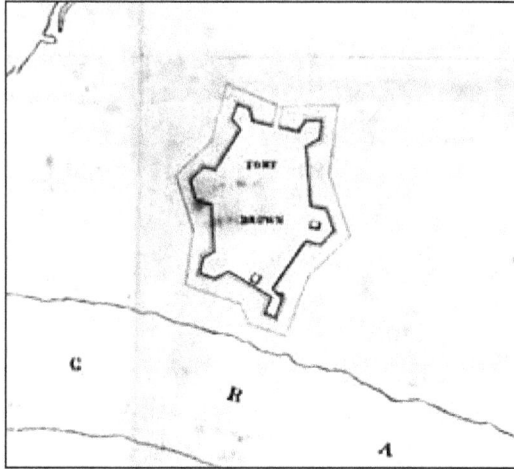
Sketch shows the shape of Fort Brown

War, Taylor lost only 150 men to 1,200 Mexicans killed or wounded.

The men at Fort Texas lined the ramparts to watch Mexican troops retreat across the river, chased by Taylor's dragoons. The bombardment of the fort ceased.

Taylor's returning troops were astounded, Whiting wrote, at the destruction in the fort, which was plowed and furrowed by exploding shells and bombs. Their baggage and bedrolls, used for bomb shelters, were piles of ruins.

On May 17, 1846, Matamoras surrendered and Arista's forces retreated toward Monterrey. Taylor ordered Fort Texas renamed Fort Brown in honor of Maj. Jacob Brown. The town that grew up around the fort became Brownsville. Capt. Daniel Powers Whiting went on to fight in the battles of Monterrey, Veracruz and Cerro Gordo. The Mexican War veteran died on Aug. 2, 1892, in Washington. He was 85.

LAST BATTLE OF CIVIL WAR

John Salmon Ford's duty, as adjutant to Jack Hays in the Mexican War, was to send out death notices. He would write "Rest in Peace" at the bottom of casualty lists, which was shortened to "R.I.P." Someone started calling him "Old Rip." After the war "Old Rip" became a captain of Rangers and when Texas seceded from the Union, he was named chief of conscription, in charge of rounding up draft-dodgers. In 1863, Ford was appointed to command a regiment of Texas cavalry — which he called the Cavalry of the West — made up of young boys and old men and home militia operating in the border region. Ford was promoted to brigadier general in 1864.

Ford was in Brownsville in March 1865 when Union Gen. Lew Wallace, who would later gain fame as the author of "Ben Hur," came to Brazos Santiago. Wallace sent a message to Confederate Gen. James Slaughter, seeking a conference. Slaughter agreed to meet Wallace at Point Isabel and he took Rip Ford with him.

The subject was the possibility of concluding an informal, separate peace between Union and Confederate forces in South Texas. Wallace said it was useless to continue to fight on the Rio Grande. Slaughter and Ford said they had no authority to act unless they received instructions from Confederate superiors. Still, Ford left the meeting with the understanding there would be a peaceful co-existence on the border based on a gentlemen's agreement. Confederate

389

superiors in the Trans-Mississippi Department were furious that Slaughter and Ford discussed reaching an understanding without proper authority.

Not long after that, on April 9, Robert E. Lee surrendered at Appomattox. The news didn't reach South Texas for some time. On May 11, Col. Theodore Barrett, commander of the federal encampment on Brazos Island, sent a detachment of 300 men to take possession of Brownsville. The detachment was made up of black soldiers from the 62nd U.S. Colored Infantry and Company A of the Second Texas U.S. Cavalry, under the command Lt. Col. David Branson.

On May 12, Branson's men routed a Confederate outpost at Palmito Ranch, 12 miles east of Brownsville, near the old Mexican War battlefield of Palo Alto. The outpost was manned by Confederate cavalry commanded by Capt. George Robinson. Later that afternoon, Robinson's troops began to skirmish back toward their former position. The federals, assuming the Confederates got reinforcements, fell back four miles east.

Rip Ford received word that Union forces had attacked Robinson's outpost. He ordered Robinson to hold his ground.

Over supper, Slaughter and Ford talked about what to do. There is no hint in Ford's memoirs that they knew the war was over. While both were brigadier generals, Slaughter was senior and in command. Ford asked Slaughter:

"General, what do you intend to do?"

"Retreat," Slaughter said.

"You can retreat and go to hell if you wish," Ford said he told Slaughter. "These are my men and I am going to fight."

Slaughter reluctantly agreed to resist the federal advance and said he would meet Ford next morning on the parade grounds at Fort Brown to march out to repel the enemy.

Next morning, Ford waited until almost noon with no sign of Slaughter. Ford, at the head of 70 men and a battery of six 12-pounders, marched to the scene of the previous day's battle, not far away, and took command of Robinson's troops. Ford observed the federal position, placed his batteries to block the road, deployed his forces, and told his troops, "We whipped them before. We can whip them again."

Artillery fire was directed at the Union position and skirmish firing became brisk. As the Confederates charged, Union troops began to run. They continued to retreat pell-mell until they reached Brazos Island, seven miles away. Ford, in a wry understatement, said they left the battlefield "in a rather confused manner."

The Confederates halted near Boca Chica Pass. At sundown, Confederates and Yankees moved out in skirmish formation. A Union soldier, John J. Williams, a private in the 34th Indiana, was killed. His family later received a medal honoring him as the last soldier killed in the Civil War.

As the sun went down, an artillery shell fired from the Union guns struck near the Confederate position. A Confederate soldier in his teens — using "a very profane expletive for so small a boy" — fired his rifle in the general direction of the darkening dunes at Boca Chica. It was the last shot fired in the Civil War.

In this affair, wrote Ford, the federals lost 25 to 30 men killed and wounded and 113 prisoners. Ford's losses were five wounded, though he may have understated his casualties. Later accounts said Ford learned of Lee's surrender and the downfall of the Confederacy from prisoners taken in the battle. The federals said they thought the Confederates knew the war was over and that they were sent to take possession of Brownsville, not expecting to meet any resistance.

While news of the Confederacy's demise did reach some places along the border before the fight, whether Ford knew it is another question. Some believe the last battle was fought because Ford didn't like the idea of his men surrendering to black soldiers in the Union Army.

It has also been pointed out that if Ford's command continued to resist, a valuable consignment of cotton could be moved across the river into Mexico to avoid confiscation by Union troops. Richard King and Mifflin Kenedy, cattle ranchers and Rio Grande steamboat owners, had an interest in this cotton. The two men piled up fortunes from cotton traffic during the war.

Tom Lea in "The King Ranch" had the right take on this, I believe. He wrote that Yankee speculators persuaded Barrett, the Union commander at Brazos Santiago, to capture Brownsville so the Union quartermaster could then sell the cotton as contraband with a good profit for the Unionists involved. The plan, wrote Lea, "took no account of Rip Ford, who cared very little about the fate of CSA cotton but a great deal about any violation of the pledged word of the (Lew) Wallace truce."

Whether the fight was a result of a misunderstanding on both sides, or whether it was calculated to give the Confederates time to move cotton to safety across the river, whether it was the result of a violation of a gentlemen's agreement, are questions best left open until more evidence is found. But the Palmito Ranch skirmish between Old Rip's troops and Union soldiers from Brazos Island was the last battle of the Civil War.

CONFEDERATES FLEE TO MEXICO

After Robert E. Lee surrendered at Appomattox, a group of Confederate officers decided to ask for volunteers to cross the Rio Grande, conquer the country up to the Sierra Madre mountains, then form their own government. The officers asked Gen. Simon Bolivar Buckner to command them. As Buckner delayed in giving an answer, the Confederate troops drifted away, most returning home, and there were no volunteers for the Sierra Madre venture. Several Confederate officers decided to go anyway.

In Austin, Gov. Pendleton Murrah, the 10th governor of Texas, discussed a plan of exile with Gen. Alexander Watkins Terrell on June 17, 1865. They feared the victorious Yankees would exact revenge against Confederates of high rank. During the war, Terrell led the 34th Texas Cavalry — Terrell's Texas Cavalry — in the Red River Campaign in northern Louisiana.

When Terrell's party left for Mexico, Gov. Murrah, though he was in bad health, went along. He died of consumption at Monterrey on Aug. 4. At San Antonio, the Texas Confederates joined others fleeing into exile from Louisiana, Kentucky, and Missouri. The Confederate refugees included prominent politicians, such as Gov. Henry Allen of Louisiana, Thomas Reynolds of Missouri, former Governors Trusten Polk of Missouri, Charles Morehead of Kentucky, Thomas Moore of Louisiana, and Edward Clark, who completed Sam Houston's term.

Besides Terrell, there were several Confederate generals and colonels, including J. B. Magruder, William Hardeman, Wilburn King, all from Texas. There were also Sterling Price, E. Kirby Smith, Thomas Hindman of Arkansas, William Preston of Kentucky. From South Texas, there were Gen. Hamilton Bee and Col. P. N. Luckett. Many prominent families went south, some with their slaves.

When Terrell's party reached Roma, they learned that Union cavalry was approaching with orders to capture or kill Confederates trying to enter Mexico. They raced to reach a ford on the river above Roma ahead of Union pursuit and crossed into Mexico.

Henry Maltby's newspaper, *The Ranchero*, which had been at Corpus Christi but was moved to Matamoros, reported on July 23, 1865 that "a large number of distinguished Confederates have passed through Monterrey for the city of Mexico."

Gov, Murrah, before he died, gave Terrell a letter of introduction to Maximilian, the French-imposed emperor of Mexico. Terrell carried the letter, wrapped in oilcloth, in one of his boots. Murrah asked Maximilian for consideration for Terrell and William Hardeman, who were instructed to look for a suitable place where Confederate exiles could settle.

Gen. Terrell rode to Mexico City and was granted an audience with Maximilian at the emperor's residence at Chapultepec Castle. Maximilian gave him the rank equivalent to colonel in the French army in Mexico. Gen. Magruder, George Flournoy, and William Hardeman, known as "Gotch," also served in Maximilian's army. In respect to Terrell's mission, Maximilian opened Mexico to colonization by former Confederates. He granted them freedom of worship, exempted them from paying taxes for a year, and offered each head of family 640 acres of land. He even allowed them to keep their slaves in an "apprenticeship."

Confederates in exile found various occupations in Mexico. Wilburn Hill King, who had also fought in the Red River campaign, began a sugar plantation. Gov. Henry Allen of Louisiana established an English-language newspaper called the *Mexican Times*. Matthew Maury, the first naval officer of the Confederacy, was appointed commissioner of colonization. John Henry Brown, the later historian, was chosen to survey lands for colonization.

Hamilton Bee planted cotton. Sterling Price built a bamboo house and tried his hand at becoming a coffee planter. Hindman also started a coffee plantation. They found farming difficult in a land overgrown with bamboo and banana. Growing coffee was also hard since it took years to reach maturity.

The most prominent Confederate colony was at Villa Carlota, named for the Emperor's wife, west of Veracruz on the road to Mexico City. It was described as a poverty-stricken village of crudely made clapboard houses and crumbling adobe, with loose pigs foraging in the yards. Many Confederate expatriates lived in the vicinity. Another colony was at Tuxpan, between San Luis Potosi and Tampico. Other Texas families located in Monterrey, Saltillo and Mexico City.

J. Williamson Moses, a former Ranger and a mustanger in South Texas, went to work operating a steam engine at a sawmill near Saltillo. In his memoirs, Moses wrote that there were many Texas families living in Mexico after the war. "We did sometimes hear the English language and could bring up home subjects." Moses found the people of Mexico "generally, almost universally, kind and considerate," though it was a dangerous and unstable time. Maximilian's regime, backed by French forces, was under attack by Benito Juárez and his ally Porfirio Diaz. In the

Alexander Watkins Terrell fled to Mexico and joined Maximilian's army after the Civil War. He returned to Texas in 1866.

fighting, Maximilian was cornered and captured at Querétaro. He died on June 19, 1867 before a firing squad at Cerro de las Campanas — "Hill of the Bells." His imperial reign lasted three years and this brought an end to the French attempt to rule Mexico by proxy.

Juárista soldiers, flush with victory, attacked and burned the Villa Carlota. After Maximilian's execution, most Confederate exiles returned to the U.S. Having backed Maximilian, they were the losers in another civil war — and exiled a second time.

Terrell slipped out of Mexico posing as "Colonel Monroe." He wore a sombrero and faded gray uniform and returned to Texas. Terrell went on to a distinguished career. He was elected to the Texas Legislature, authored legislation to build a new state capitol, served as U.S. envoy to the Ottoman Empire and, as a university regent, became known as the father of the University of Texas. Terrell died in 1912 and was buried in the State Cemetery in Austin.

PREACHER IN THE WILDERNESS

In April 1838, a party of surveyors and land agents camped at the site on the shore where Corpus Christi would be built. Among the land agents was Baptist preacher Z. N. "Wildcat" Morrell.

Morrell, who called himself a cane-brake preacher, moved his family from Mississippi in 1836. They reached Texas at the time of the battle of San Jacinto. He started to farm at the Falls of the Brazos, settled by the Robertson Colony. Rangers stood guard while Morrell plowed fields and planted corn. They were always threatened by Indian attack. When he could, Morrell would preach a sermon, usually in a log cabin with a dirt floor.

After several Indian attacks, Morrell moved to Washington-on-the-Brazos and opened a store. He held prayer meetings in an old house. Saloon-goers would hold an opposition prayer meeting, with mock hymn-singing with naughty choruses followed by the taunting question of, "Brother, are you saved?" They would huddle outside Morrell's meeting place and hold a chicken by its neck to make it squawk. Morrell finally smashed one of them over the head with a heavy cane and the mockery stopped.

Morrell invested in land certificates given to furloughed soldiers by the Republic of Texas because it had no money to pay them. Land certificates could be bought for next to nothing; the holders of certificates could claim unclaimed land in the public domain.

Morrell and three land agents took a trip to the Corpus Christi area to survey unclaimed lands. At Goliad, they saw the breastworks from 1836, two years after Fannin and his men were "butchered in cold blood." There were only two or three Mexican families and about as many Irish in Goliad.

Morrell's party found the village of San Patricio deserted; it was abandoned during the Revolution. They met up with a party of eight surveyors and rode on to Corpus Christi Bay.

"We saw no indication of any former settlement at this place," wrote Morrell, "but were informed by an Irishman accompanying the surveyors that this was the point at which the (former) colony of San Patricio procured its supplies."

As surveyors worked, Morrell and another land agent, Matthew Burnett, rode southwest to get a view of the country. They passed the Salt Lake and saw mustang horses and wild game of every kind. They found fresh water and good grass for their horses and camped for the night. Next morning, they went to kill one of the wild cattle to replenish their meat supply. As they rode toward a bunch of cattle, and got close enough to shoot, they saw an Indian on horseback. Burnett raised his gun to shoot, but Morrell stopped him.

"We were in no danger, could not plead self-defense, and in the commission of a deliberate murder I feared the judgment of God." They got close enough to talk. The Indian was a Karankawa boy. Morrell told him in Spanish they were friends. The Indian pointed to his camp and tried to get the two men to follow him.

Morrell was worried about the rest of their party, 40 miles away. They rode as fast as they could back to the camp. They rode into camp and found the surveying party surrounded by 40 Karankawa warriors from the tribe the young boy belonged to. The Indians had already disarmed

Rev. Z. N. Morrell, a pioneer Baptist preacher, rode with Jack Hays in the battle of Salado Creek in 1842.

the surveyors and took their horses. The Karankawa boy pointed out Morrell and Burnett as the men who befriended him. "He recognized us, ran up smiling, as glad as if he had met relatives. Peace was made. Horses, guns, blankets, and everything was given up, and a treaty was made. I thank God that my motto ever was, even among Indians, not to kill except in self-defense." Morrell agreed to take a letter to Sam Houston asking him to recognize the treaty they made.

It appears that Morrell owned two tracts of land on the west side of the Nueces River, surveyed in 1838, land now occupied by the city of Corpus Christi. Morrell apparently traded the Corpus Christi land for a homestead site on the Guadalupe River above Victoria.

399

Two years later, Morrell fought in the battle of Plum Creek. This was after a large Comanche war party sacked and burned the little town of Linnville on Matagorda Bay. When the battle was over, Morrell heard a woman screaming from the bushes. She was trying to pull out an arrow from her breast. Morrell put down a blanket for her to rest on, using his saddle for a pillow.

Two years after Plum Creek, Morrell rode with Jack Hays in the battle of Salado Creek that defeated Gen. Adrian Woll's invaders. As Woll withdrew, his troops came upon Capt. Nicholas Dawson, who was bringing 53 men to join the Texas forces. They raised a white flag, but were cut down by Woll's artillery. Only 15 of Dawson's 53 men survived. Morrell went to the scene of the slaughter, knowing his son was with Dawson's men. He turned over bodies looking for his son. "Thirty-five dead bodies of friends lay scattered and terribly mangled among the little cluster of bushes on the broad prairie," Morrell wrote. "I recognized the body of nearly every one. Here were men, heads of families, their wives now widows and their children orphans; and here, too, lay dead the bodies of promising sons of my neighbors. I drew a pencil from my pocket and wrote down the names of the dead, so that I might make a correct report to the bereaved."

Rev. Z. N. "Wildcat" Morrell founded one of the first Baptist churches in Texas. He was a pioneer Indian fighter who could quote Scripture while loading his rifle. He never missed an opportunity to preach a sermon or to join in the defense of settlers on the frontier. To learn more about Z. N. Morrell, read his "Flowers and Fruits in the Wilderness."

INDEX

Fort Bend County 338
Fort Brown (see also Fort Texas) 100, 297, 299, 388
Fort Esperanza 101, 102, 103, Map 106, 375
Fort Gibson 298
Fort Jesup, La. 233
Fort Merrill 149
Fort Meyer 300
Fort St. Louis 213
Fort Semmes 74, 100, 101, 103, 106, 153, 375
Fort Smith 298
Fort Sumter 274, 275
Fort Texas 385-387
Fort Whiting 298
Fort Worth 157
49'ers 59, 74
Foster, James 230
Fox, Monroe 141
Fredericksburg 373
Fremantle, Arthur James Lyon 93
French, George 90
Friend & Cahn Bank 88
Fuller, Theodore 188
Fullerton, Capt. 320
Fulton, George Ware 71, 72, 108
Fulton Mansion 108
Fulton (town) 72
Furman, Edward 166

Gallagher Ranch 143
Galveston 1, 22, 41, 45, 193, 309, 318, 319, 375
Galveston News 11
Galveston Ranch 202
Galvez, Bernardo de 127, 227
Garner, John Nance 1, 329, 332, 339
Garner, Jim 79
Garza, Ben 223
Garza Falcón, Blas de la 381
George Evans Elementary 147
Gerhardt, Minnie 144

Gettysburg 93, 321
Giles, Alfred 132, 136
Gillespie, Richard 354
Gilliland, Maude (Truitt) 13-16, Photo 15, 215
Gilpin, H. A. 21, 43, 51, 273
Gipson, Fred 292
Gipsy (ship) 80, Photo 82
Givens, Royal 89
Glover, Rufus 127
Goliad 32, 33, 103, 116, 117, 193, 231, 262, 263, 350, 382, 398
Gonzales, Tex. 305
Goodnight-Loving Trail 128, Map 129
Gordon, J. Riely 133, 136
Govatos, John 255, 256
Government Wharf 250
Gradwhol's Shoes 88
Graham, John 274, 358
Grande, Ben 218, Photo 220
Grande, Frank 218
Grant, Mary (see Anderson)
Grant, U. S. 249, 301-304, Photo 303, 382
Gravis, Charles 151, 152, 357, 360
Gravis, Frank 151, 152, 357, 360
Gravis, Irenah (see Berry)
Gravis, John A. F. 357
Gray, Mabry B. "Mustang" 28, 197-200, Sketch 200, 235
Gray's Ranch 197
Greasy Rube 200
Great Depression 5-8, 143, 167, 223, 243
Great Western (Sarah Bourjett) 298
Green, Joseph F. 110, 114
Greer, James Kimmins 54
Gregory, Tex. 202, 211
Gregory, Frank 127
Griffin, M. A. 187
Grim Ranch 203, 346
Grimes, William B. 230, 232

411

Lichtenstein, Albert 64
Lichtenstein, Morris 87, 89
Lichtenstein, Morris, Jr. 248
Lincoln, Abraham 9, 60, 99
Linn, John J. 21
Linnville 373, 400
Lipantitlán 57
Little Rock 298
Live Oak Peninsula 69
Live Oak Point 22, 69-72, Sketch 72, 325
Lively (unknown) 67
Liverpool 30, 45
Lone Star Fair 59, 74, 250, 306, 317, 318, 325
Lone Star Hook & Ladder Co. 238
Lone Star Margaret (yacht) 80, Photo 82
Long, Hugh 221
Long Scotty 33
Long Shirt, Comanche chief 58
Longstreet, James 304
Lookout Peninsula (Lamar) 69, 70, 123, 271
Los Alamos, N. M. 224
Los Algodones 93, 94
Los Horcones Ranch 331, 339, 343, 344
Los Patrios 266, 267
Lott, Uriah 10, 139, 181
Louisiana (steamer) 34
Lovenskiold, Charles 9, 10, 161, 162, Photo 164, 237
Lowman, Al 97, 98, Photo 98
Loyd's Pavilion & Pleasure Pier 166, 255, Photo 259
Luby, James O. 335
Luby, J. P. 372
Luckett, Philip N. 226, 394
LULAC 223
Lyons, DeWitt 124, 270
Lyons, Lucy (Boatwright) 124
Lyons, Warren 124, 125, 270
Lyonsville 124

Luling, Tex. 241

Madero Revolution 16
Magnolia Mansion 131, 133, Photo 135
Magruder, John 304, 394
Male & Female Academy 89
Maltby, Bill 11, 100
Maltby Circus 250
Maltby, Henry 193, 194, 227, 273, 275, 276, 394
Mann's red house 163, 250, 251, 357
Mann, Walter 101
Mann warehouse 34
Mann's Wharf 255
Mann, William 72, 133, 249
Marcy, William 326
Marion, Iowa 101
Market Hall 89, 121, 122, Photo 122, 164, 235, 237-240, Photo 239, 358
Market Saloon 219, 220
Market Square 121, 153, 165, 237-240
Marsh, Jane 162
Martinez, Maximo 96
Mary (ship) 310
Mason, Bill 342
Matagorda Bay 83, 373, 400
Matagorda Island 101, 103, 157, 275, 337, 374, 375
Matagorda Peninsula 36, 69
Matamoros 26, 27, 42, 60, 65, 70, 74, 91, 93, 94, 194, 227, 235, 265, 308, 361, 385
Matamoros Road 91
Mathis 214
Mathis Dam 222
Maverick, Mary 351
Maximilian, Emperor 394, 396
Meade, George 304
Meansville 322
Medina Bus Line 120

412

413

415

416

OTHER BOOKS FROM NUECES PRESS

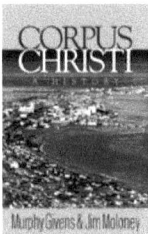

www.ingramcontent.com/pod-product-compliance
Lightning Source LLC
Chambersburg PA
CBHW060418100426
42812CB00030B/3232/J